American Political Fictions

American Political Fictions

War on Errorism in Contemporary American Literature, Culture, and Politics

Peter Swirski

palgrave
macmillan

AMERICAN POLITICAL FICTIONS
Copyright © Peter Swirski, 2015.

First published in 2015 by PALGRAVE MACMILLAN® in the United States—a
division of St. Martin's Press LLC, 175 Fifth Avenue, New York, NY 10010.

Where this book is distributed in the UK, Europe, and the rest of the world, this
is by Palgrave Macmillan, a division of Macmillan Publishers Limited,
registered in England, company number 785998, of Houndmills, Basingstoke,
Hampshire RG21 6XS.

Palgrave Macmillan is the global academic imprint of the above companies and
has companies and representatives throughout the world.

Palgrave® and Macmillan® are registered trademarks in the United States, the
United Kingdom, Europe and other countries.

ISBN: 978-1-137-51888-0

Library of Congress Cataloging-in-Publication Data

Swirski, Peter, 1966-
  American political fictions : war on errorism in contemporary American
literature, culture, and politics / Peter Swirski.
      pages cm
    Includes bibliographical references and index.
    ISBN 978-1-137-51888-0 (hardback : alk. paper) 1. Political fiction,
American—History and criticism. 2. Politics and literature—United
States. 3. Narration (Rhetoric)—Social aspects. 4. Mass media—Political
aspects—United States. I. Title.
    PS374.P6S87 2015
    813.009'358—dc23

                                                              2014049901

A catalogue record of the book is available from the British Library.

Design by Amnet.

First edition: June 2015

10 9 8 7 6 5 4 3 2 1

The most important thing for us is to find Osama bin Laden. It's our number-one priority, and we will not rest until we find him.

—George W. Bush, September 13, 2001

I don't know where he is. I have no idea, and I really don't care. It's not that important. It's not our priority.

—George W. Bush, March 13, 2002

Dedicated to friends and colleagues
in the English Department at UMSL

Contents

List of Figures   xi

Introduction: Artists and Con-Artists   1

1   A Picture Is Worth a Hundred Thousand Words:
Joseph Heller, *Picture This*   19

2   No Child Left Behind: Tim LaHaye and Jerry B. Jenkins,
Left Behind: A Novel of the Earth's Last Days   49

3   A Planet for the Taking: Alistair Beaton, *A Planet for
the President*   79

4   (R)hyming (A)merican (P)oetry: Various Artists   107

5   The Left Wing: Aaron Sorkin, Lawrence O'Donnell, Jr.,
Eli Attie, et al., *The West Wing*   137

Notes   167

Bibliography   175

Index   199

List of Figures

0.1	Ride 'em Cowboy!	7
0.2	The Government's Idea of Probity	12
1.1	Constitutional Mythomatics	30
1.2	War is Business	43
2.1	If Jesus Were GOP . . .	56
2.2	Rightwingers and Leftwingers Going Nowhere	67
3.1	Mr. Bush . . . Tear Down This Wall!	90
3.2	Dnal-sdrawkcab	95
4.1	My Turf	112
4.2	Human Evolution	132
5.1	Speak Softly and Carry a Big Shovel	147
5.2	Money Talks, Bullshit Walks	153

Introduction

Artists and Con-Artists

A Quantum of American History

I was not lying. I said things that later on seemed to be untrue.

Richard Milhous Nixon

In the last year of the nineteenth century, the commissioner of the United States Patent and Trademark Office penned a memorandum to President McKinley advising him to close the office. His rationale? Everything that could possibly be invented has already been invented. Imagine that: a top-level federal bureaucrat composes an effective suicide note in which he recommends sacking himself and his underlings in the name of reducing redundancy and trimming the budget.

The story was so good that for decades it made the rounds in the media, first by word of mouth, then mouse, with everybody milking it for maximum effect. In May 1987 Ronald Reagan's speechwriters even worked it into an address that the president—a lifelong apostle of small government, except when it came to matters of defense—gave to graduating students in a local high school in Chattanooga, Tennessee. Once the story had received a thumbs-up from the Office of the President of the United States, it picked up even more momentum, gaining in stature every time it was trotted out as a quantum of American history by amateurs and *The Economist* alike.[1]

Except it was nothing of the sort. The public officer who was alleged to have so ill-counseled McKinley was Charles Holland Duell, head of the Patent Office from 1898 to 1901, before he moved to private legal practice and then to the federal bench. The problem is that there is not one shred of evidence that Charles Holland Duell has ever written anything resembling the memorable memo. In spite of a century of endorsements going all the way up to the Oval Office, the story has zero basis in historical fact. It is apocryphal. It is made up. It is, in short, a great piece of American fiction.[2]

Organized politics is, of course, not the only wellspring of enduring political fiction. At a far remove from the White House and the Patent and Trademark Office lies a different kind of political make-believe: American literature that, instead of practicing art for art's sake, practices grassroots democracy. Judging by the number of critical encomiums, to this day the quintessential example of this variety of political fiction is the muckraking classic of American letters, Upton Sinclair's *The Jungle* (1904).[3] Written by an American and published in the United States, it plots a theme that has lost nothing of its socioeconomic resonance: the plight of immigrant slave-wage earners in the turn-of-the-century slaughterhouses of Chicago.

But here problems begin to mount. To begin with, *The Jungle* is far from a typical work of fiction, having been underwritten by Sinclair's seven-week fact-finding mission to the abattoirs of Armour, Swift, and Morris as an investigative reporter for the socialist magazine *The Appeal to Reason.* So fundamental, in fact, was this documentary aesthetic to his conception of art that he made it the cornerstone of his 1903 manifesto "My Cause." Three years later, agonizing over the cuts he had inflicted on *The Jungle,* he even rued that his error lay in thinking that it is fiction that makes life, not the other way round.

Worse still, even though Sinclair's classic is typecast as a political novel, in truth it has precious little to say about politics. This is especially so in the self-censored book version canonized around the world in more than eight hundred editions. Taking the knife to almost all references to socialism and the Socialist Party of America to make *The Jungle* palatable to a commercial press, Sinclair transformed a working-class novel into an exposé of the horrors of the meat-packing industry, testified by his lament that he aimed for the country's heart and by mistake hit it in the stomach.[4]

But if equating "political" with "socially engagé" is contentious from the start, so is equating American political fiction with literature composed by Americans and published in the United States. Alistair Beaton's *A Planet for the President* (2004) is a mother of all satires on the gunboat presidency of George W. Bush and America's fixation with manifest destiny and world hegemony. Between partisan flak and demotic vernacular dished out with the flamboyance of Mark Twain in one of his hang-'em-high moods, this White House burlesque is as American as they come. Yet it was penned by a Scotsman and published outside the United States.

Historically speaking, Beaton is, of course, in some choice company. There is nothing new about American literature being written outside the country or, for that matter, by non-Americans. James Fenimore Cooper's *The Prairie,* Ernest Hemingway's *The Sun Also Rises,* and Francis Scott Fitzgerald's *The Great Gatsby,* to name only three timeless classics, were all written in Paris. Conversely, a towering monument of American letters entitled *De la démocratie en Amérique* was composed by a nineteenth-century French tourist and future deputy in the French Assembly, Alexis de Tocqueville.

When it comes to equating literary fiction with novelistic prose, the mismatch is, if anything, even more pronounced. Rap, the quintessentially American genre of poetic and musical expression, is by its very nature countercultural, oppositional, and—with a regularity that is far from accidental—political. Yet, no matter how much *eliterary* conservatives might close their ears to the greatest explosion of black poetry since the Harlem Renaissance, no one could confuse rap lyrics with narrative prose. For that matter, not even the most successful political fiction in the history of American artertainment falls under the heading of literary prose, having ruled the airwaves with a synergy of image, spoken word, and music.[5]

The West Wing liberally steeped itself in contemporary partisan politics, from the chicken-suits episode ("Freedonia"), borrowed from an Arkansas governor's 1992 election trail, down to the federal government shutdowns during his 1995 standoff against Gingrich-led House. Week after week, its high-octane fusion of political soapbox and soap opera cast its spell on umpteen million viewers during a seven-year, Emmy-studded run.

With Aaron Sorkin, the creative mastermind, deploying a cadre of researchers, writers, and consultants—including Clinton's former press secretary Dee Dee Myers, Gore's speechwriter Eli Attie, Carter's pollster and policy adviser Patrick Caddell, Democratic senatorial aide Lawrence O'Donnell—and, for a spell, Reagan and Bush I's press secretary Marlin Fitzwater and speechwriter Peggy Noonan, Reagan's chief of staff Kenneth Duberstein, Republican pollster Frank Luntz, and chief economic adviser to both Clintons Gene Sperling—this was one political fiction that did its homework.

Truth being stranger than fiction, in addition to making television history, *The West Wing* even made political history by handing a blueprint to Britain's Conservative Party for their vaunted 2006 rebellion-by-stealth against Tony Blair. On "A Good Day," from the show's penultimate season, Democratic lawmakers pretend to clear out from Capitol Hill to hoodwink the Republican Speaker into calling the vote on stem cell research under the impression that it is in the bag. "That's where the idea came from," revealed the ringleader of the British MPs who copycatted this stealth tactics. "It was directly inspired by *The West Wing*."[6]

As in the United Kingdom, so in the United States. New York Democratic representative Carolyn Maloney also adopted a real-life political stratagem from the series, although this time from the inaugural season. In "Enemies," President Bartlet falls back on his executive powers from the 1906 Antiquities Act to proclaim an environmentally sensitive region in Montana a national monument, and as such out of bounds for mining. Maloney's 2000 plea to Clinton to evoke the Antiquities Act to preserve Governor's Island (just south of Manhattan) by declaring two of its forts national monuments had been, as she cheerfully admitted, borrowed lock, stock, and both barrels from *The West Wing*.

But politics also imitates art in more disquieting ways. Just ask comedian Reggie Brown about his experience straight from Frank Capra's *Meet John Doe*. In 2011 Brown was asked to do his shtick as an Obama impersonator at the annual Republican Leadership Conference. Proving himself an equal opportunity offender, he opened with a joke that, with mixed-race parents, the president ought to celebrate only half of the Black History Month, before going after the bigwigs in the GOP: Mitt Romney, Newt Gingrich, and Tim Pawlenty. But he appears to have crossed the line when he segued into a gag about Tea Party stalwart Michele Bachmann. It was at that moment that Reggie Brown met John Doe, as the power to his mic was cut while he was ushered from the stage to swelling music.

Satire or misfire? Anti-constitutional suppression of free speech or merely questionable taste in jokes? You be the judge.

America's Finest News Source

The world is rapidly getting "Ahmadinejadized," if I'm allowed to make a joke.

Mahmoud Ahmadinejad

The central premise behind *American Political Fictions* is that approaching popular political art as an elementary expression of American democracy offers a valuable vantage point for a critical look at America's erroneous conceptions of itself. Traceable to the ubiquitous culture of spin, questions about the level of citizens' participation—or indeed, lack thereof—in the political process are really questions about the degree to which political apathy is rooted in and reflected by the culture in which we all participate.

My historical timeframe is roughly that of the last generation. A little over thirty years ago, a charismatic Republican president promised Americans hope and deliverance from the ravages of "an economic affliction of great proportions."[7] These days the promises of hope and deliverance are spouted by a charismatic Democrat. Other than that, nothing appears to have changed, right down to the ravages of an economic affliction of great proportions. This is why my inquiries into American political fictions and the political structures they describe are not only literary but also *critical*, in the sense of skeptical inquiries into the political fictions prevailing in contemporary public discourse.

Only a year after *The Closing of the American Mind*, a book that argued that higher education has failed democracy, the leading satirist of his generation set out to educate the American public about democracy by means of a "faction" that broke almost all fundamental rules of narration. Eerily, even as *Picture This* (1988) grafted events going back to Thucydides onto the military and social agenda under Reagan, Joseph Heller's novel-as-history reads nowadays as if it had been written under Bush II. A tragic constant or a quirk of history?

My two-pronged answer to this question occupies chapter 1, "A Picture Is Worth a Hundred Thousand Words." An anatomy of Heller's canons of storytelling helps me shed light on the ways in which he splices historical fact with satirical fiction to deliver his most searching sermon and his darkest comedy. And a review of the canons of experiential historiography allows me to assemble a picture of Greek, Dutch, and American varieties of democratic imperialism—a two-and-a-half-thousand-year global theater starring War and Money.

In chapter 2, "No Child Left Behind," I come to grips with the recent publishing sensation from two fundamentalist Christian ministers-turned-writers, Tim LaHaye and Jerry B. Jenkins. Their Bible-spouting sixteen-book cycle *Left Behind* (1995–2007) has by now sold an estimated eighty million copies, crossing over from the evangelical margins to the bookseller's mainstream. Cementing its commercial success, it has been adapted into movies, radio series, graphic novels, music CDs, a board game, and a video game, not to mention spawning spinoffs of its own.

Man is by nature a political animal, aphorized Aristotle more than four hundred years before Christ, and *Left Behind* brings this animal to narrative life for that segment of America that sees Reagan as Messiah and Obama as Antichrist. Ranging from the first to the last novel in the series, my discussion maps their fuzzy logic and *theologic* onto the rise of apocalyptic imagery in American public life. On a broader front, it traces the connection between Bible-inspired nonfiction and the politics of American education from the textbook wars of the 1970s to the No Child Left Behind Act and the recent Texas Textbook Massacre.

In 2004, at the height of one of the lowest spells in US history, Alistair Beaton published his most political novel in a journalistic and novelistic career defined by politics. Touted by *The Independent* as Britain's greatest living satirist, this former reporter and speechwriter for the future British prime minister poured a lifetime of partisan savoir faire into *A Planet for the President* (2004), a critically acclaimed satire about a White House plot to end all plots.

In chapter 3, "A Planet for the Taking," I dissect its nobrow poetics and shoot-from-the-hip politics in a comparative study of the Bush II and

Obama administrations. Fortified by a series of personal interviews with the author, I also interrogate the premises of topical satire in light of its historical mission to roast public figures over bonfires of their vanities. Beaton's political and environmental commitments come together in an end-of-the-world humoresque and a *catharsis* with few parallels in contemporary American literature.

In chapter 4, "(R)hyming (A)merican (P)oetry," I direct the spotlight on rap as a quintessentially American cultural formation and a quintessential form of countercultural expression. Bringing poetics and politics together allows me to document both the artistic ambitions of prophets in the 'hood and, as importantly, the commercial seductiveness of profits in the 'hood, together with the resulting tug-of-war over their politics and identity.

Bestselling or selling out? The question illuminates at once rap's lust for stardom and its commitment to political engagement on all fronts, domestic and foreign. With hip-hop turning forty and middle-aged, with the genre dominated by the tastes of white suburban consumers, and with lyricists still fighting for mainstream recognition of their political and artistic credentials, I take a closer look at why rhyme continues to pay so much and in the name of what values.

Finally, *The West Wing*. In chapter 5, "The Left Wing," I identify the correlative to this epic drama in the groundbreaking televised debate between its two presidential candidates. Recorded live during the show's final 2006 season, it fused reality and scripted TV in an open put-down of real-life electoral debates. Highlighting the democratic role of political art, I highlight the principles of democracy as political power delegated to the public, of the referendum as the basic tool of democracy, and of public education (including public edutainment) as the key to exercising that tool and that power.

My arguments are grounded in my conviction that personal and collective well-being presupposes a genuine people's democracy, not the republican excuse for one enshrined in the United States. To flesh out this point, I triangulate three varieties of democratic theory and praxis. They are exemplified by the initiative system as practiced for roughly a century and a half in Switzerland, for a century in California, and for a little over two years in the European Union in the form of its vaunted CSI: the European Citizens' Initiative.

Throughout I illustrate many of the above points with political cartoons—still another variety of American political fiction—insofar as they graphically illustrate my belief that the matters at hand are often too serious to be tackled without humor. Jokes are a serious business in politics. In the nineteenth century, Thomas Nast proved it once and for all by whipping up public sentiment and public prosecutors against Democratic Party's charismatic Tammany "Boss" Tweed. Drawing and quartering the body politic for our collective edutainment, cartoons remind us that politics and political caricatures both demand a willing suspension of disbelief.[8]

Figure 0.1 Ride 'em Cowboy! ". . . Thomas Nast proved it once and for all by whipping up public sentiment and public prosecutors against Democratic Party's charismatic Tammany "Boss" Tweed . . ."

Credit: Florida Center for Instructional Technology

As if to illustrate the point, in September 2012 satirical magazine *The Onion* stepped right on the line between political fact and fiction. Mock-advertising itself as "America's Finest News Source," *The Onion* excels in posting very funny and very fictive opinion polls. On this occasion, it reported a juicy item: "Rural White Americans [read: rednecks] Prefer the Iron-fisted President of Iran Mahmoud Ahmadinejad to Barack Obama." Taking this political fiction for a fact, the Iranian state media widely reported on the poll among sideswipes at Uncle Sam (soon followed by the North Koreans, who fell for the magazine's "sexiest man alive" piece on Kim Jong-Un).

But, as in the case of Reggie Brown, there is a darker side to all this satirical fun and games. Of late Cartoonists Rights International has issued a public warning that visual satirists are increasingly becoming targets

of escalating harassment and even prison terms dispensed by the growing league of humorless politicians. The fact that the worst of these abuses
take place outside the United States is small comfort. In the wake of the
Snowden affair, no one believes that it can't happen here, whatever "it"
might be.

We're Not Stupid

It's still about the economy . . . and we're not stupid.

Mitt Romney

No book on American political fictions would be complete without a critical look at political oratory, whether in the form of stump pledges, campaign trail rhetoric, policy papers, partisan manifestos, congressional
addresses, or occasionally even State of the Union grandiloquence. All rain
on the electorate with the avowed aim of imparting the truth, the whole
truth, and nothing but the truth. Except that, with an unfunny monotony
of a late-night sitcom, it is only a matter of time before another political
whopper is dragged into the light.

No matter if it is the pledge to close Guantanamo within a year of moving
into the Oval, the "slam dunk" case of nonexistent Iraqi WMDs, the false
truth of "I did not have sexual relations with that woman," the covert sales
of weapons to Iran to finance a war outlawed by Congress, the escalation
of "police action" in Southeast Asia, the fabrication of the Gulf of Tonkin
casus belli, the Bay of Pigs invasion of a sovereign nation, or the hand-over-
the-heart protestations of "I am not a crook." You could fill a big children's
book with the cock-and-bull stories spun by the highest office in the land.

It may be uncommon to approach White House communications as a
literary genre characterized by core thematic (free market, democracy),
stylistic (folksy, anti-intellectual), and rhetorical (religious, apocalyptic)
conventions. But *American Political Fictions* is not a common book of criticism: big on exegesis, small on analysis. Quite the reverse. It puts political
fiction under the microscope to better calibrate the nature of political spin,
which relies on poetic license as much as novelists, lyricists, or scriptwriters do. At the same time, it spares no effort to set the record straight on
Beltway fictions to better calibrate the nature and the accuracy of political
art. In short, it scrutinizes the errors of omission and commission perpetrated by both classes of producers of American political fictions: artists
and con-artists.

Intentionality is the key issue here. Writers spin their yarns to cast light
on the world of politics; politicians spin theirs to keep what they do out

of the public eye. If political art and entertainment deserve to be taken seriously, it is to the extent that they are taken seriously by the Americans who buy them—and arguably buy into them—by the millions. This entails taking the measure of the ideological agenda and rhetorical spin of such artertainment in order to extricate fact from fiction. It also entails taking stock of fairy tales spun by politicians of all stars and stripes in order to throw critical light on the popular art that immerses itself in politics. In short, it entails war on error and disinformation in the spirit of *amicus Americae, sed magis amica veritas.*

A case in point: the fiction of market economy. Even as everyone knows that American politics is all about the economy, stupid, no one is willing to admit that everyone is equally stupid. Flashback to August 1993. Newt Gingrich, the Republican leader in the soon-to-be Republican House, positions himself as the exorcist of Clinton's tax-and-budget package. The tax increase, he thunders, "will kill jobs and lead to a recession, and the recession will force people off of work and onto unemployment and will actually increase the deficit."[9] Washington experts like Phil Gramm, chairman of the Senate Banking Committee and former economics professor, echo his apocalyptic scenario with their own prophecies of gloom and doom:

> We are buying a one way ticket to recession. I want to predict here tonight that if we adopt this bill, the American economy is going to get weaker and not stronger, the deficit four years from today will be higher than it is today and not lower.

What happened was exactly the opposite. Powered by the budget, the economy racked up one hundred and fifteen months of expansion, the longest uninterrupted growth in the United States' history. Over two terms, Clinton's budgets tackled the deficit, whittled unemployment down to 4 percent, cranked out more than twenty-two million jobs—more than under Reagan and Bush I combined—and bred corporate wealth at a blistering pace (the dot-com bubble did not burst for good until 2001).

The truth is that the national economy is so enormous, so complex, and as a consequence so unpredictable that the so-called experts seldom know what they are talking about. That being the case, there is every reason to question the premises behind market economy, all the more so that Demublican administrations make a mockery of it anyway. Every time the economic chips are down, laissez-faire gets exposed for what it is: a bestselling political fiction. Not to look too far, in 2006 the bosses of the Big Three carmakers went to the White House to lobby for protectionist handouts after failing to retool from gas-guzzling minivans and SUVs and falling behind Europeans and Asians in the hybrid and economy market. Late in 2008 their socialist agenda was granted by the supposedly laissez-faire Republican administration.

At about the same time Bush II and Cheney were twisting the rubber arms of congressional lawmakers to earmark seven hundred billion dollars for a shot in the arm of financial institutions badly in need of a fix. In this way the ostensibly market-worshipping White House effected the largest intervention into mortgage companies and banks in the history of the world. Adding insult to injury, even as it saddled taxpayers with paying off these obscene sums for decades to come, it let multimillionaires like Romney and multibillionaires like Buffet skate away with the lowest taxes in the nation (in 2011 the latter publicly blasted Congress for being too billionaire-friendly).

What happened to laissez-faire? To keeping the government out of business? In 2012 stumping Romney effectively disowned the government by disowning redistribution of wealth as an "entirely foreign concept."[10] But even as the feds dole out welfare checks to corporations, free-market competition does not come into its own even at the grassroots level. In the 2012 primaries, Romney was punished by autoworkers in his home state of Michigan for voting against the bailout of the Big Three carmakers. Their protectionist vote was as all-American as the 1937 protectionist action by New York cabbies. Lobbying Tammany to cap the number of taxis, the hacks stopped would-be competitors from entering the market and lowering fares, thus hurting both the paying public and the Depression-era jobless seeking work in the taxi trade.[11]

Giving the lie to the economic pieties on which the country stands, historian Charles Austin Beard even documented the degree to which both the Constitutional Convention and the Constitution itself had been framed by the back-slapping, cigar-chomping, bond-and-stock holding interests of its elite signatories. George Washington, for example, had been both the largest landowner throughout the thirteen colonies and the fiercest lobbyist for federal reparation of war losses, starting with his own. His demands were granted by the same protectionist racket that has been preaching the free-market gospel ever since.

This is not to gainsay that the "invisible hand" of Smith and Ricardo can regulate free-market competition the way they say it should. But it will do so *if and only if* a number of conditions are in place, beginning with the presence of multiple, independent, rational wealth-maximizers who have unhampered access to accurate information about the perfectly transparent market. All must trade on equal terms, with no barriers to impede the stream of new buyers and traders, and none must be powerful enough to skew the market by influencing the price.

When, if ever, did even these basic preconditions hold true in the United States or, for that matter, anywhere in the world? Naturally, next to the ossified economies of the former Soviet Union, the American market *is* free. Like in academia, it is all a matter of degree. But, propaganda aside, the national economy is regularly planned, overseen, intervened in, and bailed out in keeping with the regulatory policies jointly enforced by the feds and the Fed.

Yet, just like the fiction of the closing of the Patent and Trademark Office, the fiction of the self-regulating market gains in stature each time it is mouthed by politicians or their economic entourage, irrespective of whether they have actually read Adam Smith or not. Those who do are wont to discover that, even as he extolled the aggregated wisdom of the marketplace, the Scottish economist insisted that essential public good required a strong government, a fact conveniently ignored by neoliberal (in today's parlance, neoconservative) free-market ideologues.[12]

The taxpayers are, of course, reluctant to pass judgment on the economists, because they feel—and are made to feel—that they are not smart enough to wrap their heads around the math and the jargon. As a result, when a microphone is shoved under their noses, John and Jane Doe fall back on soundbites about the invisible hand or about less government in business and more business in government. Meanwhile, deregulation of banking and financial markets paves the way for meltdowns that regularly wipe out trillions of dollars in shareholder value and reveal palliatives about free market for what they are: great American fictions.

Yertle the Turtle

> Every gang every crew every set (that's political)
> Every bang every truce ever set (that's political)
> Every claim of the truth ever said (that's political)
> You can't escape the physical everything's political.

dead prez

Blog after blog, post after post, citizens' forums paint politicians as a miracle of evolution. Humanlike on the outside, they are all shellfish on the inside—no brain, no guts, no spine. Also like shellfish, they evince little evidence of being concerned with abstract notions such as probity and rectitude, in defiance of the public's interest in candidates' reputation for both.[13] No wonder that George Carlin used to get so many hoots out of his Political Calculus 101: if honesty is the best policy, by elimination dishonesty must rank a respectable second-best.

To be fair, a share of the blame belongs to the public. Crowds expect to be flattered, and candidates are only too eager to oblige. Many citizens realize deep down that they are listening to generic pablum that politicians

THE GOVERNMENT'S IDEA OF PROBITY

Figure 0.2 **The Government's Idea of Probity** ". . . Like shellfish, they evince little evidence of being concerned with abstract notions such as probity and rectitude . . ."
Credit: Grea

spout off to all assemblies and individuals they encounter. But apparently it is still gratifying to have them go to all this trouble to pretend they care. Blame the politicians for lying through their teeth; blame the public for showing up to listen.

Flouting the frequently invoked, if seldom examined, opinion that political artertainment makes for bad art and even worse entertainment, some artists have long been meting out poetic justice to the calculated inexactitudes and outright dishonesties of the bipartisan spin machine known as the government. In the very year he penned his political classic *Animal Farm*, George Orwell entreated all to do just that, with the reminder that the attitude "that art should have nothing to do with politics is itself a political attitude."[14]

Since then, his call to arms has been echoed by intellectuals of all stripes, beginning with dead prez—a New York rap duo of stic.man and M-1—who propagated it with an intensity more typical of cultural studies departments, where it has long been taken for granted that "all texts are ultimately political."[15] Other academics have gone so far as to proclaim that just because "judgments about quality are being made" in television programming, this makes them "invariably political." This urge to politicize, politicize, politicize has spread even to journalism, where, half a century after Orwell, J. Herbert Altschull restated in *Agents of Power*, "To take sides for a certain political point of view is to be clearly political."

All this is very true—except that equating politics with a political attitude opens the door to equating it with practically anything under the sun. A textbook example of how watered down the "P word" has become in contemporary literary culture comes from that august tastemaker *The Times Literary Supplement*. Not long ago it carried a review of a new collection of stories by an American writer, Lorrie Moore. Wasting no time to fire the Big Bertha, on page one the reviewer pronounced the leading story in the collection "overtly political."[16]

To the unsuspecting reader, them fighting words might summon a vision of America's elected heavyweights, partisan kingpins, or legislative playmakers hashing out their agenda in the service or disservice of the nation. Not so. As the review makes clear, the story has actually zero to say about the political process as practiced by individuals whose job titles attest to their involvement in politics, be they politicians, Hill pundits, PAC strategists, or political scientists. What makes it overtly political, then? The gloss is nothing short of banal: it concerns itself with racial, social, and economic iniquities. So does, of course, "Thidwick the Big-Hearted Moose" and "Yertle the Turtle," not to mention almost any work of literary fiction. It may come as a surprise that Dr. Seuss wrote overtly political fiction, but then *ex falso quodlibet*.[17]

Analogous examples of critics pouring water into political wineskins are too many to enumerate. For every politically hard-nosed writer like Gore Vidal, there are dozens of literary exegetes ready to slap the label on almost any kind of cultural artifact in the name of radicalizing academic discourse and, presumably, making it less irrelevant to society at large. Unfortunately, as more and more of contemporary culture undergoes this kind of facelift—these days it is fashionable to discourse on the politics of ecocritical mythography, transgender erotica, or even consumer product advertising—the term loses any meaning whatsoever.

The flip side of this process is the marginalization of literary and cultural studies that actually have something to say about politics. This, in turn, feeds back into mainstream American culture where feel-good films such as the 2008 biopic *Che* are mistaken for political art. In reality, in making a biography of a fanatical political revolutionary, Soderbergh and his scriptwriter succeeded in turning Che's memoirs into a near-impossibility: a four-hour film almost entirely devoid of politics.[18]

On an even larger scale, the attenuation of politics in today's culture and cultural criticism plays right into the hands of social engineers who would keep politics away from the public eye and the public away from politics. To counter this, much as I did in *Ars Americana, Ars Politica* (2010) and *American Utopia and Social Engineering* (2011), I revert to the core meaning of "political" in examining some of the best and worst examples of political fiction in today's culture.

Dividing my attention between the bestsellers that take aim at American politics and their political targets, I broaden the meaning of "American" by paying tribute to one of the funniest and darkest American satires to appear both in and out of the United States. I retool the meaning of "political" by pushing into partisan—both left- and rightwing—territory in pursuit of popular art that flies its party colors with unrepentant pride and prejudice. And I forge a more comprehensive notion of "fiction" by branching out into literary faction, lyrical poetry, and TV drama, to say nothing of the make-believe that streams out of the White House and the Hill in the guise of policy.

My goals transcend, of course, merely rewriting the book on American political fiction. By elucidating the ideological underpinnings, cultural manifestations, and democratic essence of contemporary political art, I hope to forge a more comprehensive picture of the partisan culture on which such art feeds. By studying political make-believe in all of its shapes and hues, I hope to forge a more comprehensive picture of contemporary American culture and perhaps even America itself.

As with all interdisciplinary ventures, there are inherent hazards. Upon finishing *American Political Fictions*, some literary scholars may conclude that there is more politics and political history here than they bargained for, even as historians and political scientists may object that there is too little. Be that as it may, I am encouraged in my undertaking by finding an ally in a most unlikely place: the Pentagon. This is because, odd as it sounds, of late the US military establishment has been commanding soldiers on active duty, war vets, officials at the Department of Defense, and even sitting politicians to embrace political art.

Back in 2009 London theaters put on a twelve-play cycle called *The Great Game: Afghanistan,* which dramatized sundry periods of the blood-soaked history of Western military interventions. In 2011, at the order of the Pentagon brass, the entire dodecalogue was restaged in Washington, DC, in a belated effort to teach Americans something about the country they had been occupying longer than the Soviets had during the 1980s. "There is an assumption," conceded the Defense Department spokesman in defense of this new *militerary* policy, "that the arts and our men and women in uniform are from different planets. It's not the case."[19] Art arm in arm with the arty? Politics does make strange bedfellows.

Who's Who in Washington

See, in my line of work you got to keep repeating things over and over and over again for the truth to sink in, to kind of catapult the propaganda.

George Walker Bush

Being taken seriously by five-star generals is far from the only reason for taking popular culture seriously. Read, listened to, and watched by millions of potential voters, bestsellers that programmatically immerse themselves in politics ought to have a measurable impact on public opinion in the country. The nature, efficacy, and most of all accuracy of such mass political education should be of profound importance not just to political analysts, but to literary and cultural ones as well.

Examples of literary fictions turning real lives around are as many as one cares to enumerate, beginning with Sinclair's *The Jungle*. That said, not many can match the career of the novel that, in the apocryphal words of that illustrious literary critic Abraham Lincoln, started the Civil War. Derided by the highbrows for its mawkishness, *Uncle Tom's Cabin* cashed out abolitionist politics in common emotional currency to more effectively (and affectively) shape public opinion. And shape it it did, snapped up by the end of the first week by no less than ten thousand readers and by the end of 1852 by three hundred thousand—all this in a nation of barely thirty million. Outselling literary rivals, such as Caroline Lee Hentz's *Plantern's Northern Bride*, which depicted slavery as a just social order, it left their political points in the dust.

The same political-and-popular formula that made *Uncle Tom's Cabin* the blockbuster of the nineteenth century reprises its winning ways in the twenty-first. From the rightwing *Left Behind* to the leftwing *The West Wing*, today's bestsellers freely mix partisan commitment and mass-market penetration. In the process, they turn liberals such as Michael Moore into political superstars, Democrats such as the former *SNL* comedian Al Franken into US senators, and Republicans such as Stephen Colbert into satirical lightning rods for super-PACs and other quirks of America's electoral campaigns.

Be that as it may, some academics remain reluctant to take seriously the contemporary crop of popular artists with a cause. Indeed, these days one has to turn to political scientists for substantive discussions of politics in mass culture—chiefly, it appears, Hollywood cinema and network television.[20] Is it because, even as popular writers grind their political axes, they cheerfully aim to entertain as much as to elevate? Is it because their political thrusts and rhetorical feints are contrived to stir emotion as much as reflection? Is it because, with sophisticated arguments rubbing elbows with argumentative sophistry, much like politicians themselves, they turn today's political culture into a checkerboard of fact and fiction?

Whatever the reasons, instead of being applauded for combating political apathy, popular creators routinely come under fire for allegedly pandering to the lowest cultural denominator. Granted, not all paperbacks aspire to make aesthetic and political waves. But counterexamples to the stereotype are as easy to find as a controlled substance in a congressman's pocket. Steve Alten's *The Shell Game* (2008) is only one of a crop of contemporary pulp fictions to sport a bibliography and copious annotations designed to educate readers about which parts of the story are *non*fiction.

The same mélange of nobrow poetics and politics drives *The Race*, one of the publishing novae of the last decade. Listing the political insiders consulted for the book, the author, a former SEC's liaison to the Watergate special prosecutor, compiles a virtual *Who's Who in Washington*: Newt Gingrich, John McCain, Governor Mark Sanford, Secretary of State James Baker, Congresswoman Stephanie Tubbs Jones, and Congressman James Clayburn, not to mention rows upon rows of strategists, spin-sters, consultants, pundits, journalists, academics, scientists, and military officers.

Praised both by Bill Clinton and by the conservative *Spectator*, *The Race* highlights a crucial point about popular culture as an instrument of mass political education. Even as organized politics is increasingly spurned by the public as the enclave of professional manipulators and power-greedy opportunists, political entertainment and edutainment draws audiences in the tens of millions. In the process it begins to take over several key roles traditionally played by political campaigners and the public media: those of information bearers, partisan critics, grassroots educators, and mobilizers of public opinion—in short, the roles of watchdogs and guardians of democracy.

And just in time, it seems. After all, reflecting the death of the humanities in general, some American schoolchildren are no longer required by their curricula "to recall any specific event or person in history."[21] Moreover, it is the mythopoeic version of history that students are not expected to recall, not the politically correct (and, at the same time, politically incorrect) one preserved, for one, in the voluminous correspondence between John Adams and Thomas Jefferson. Away from the public eye, the Founding Fathers take these truths to be self-evident that, as natural aristocrats, they are better suited to wield political power than other men. Or so they say.

Not surprisingly, to balance the sometimes heavy political superstructure, popular creators always look for ways to lighten the ballast and quicken the pace. Political discourse laced with socioeconomic history is, after all, hardly a recipe for box-office success. All too frequently, art engagé groans under the weight of gravitas, ending up preaching to academics while the congregation wanders off in search of lite entertainment. Realizing this, in a quintessential nobrow fashion, the writers whose works lie at the heart of *American Political Fictions* court the paying public with furious politics and fast rhetoric.[22]

Bristling with economic statistics and partisan polemics, they challenge the stereotype of mindless blockbusters. Grafting political content onto popular entertainment, they exemplify the power of engagé art that resonates with mass audiences. Today, when politics-as-usual has alienated so much of the American electorate, it is often popular artists who stoke public interest in matters of government. Reaching tens of millions of readers, viewers, and listeners, they redefine not just the mass cultural but also the mass political frontlines of America today, proving that in some cases, at least, there is little virtue in dividing culture into art and bestsellers.

Even as the works themselves are always my primary focus, in every case I spare no effort to situate their content in context. Inevitably, seeking to evaluate both how this content is communicated in artistic terms and to what partisan ends, there may be a price to pay in terms of bibliographical nuance. My hope is only that the gains outweigh the losses and that what may be occasionally forsaken in particulars is recouped in perspective and clarity. Today, among mounting disciplinary divisions and, consequently, limited visions, the need for a broader perspective on American populist art and elitist politics is greater than ever.

A Picture Is Worth a Hundred Thousand Words

Joseph Heller, *Picture This*

Keffiyeh in the Knesset

History is bunk, says Henry Ford, the American industrial genius, who knew almost none.

Joseph Heller, Picture This

In 1961 a first novel by a then unknown writer won the National Book Award, edging out another first novel by a then unknown writer. But while few readers today remember the winner, Walker Percy's existential novel *Moviegoer*, with every year the runner-up looms bigger than ever. With tens of millions copies sold in every corner of the world, with translations ranging from Chinese to Finnish, *Catch-22* has even wormed itself into everyday language, boasting entries in English dictionaries from *Webster's* to the *OED*.

A modern classic and a staple of college literary curricula, it is also—in spite of its pacifist tenor—required reading at the US Air Force Academy, which in 1986 even sponsored a symposium to mark the quarter-centenary of the book's release. This last accolade sounds less peculiar in the light of the little-known fact that, for the 1970 film adaptation, Hollywood assembled not only a cast fronted by Alan Arkin, Orson Welles, Martin Sheen, Martin Balsam, John Voight, and Bob Newhart, but also the twelfth largest bomber fleet in the world.

Much of this enduring success can be attributed to Heller's reader-friendly aesthetics: acerbic humour, immaculate and complex plotting, pleiades of oddball characters, and an almost rapperlike countercultural iconoclasm. But, at the end of the day, the reasons for its abiding place in the twentieth-century zeitgeist have more to do with history than with literature. Ostensibly set during the Second World War, *Catch-22* came to epitomize so much of the decade it ushered in because it so uncannily presaged the mindset of the Vietnam War. Little wonder that, while the Kennedy, Johnson, and Nixon administrations waged war to make peace, pacified Vietnamese villages in order to save them, debased language into a public relations spin-cycle, and turned the Cold War into a *comedie bouffon*, Americans turned en masse to their up-and-coming master of black comedy.

More than a decade later, amid the chaos of Nixon's impeachment and resignation, Christopher Lehmann-Haupt reviewed another book of Heller's for *The New York Times*, predicting that *Something Happened* would be to the 1970s what *Catch-22* was to the 1960s: rooted in history, visionary about the future. Were he writing at the end of the 1980s, he could have said the same things about *Picture This*, a historical tour de farce written after eight years of Reagan that reads today as if it had been written after eight years of Bush II. This prophetic intimation of the future past is one compelling reason to revisit this extraordinary novel from the writer who passed away in 1999, after completing his farewell *Portrait of an Artist, as an Old Man*.

In *Picture This* Heller breezes through two and a half millennia of history, politics, economics, and art to deliver his most searching sermon and his darkest satire. Exhuming long stretches of Western history, ancient and modern, time and time again he fast-forwards to his Reagan-era present, splicing history and literature into a novel type of narrative: *historature*. Naturally, the cynic in him has few illusions about the efficacy of art—or, for that matter, history—against ignorance, apathy, or worst of all, television. If there was never another novel written, he shrugged in a 1971 interview, "no one would care. But if there was no more television, everyone would go crazy in two days."[1]

In *Picture This* his cynicism is equally corrosive. You will learn nothing from history that can be applied, he tells his readers, so don't kid yourself into thinking you can. Yet the artist in him belies the cynic. Having conceded previously that he was no good at writing nonfiction, he yokes his genius for the surreal to the retelling of sober fact. Having confided elsewhere that the easiest part of writing for him was the dialogue, he now crafts a novel-as-history—or history-as-a-novel—with scarcely any dialogue at all. Having traded ink for acid, he takes the artistic risk of his career by composing a *summa historiae* that stands out from his oeuvre like a keffiyeh in the Knesset.

In the autumn of his career, like the elder, more vitriolic Twain, Heller takes on a subject of epic proportions: the American empire. On a narrative canvas befitting his ambitions in size, he clothes Periclean Athens and the seventeenth-century Dutch Republic in military fatigues in order to juxtapose their spectacular rises and even more spectacular falls with the state of the American union. He is, to be sure, too canny a historian to shut his eyes to the differences among the three superpowers. But the stirring consonance of his comparisons suggests that the differences may be only superficial, and the analogies profound. Shuttling back and forth between the internecine wars on the Peloponnesus and the colonial heyday of the Dutch East India Company, *Picture This* lives up to its author's catchphrase of being a book about money and war. Recto and verso of the same political coin, these twin engines of history impose an almost classical unity of theme on what some critics panned as a scattershot (not to say scatterbrain) book.

Is Heller a prophet? Or is it just that we don't care to learn from history? In the year that *Picture This* came out, the author himself favored the latter alternative: "No one can change history, but it keeps on repeating."[2] Indeed, the pity and pathos that permeate the book arise from his focus on the historical invariants in human affairs, particularly when it comes to politics, war, and money. Barring military technology and the means of economic production, precious little, after all, has changed since the Golden Ages of the Greek and Dutch republics.

"I went back to ancient Greece because I was interested in writing about American life and Western civilization," explained Heller in an interview with Bill Moyers. "In ancient Greece I found striking—and grim— parallels."[3] And if his literary thesis is right—if the historically dissimilar superstructures are driven by the same political and military engine— *Picture This* goes a long way to explaining why Americans regularly find themselves at war with countries many could not even place on the map.

The Rise of the Dutch Republic

The bust of Homer that Aristotle is shown contemplating is not of Homer. The man is not Aristotle.

Joseph Heller, Picture This

Wearing the chiton of Cassandra under the burgemeester's finery, Heller tops both with a jester's cap and proceeds to dismember three different bodies politic that, as he is at pains to portray, have fallen prey to imperial hubris. That is why behind his satirical *récit* of the history of the ancient Greek imperial democracy and the Dutch corporate regime—peppered with his puckish, other times scathing, ad libs—always lurk the decades that belonged to John F. Kennedy, Lyndon B. Johnson, Richard M. Nixon, Gerald Ford, Jimmy Carter, and Ronald Reagan.

Stitching these disparate epochs and geographical locations is the painting depicting one of the world's greatest philosophers, executed by one of the world's greatest painters, purchased in 1961 by one of the greatest American museums for then the greatest sum of money ever spent on a work of visual art. The end result is a narrative structure perfected already in *Catch-22*: time-warped chronology that mixes and remixes cyclically amplified flashbacks and flashforwards to a handful of central events, the book's structural and thematic leitmotifs.

One of these is the life and death of Socrates: soldier, cynic, philosopher, and gadfly on the Hellenic body politic. Another is the destructive and, as Heller goes to extraordinary lengths to document, self-destructive succession of wars between Athens and Sparta. Finally, there is the genesis in 1653 of the painting *Aristotle Contemplating the Bust of Homer* by Rembrandt van Rijn and its subsequent vagaries on the international art scene.

Even without Heller's sardonic asides, it does not take a degree in history to recognize in the sundry episodes from the lives of the Greek and Dutch empires the archetypes of the Cold War, the Vietnam War, the conservative revolution under Reagan, and—uncannily—the neoconservative revolution under Bush II. Projected onto a canvas at once panoramic and intimate, the fates of the three empires are catalysts for the author's ruminations on the nature of democracy, war, law, art, money, and not least, human nature.

Heller's chronological jump-cuts underscore the common fate of republics that come down with an acute case of manifest destiny. The historical fact that in 1609 Henry Hudson seized a prime chunk of real estate on North America's eastern seaboard in the name of the Netherlands only tickles his sardonic bone. So does the fact that mercantile Holland was in its time as fearsome a commercial power as is the United States today. And that, enshrined as the democratic torchbearers of the Western civilization, both Athens and America got there on the backs of political demagoguery, domestic slavery, and overseas militarism.

Heller takes no prisoners when savaging the disparities between accepted historical pieties and the actual historical circumstances. So overriding, in fact, is his allegiance to history that some reviewers were scratching their heads over whether Heller's novel was a novel at all, as opposed to "a history text in which the pages have been scrambled."[4] In the face of a syncretic satire like *Picture This,* one can, of course, debate where solid fact ends and poetic licence begins. But there is no debating that what holds its thirty-seven chapters together is not a conventional hero or storyline, but a sense—and the senselessness—of history.

Heller cribs from a staggering number of sources, from Plato's *Apology*, *Laws*, *Republic*, *Seventh Epistle*, and *Symposium* and Aristotle's *Poetics*, *Metaphysics*, and *Ethics*, to Xenophon's *Hellenica*, Diogenes Leartius's *Lives of Eminent Philosophers*, and Plutarch's *Parallel Lives*—not to mention Hesiod, Aristophanes, Aeschines, Homer, and who knows who else. As if that were not enough, he lifts entire sections almost verbatim from Thucydides's *History of the Peloponnesian War*, particularly on the bloodbath of the city of Corcyra, the deliberations leading to the massacre of the island of Melos, and the calamitous campaign of Athens against Syracuse.

His portrait of Rembrandt and his times, on the other hand, owes at least as much to Gary Schwartz's *Rembrandt: His Life, His Paintings*, Paul Zumthor's *Daily Life in Rembrandt's Holland*, Simon Schama's *The Embarrassment of Riches*, and John Motley's more than a century old yet still unsurpassed treatise *The Rise of the Dutch Republic*. Little wonder that in the face of this cornucopia, some literary critics threw up their hands in despair, sounding for all the world like Mordecai Richler when he grouched that Richard Condon's political satires were not so much to be reviewed as counter-researched.

True enough, *Picture This* flouts every rule taught in creative writing classes. Piling fact upon fact and trivia upon trivia, it wastes no opportunity to digress into—among a myriad others—thumbnail biographies of Alexander the Great, William of Orange, Philip II, or Spinoza among disquisitions on curing herring, the invention of the telescope, and the Dutch shipbuilding industry, not to mention Rembrandt's birthweight, schooling, marital and extramarital life, and even such crumbs of art history as the fact that the corpse in Rembrandt's *The Anatomy Lesson of Dr. Nicolaes Tulp* was that of a man hanged for stealing a coat.

At first blush all this may seem just a slapdash inventory of historical ins and outs, no more than narrative fodder for the author's irrepressible rhetorical flourishes and ironic editorializing. Heller's ruminations on his craft, however, offer good reasons to believe that this free-associative exterior hides a studious design. "I tried to avoid . . . the conventional structure of the novel," emphasized the author of *Catch-22*. Seemingly unstructured and repetitive, all the incidents were meticulously plotted "to give the appearance of a formless novel."[5]

This is not to deny that the book elevates redundancy, be it in the form of repetition, refrain, periphrasis, or amplification, to the status of a major structural tenet. Stylistically, however, like old-school rap it practices minimalist aesthetics. Staccato sentences are frequently chiseled down to a single line and paragraphs dramatically lineated to highlight, or just give breathing room to, a relentless barrage of history at its most absurd.

Look at this embarrassment of riches through one eye, and you will see what Heller himself dubbed tongue-in-cheek as excessive excess.[6] Look through the other, and you will discern exquisite dramatic counterpoint, tragicomic fusion, and ontological syncretism from a writer of superlative literary credentials: Ivy League MA in literature, Fulbright and Christensen scholarships at Oxford, and Distinguished Professorship of English at the City College of New York. To be sure, no one would ever accuse *Picture This* of being a swashbuckling adventure à la Alexandre Dumas *père*. But neither is it tedious and static, as at least one critic railed in a fit of pique at its unorthodox design.

Heller is never happier than when serving history with a twist, typically by resorting to an ironic conceit, anachronistic paraphrase, or *reductio ad absurdum*. His pages are peppered with politically incongruous one-liners, such as, "One of the effects of capitalism is communism" (89). At the opposite end of the scale, he luxuriates in complex dramatic scenes that illustrate how, compelled by strategic, political, or just economic expediency, imperial history then and now looks like one gigantic catch-22. His emotional palette, too, swings from solemn, as during the kangaroo trial of Socrates, to surreal, as when aged Rembrandt muses on the payoffs of imitating paintings by his apprentices which, although imitations of his own, are deemed by the paying public to be more Rembrandt-like.

MiniTrue

> The Greek physician and writer Galen, living in Rome in the second century after Christ, reports that libraries there were already paying high prices for manuscripts by illustrious figures from the past, creating a market with rich rewards for spurious documents by skillful forgers. The document in which Galen says this may be spurious.
>
> *Joseph Heller, Picture This*

Even as Nabokov denigrated the mingling of fiction and fact as mangling of both art and truth, Heller could not care less. His title is the best case in point. A double entendre, it plays on Rembrandt's historical picture and on our capacity to picture things that are not—the prerogative of fiction. Rembrandt's painting of Aristotle contemplating the bust of Homer is, of course, real enough, but since no one has any idea what the historical Aristotle looked like, the artist had to invent his likeness, much like that of Homer, of whom nothing is known except his name.

As for the one and only figure in *Picture This* who approaches the stature of a hero, although there exist historical accounts of him from Plato himself, the latter met Socrates only briefly, only as a young man, and only when the sage was already past sixty. To conclude that the younger philosopher's picture of the older one might be a composite of fact and fiction would be a truism. The ontological distinction between fiction and nonfiction indeed obscures the fact that novelists and historians alike employ the gamut of rhetorical and stylistic devices to convert readers to their point of view. To muddy the ontological waters even further, the historical roots of faction go back more than two thousand years prior to the New Journalism of Tom Wolfe and the nonfiction novels of Truman Capote.

One of its most renowned practitioners was, in fact, none other than Heller's narrative model from antiquity, Thucydides. Availing himself of what today we might call ethnographic fieldwork, including personal interviews with the historical figures of whom he wrote, the Greek historian regularly indulged in all manner of rhetorical and satirical tropes to relay the cruelty and senselessness of wars between Mediterranean superpowers. Varying in tone between magisterial and personal, like the author of *Picture This*, Thucydides also did not shrink from judging the merits of historical personages and events.

Taking issue with any number of inherited clichés, he did not spare even the Trojan War, the darling of ancient chroniclers that, he insisted, "falls short of its fame and the prevailing traditions to which the poets have given authority."[7] Nor did he shy away from putting words in people's mouths, albeit strictly in accordance with their historical background and personality. "My habit," he conceded, "has been to make speakers say what was in my opinion demanded by the occasion, of course adhering as closely as possible to the general sense of what they really said."

A narrative historian of power politics who employed dramatic attribution to make his themes—be it war, government, or the state of the empire—more salient, Thucydides may differ from Heller in emphasis, but hardly in substance. The latter's Aristotle, for example, seems to have all the fun in the world when he harnesses the Socratic method, as described to us by Plato himself, to poke holes in the latter's blueprint for a just government in a textbook example of historical attribution:

> "In my virtuous communist republic, it will be the role of the individuals to do the bidding of the state."
>
> "And if people don't agree?"
>
> "They will be oppressed, for the good of the state. The Guardians will make them."
>
> "Who will make the Guardians obey?" inquired Aristotle. "Where is the stronger force to compel them?"
>
> "What difference does it make?" said Plato, vexed. "What people do in this world is of no consequence."
>
> "Then why are you bothering? Why are we talking? Why did you write your *Republic*?" (281)

It is, of course, ironic that the very empires that permitted Thucydides and Heller to crucify them in writing, afforded them so much to crucify. In his classic of political philosophy, *The City and Man* (1963), Leo Strauss even remarked on the fact that Thucydides's philippics were curiously tolerated by the authorities, most probably to provide a social vent that would leave their imperial ambitions intact. More contemporarily, novelist and historian Tom Holt appended a comic chorus to this thesis in his twin satires of the Periclean city-state, *Goatsong* (1989) and *The Walled Orchard* (1990).

To his credit, Heller takes full account of this irony by turning the tables on himself. Writing history, writing about history, or writing about writing about history perforce entails making choices not only about causality, but equally about context. Even the most conscientious chronicler must, after all, select and collate his data and at times make conjectures about them, raising the question of what stays on the cutting-room floor. Be that as it may, Heller's stance never wavers: much as we need history, we need truth even more.

Had he lived to our millenium, he would have been dismayed to learn how right he was, and how his Hellenic, Dutch, and American case studies are mirrored around the world. The French government, for example, proved itself an apt pupil of the White House, which had fought the entire Vietnam War without a declaration of war, calling it a "police action" instead. Only in 1999 did the Palais de l'Élysée publicly acknowledge that its brutal eight-year campaign to suppress Algerian independence *was* a war rather than, as it had previously maintained, an operation to maintain order.

But echoes of the Orwellian MiniTrue do not stop there. In 2005, to howls of derision from former colonies seconded by historians abroad and at home, the French parliament passed a vote to uphold a law that had for decades ordained the history textbooks to drum up the benevolent side of the country's colonial rule. Eventually, the brouhaha reached such a crescendo that the offensive statute was abrogated, but the moral is not difficult to extract: new and improved history is only a vote away.

The French Republic is not alone in taking such procrustean liberties with history. There is no need, either, to roll call the universally reviled monsters from twentieth-century history, from Hitler to Stalin, Mao, Pol Pot, or al-Bashir. In *The Clash Within* (2007) Martha Nussbaum made a compelling case for how the democratically elected Hindu Right—the BJP (Bharatiya Janata Party) and its allies—is busy rewriting big chunks of Indian history with the goal of elevating Hindus at the expense of Muslims.

In Taiwan, for reasons rooted in their struggle for international acceptance as a sovereign democracy, the authorities have of late excised the name of Chiang Kai-shek from streets and even the national airport. Chechen militias used to be hailed in US political circles as freedom fighters before becoming rebranded as terrorists when Bush II needed Russian compliance in the Security Council for his wars in Asia. In 2007 violent protests erupted in Okinawa against Japanese orders to doctor high school history books that teach how the World War II Japanese army ordered Okinawans to kill themselves, rather than surrender.

In 2012 the Afghani education ministry endorsed a new history curriculum that wipes out nearly four decades of the country's war-ravaged past. Not a word about the bloody coups of the 1970s, the Soviet occupation of the 1980s, or the subsequent Moscow-installed puppet regimes in Kabul. Not much more on the merciless civil war between the mujahideen factions of the 1990s, the rise of the tyrannical Taliban, and the illegitimate US and NATO suzerainty throughout the 2000s and 2010s. In 2013 North Korean state media removed almost their entire online archive following the execution of a top politician who had fallen out of favor with the regime headed by his nephew, the ruling dictator Kim Jong-un. Out of sight, out of mind. Samuel Butler was right: even if God cannot alter the past, historians can.

Imperial Democracy

> In the ancient Athens of the past, only the rich had the right to hold public office. Now every male citizen had that right, but the poor, of course, could not afford to, and power remained where it had always been, with the noble and the wealthy, who were often the same. Now citizens of Athens were free to choose the oligarchs who would rule them.
>
> *Joseph Heller, Picture This*

In *Poetics* Aristotle professed poetry to be a more noble enterprise than history, inasmuch as poetry tends to express universal truths, whereas history only the particular. *Picture This*, whose working title was *Poetics*, adopts an even better known dictum of Aristotle's for an epigram: "Tragedy is an imitation of an action." Rather than mimetically, however, it interprets Aristotle's words historically. Tragic, indeed, are the cycles of political actions that bore no fruit in the past and which, by force of imitation, are foredoomed to sterility in the future present. The most poignant moments in Heller's novel owe much, in fact, to the blend of Olympian detachment and intense compassion with which he surveys the fates of individuals in societies that, notwithstanding invocations of democracy and liberty, seldom afford opportunity to practice them.

Ancient Athens may be venerated today as the premier democratic state, and democracy itself as its premier legacy, but the lion's share of commentary from antiquity is, in fact, highly critical of both. Plato himself warns that, being principally accountable to the untutored and impulsive multitude, democracy opens itself to bigotry and ignorance. Heller's Socrates is entirely faithful to his historical archetype when he rails against the premise that democracy necessarily brings unity, coherence, contentment, good government, intelligence, equality, fairness, justice, honesty, peace, or even political freedom. As if to illustrate the truth of his words, Socrates was sentenced to death for political unorthodoxy by the Athenian democrats.

Two and a half thousand years of subsequent history have done nothing to disprove Winston Churchill's contention that democracy is indeed the worst form of government, except for all those other forms that have been tried from time to time. Even at best, modern democracies often condemn their subjects to unhappy mediocrity. At worst, they are no more than politically correct figleaves sustained by internal and external (propagandist and paramilitary) coercion. Plato was correct to caution that the emotional—which is to say antirational—propensities of the *demos* can be exploited all too easily. Naked facts and rational arguments seldom prove equal to the manicured iconography and disinformation of public-relations spinners in the employ of democratically elected autocrats.

Yet the philosopher passed in silence over the fact that propaganda may be a necessary evil in political life, if only because, more than judicious suasion, it is capable of instilling emotional resonance.[8] Injected into national mythology, it is capable of offering solace, instilling psychological cohesion, and even eliciting self-sacrifice in times of trouble. This is why reformist campaigns that attempt to refocus political debates from personalities to issues always face an uphill battle. This is why the machinery of political management is geared not toward the truth but toward the candidate. This is why political fairy tales, so long as they are emotionally satisfying, oftentimes prevail over historical facts.

Historically, after all, democracy was a child of realpolitik. In the fourth century BC, with the Ionian and Aegean regions balkanized into hundreds of city-states ruled by oligarchies or monarchies, Pericles's *demokratia*, or people's power, put an end to the privileges of the Areopagus, transferred the legislative authority to the Assembly, and enfranchised every adult male citizen to participate in public affairs. Yet from the start, participation in democratic self-rule was strictly limited. Women, slaves, and foreign-born Athenians were excluded outright, at a stroke shrinking a city-state of under two hundred thousand to no more than thirty thousand. Furthermore, even as most public officials and jurymen were indeed selected by lot, the impecunious could ill afford to hold office, because they needed to make a living.

The principle of "power to the people" translated, in practice, into "power to a thousand powerful men at the top." Not much has changed since that time, either. From Adams to Jefferson, the founding generation of American nation-builders, for example, also took it for granted that political leaders of the new state would be harvested from the upper rungs of the colonial ladder. Remixing Plato's myth of a virtuous tyrant in neo-classicist rhetoric, they thought they would be men like themselves: well-born, well-bred, and well-to-do, all of which would somehow ensure that their service would be virtuous.

With history as a witness, virtue in American politics has been in rather conspicuous abeyance, routinely shortchanging the public with gamesman-ship in lieu of statesmanship. The mythos of high morals in high office was debunked already by Plutarch, who went as far as to aphorize in *Parallel Lives* that people would be far happier if kings were philosophers and phi-losophers kings. The Athenian democracy may have produced the most delicious honey, he conceded in his biography of Dion—student of Plato and an unvirtuous tyrant of Syracuse—but also the most deadly hemlock.

Periclean Athens has bequeathed us the ideal of a democratic polity, and the United States has carried this progressive, egalitarian torch for-ward. But, in an irony that plays straight into Heller's hands, modern his-tory records that, just like America in its time, Athens founded its ideals on "cruel and imperial domination, the slaughter and enslavement of its wartime opponents, the occasional genocide of another *polis*, not to men-tion the ownership of tens of thousands of domestic and industrial slaves."[9]

How easily one can fall afoul of American-style liberty is exemplified by the experience of arguably its greatest scientist. In February 1950, fore-shadowing by a decade Eisenhower's own warning to the nation, Albert Einstein went on television to condemn the de facto military government within the American government. Much like *Picture This*, his portrait of the United States has lost nothing of its sting today:

> Concentration of tremendous financial power in the hands of the military, militarization of the youth, close supervision of the loyalty of the citizens, in particular, of the civil servants by a police force growing more conspicuous every day. Intimidation of people of independent political thinking. Indoc-trination of the public by radio, press, school. Growing restriction of the range of public information under the pressure of military secrecy.[10]

The next day after the broadcast, J. Edgar Hoover dispatched a top-secret memo to all FBI offices, authorizing a hunt for any and all defamatory information on America's leading physicist and pacifist. This official smear campaign to paint him as a communist lackey, even a spy à la Klaus Fuchs, lasted until Einstein's death in 1955, by which time Hoover's file had grown to more than eighteen hundred pages of defamatory allegations and alleg-edly subversive statements. Just another brick in the wall of what half a century ago historian Richard Hofstadter identified as the paranoid style in American politics—reincarnated under Bush's and Obama's citizen meta-data-spying NSA.

The Patriot Act

> There is full freedom of expression. An unorthodox view can be expressed, provided it is an orthodox unorthodoxy.
>
> *Joseph Heller, Picture This*

A paranoid government—or, perhaps more ominously, one for whom it is merely convenient to appear so—is a familiar spectacle in the post-9/11 world. It brands contrary opinions disloyal, un-American, and a threat to the democratic order. It hyperbolizes dissent into a near-omnipotent enemy against which the populace is conditioned to stay constantly on alert, or risk a calamity of biblical proportions. Against such traitorous and seditious elements, all measures become justified and moral.

To ward off these apocalyptic threats to democracy, the government may even pass undemocratic legislation, such as the 2001 Uniting and Strengthening America by Providing Appropriate Tools Required to Intercept and Obstruct Terrorism Act. Better known as the Patriot Act, it paved the way for indefinite detention, extraordinary rendition, suspension of habeas corpus, and fullscale military invasion. Its precursor, Woodrow Wilson's 1918 Sedition Act, itself unconstitutionally suppressed free speech and hung a penalty of twenty years in jail for disloyalty to America, the flag, the government, or—the irony of ironies—the Constitution.

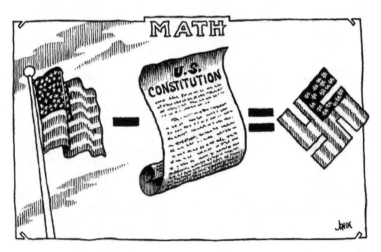

Figure 1.1   Constitutional Mythomatics ". . . Better known as the Patriot Act, it paved the way for indefinite detention, extraordinary rendition, suspension of habeas corpus, and fullscale military invasion . . ."

Credit: John Jonik

The precursor to Wilson's Sedition Act was the Sedition Act of 1798, signed into life by President Adams and upheld by his successor, Jefferson, who, even as he drafted resolutions that denounced the Act with one hand, used the other to sign executive orders using it to prosecute his own opponents. Had his authorship of these pamphlets ever become known, Jefferson himself would have been liable for prosecution for false, scandalous, and malicious writing against the government or certain officials.

In short, a classic case of What-You-See-Is-What-You-Get: manufacture enemies out of thin air, who subsequently have to be acted against on suspicion that they may act on their suspicion of your suspicion. Decades before 9/11, one clinical psychologist has diagnosed the mindset behind Bush and Cheney's keep-'em-terrorized-with-permanent-orange-level-alerts behavioral conditioning on the national scale. "Paranoid people live in readiness for an emergency. They live in a more or less continuous state of total mobilization in which catastrophe is always imminent."[11]

Every American generation is conditioned anew to fear the bogeyman. During the Cold War, which hardly ended with the collapse of the Berlin Wall, that role was foisted on the erstwhile military ally who had lost twenty million people in what the Russians refer to as the Great Patriotic War, and was itself paranoid about security. Only in 1984 did the CIA quietly own up that their data on the military spending by the Soviet empire had been systematically falsified.[12]

Heller misses no opportunity in *Picture This* to savage such expediently orchestrated political paranoia. "Whose side are you on?" snarls the closest thing to Bush II, the democratically elected autocrat Cleon, at lone antagonists to his warmongering. Like Cindy Sheehan, vilified for her peace vigil outside Dubya's White House after her son's combat death in the Iraq War, a lone moderate who objects to the extermination of the city of Mytilene is spat on as "un-Athenian, a bleeding heart, and a knee-jerk liberal" (91).

When Heller's Anytus describes the pro-war-or-pro-peace-but-nothing-else hysteria choking Athens, he describes the Cold War secretary of state John Foster Dulles, who in 1954 browbeat Vietnam with a threat that if it was not 100 percent behind America, it was 100 percent against it. Presciently, Heller also describes Bush II's 2001 speech to the joint session of Congress. which put the world in its place with, "Every nation, in every region, now has a decision to make: Either you are with us, or you are with the terrorists."[13]

Such zero-sum, with-us-or-against-us demagoguery serves to obscure the complex worldwide web of reciprocal interdependence that has been the engine of commerce and progress since time immemorial. And it is meant to do so. Bush II's hysterical ultimatums conditioned the fear-whipped American public to buy the fictions of Iraq's WMDs and Saddam's links to al-Qaeda in a prelude to the military invasion and occupation born of naked cupidity. Might makes right, and imperial agitprop lies only a small step away from outright coercion. This plays right into the hands of the White House, whose 2002 National Security Strategy elevated paranoia to the status of a political doctrine:

> We must adopt the concept of imminent threat to the capabilities and objective of today's adversaries. The United States has long maintained the option of preemptive actions to counter a sufficient threat to our national security. The greater the threat, the greater is the risk of inaction—and the more compelling the case for taking anticipatory action to defend ourselves, even if uncertainty remains as to the time and place of the enemy's attack. To forestall or prevent such hostile acts by our adversaries, the United States will, if necessary, act preemptively (15).

Democracy, as Heller illustrates on every page, does not automatically guarantee good government and world peace. Pericles was not only the founding father of democracy and an outstanding statesman, but also an imperial tyrant fixated on waging politics by Clausewitz's other means—so much so that the golden age of Pericles began with fifteen years of war and ended with one that would last twenty-seven. Thucydides, who otherwise extols Pericles's uprightness and judgment, concurs: "Athens, though still in name a democracy, was in fact ruled by her first citizen."[14] How much has changed since then?

Much ink has been spilt of late over the growing disequilibrium between the three branches of government, caused by a steady aggrandizement of presidential powers at the expense of congressional ones. The most fundamental among them is, of course, the power to take the country to war. Constitutionally the power to *declare* war is vested solely in Congress. The Commander–in-chief is supposed to carry out the policy dictated by the people's representatives. That said, presidents could always wage war without declaring one. According to Dick Cheney himself, from Jefferson on, the White House has deployed troops abroad more than two hundred times—on average once a year.[15] Of the twelve full-scale wars in that figure, only five were declared by Congress. In 1973, the War Powers Act rubberstamped this track record by permitting the Commander-in-chief to send troops abroad for up to sixty days (with an additional thirty-day withdrawal period) without prior congressional consent.

The Gettysburg Address assures Americans that they enjoy a government of the people, by the people, for the people. But march and blog as they might, the people do not get a chance to vote down the military quagmires in which their government embroils them. Nor do their elected representatives. Each of America's post-WWII fullscale wars—Korea, Vietnam, Iraq, Iraq Redux—went ahead without Congress's authorization. In February 2003 ten million people in sixty countries united to protest the White House's imminent paroxysm of belligerence. Rome alone saw three million protesters pass through its narrow streets, putting it in *Guinness World Records* as the largest antiwar rally in world history. In the United States, protesters voted with their feet in a hundred and fifty cities. The invasion of Iraq went ahead anyway.

Who needs the people anyway? In October 2002 the American people's representatives passed Joint Resolution 114, by means of which they divested themselves of their constitutional power by authorizing the president to use the nation's armed forces as necessary and appropriate. Like an imperial monarch of yore, Bush II got the mandate to use the American military practically at his discretion.

Before the 2003 invasion, a prominent US senator went public with a heartwarming fairy tale that "Saddam's fall would touch off a wave of democratic reform in the region."[16] Shaking his head at such naïve or just self-serving ahistoricism, Heller puts American gunboat diplomacy in perspective by pointing out that from Athens to Syracuse by oar and sail "was just about equivalent to the journey by troopship today from California to Vietnam, or from Washington, D. C., to the Beirut airport in Lebanon, or to the Persian Gulf" (198).

This matter-of-fact geographical juxtaposition captures a horrific constant in human affairs. Like the United States and Vietnam or the United States and Iraq, Athens and Syracuse were neither territorial nor commercial rivals, nor did they want any part of the land of the other. Queried why he bullied the Assembly into invading the nonbelligerent Syracuse, Heller's Alcibiades makes no bones about the fact that it was to attract attention to himself, make a profit, and display the glory of Athens. His justifications are as laughable as the fictions manufactured in our time by George W. Bush, Dick Cheney, George Tenet, Donald Rumsfeld, John Ashcroft, Colin Powell, and Condoleezza Rice.

Benevolent Hegemony

If another President faked another Gulf of Tonkin incident, there would still be only about two Senators voting against the resolution, and they'd be tossed out in the next election.

Joseph Heller, Playboy interview

"Who can doubt that there is an American empire?—an 'informal' empire, not colonial in polity, but still richly equipped with imperial paraphernalia: troops, ships, planes, bases, proconsuls, local collaborators, all spread around the luckless planet?" asked historian Arthur Schlesinger at the peak of Reagan's presidency.[17] Certainly no one in the Bush White House. "We're an empire now," proclaimed a senior aide to the president in 2004, adding with bravado rooted in history scorned, "We're history's actors."

Not that either claim is in doubt. As Charles Krauthammer notably argued in the early 1990s on the pages of *Foreign Affairs*, the implosion of the USSR left the United States in a unipolar moment in which it could dominate the world economically, militarily, and technologically like no other nation since the late Roman Empire. Not to look too far, shortly after the dismantling of the Soviet Union, the United States had the IMF and the World Bank rewrite Russia's economic statutes to grease the skids of its transition to capitalism and, coincidentally, open access to the new regime's markets and oil.

In the late 1990s, as Heller was crafting *Portrait of an Artist, as an Old Man*, two neocon ideologues rationalized imperial domination into what has since become the bedrock of the American political canon. Reviving Plato's myth of a virtuous tyrant—while turning a blind eye on how easily the myth was crushed already by Aristotle—William Kristol and Robert Kagan propounded that, in this novel geostrategic configuration, the United States should exercise "benevolent hegemony."[18] As in Plato's republic, the bottom line of this virtuous tyranny was to be military. Two strategic documents, the 2000 National Security Strategy and the 2004 National Military Strategy, delineated the terms of the Pax Americana. Its bottom line? Full Spectrum Dominance: armed capability sufficient "to defeat any adversary and control any situation across the full range of military operations."

What Heller did not say is that, contrary to what most Americans believe, even under the untrammelled defense budgets of Bush II and Obama, the self-appointed Globocop does not enjoy undisputed supremacy in firepower. Putin's Russia has the regularly upgraded ICBMs. China has its own nukes, not to mention a colossal army and navy (the latter beefed up recently with its first refurbished Russian carrier). Iran has domestic-made missiles and, down the road, fission devices. North Korea has both. Vietnam has jungle fighters. Iraq and Afghanistan have seemingly endless cadres of suicide bombers.

What the United States possesses, in distinction to them all, is enormous economic muscle with which to finance conventional forces that can be airlifted or shipped across the world. This is enabled by a neocolonial network of military real estate maintained to safeguard its global interests. As per the Pentagon's 2003 "Base Structure Report," the generals own or lease more than seven hundred overseas bases in one hundred and thirty countries around the world. This is not counting six *thousand* military bases in the United States, its territories, and protectorates.[19]

Mind-numbing as these figures are, even they fall far short of the actual number of military installations the United States operates globally. The

Defense Department report does not, for example, account for a configuration of new bases in Afghanistan, Iraq, Israel, Kuwait, Qatar, Kyrgyzstan, and Uzbekistan—a gigantic post-9/11 buildup through the so-called arc of instability. Meanwhile, weapons trade remains the staple of the economy, with US exports of military hardware dwarfing those of any other nation.

Indeed, American foreign policy, as triangulated by the White House, the Pentagon, and the Bechtel/Boeing/Halliburton/Chevron/Lockheed Martin lobby, demonstrably has led to higher instability in the world. There is no need to rehash the awful truth of the United States arming and financing militant Islamists like Osama bin Laden and militant secularists like Saddam Hussein all through the 1980s. In 2006 alone, at the peak of the War on Terror, the Department of State reported that acts of terrorism shot up worldwide by 25 percent.[20]

Heller quips in *Picture This* that, since the renaming of the Department of War to the Department of Defense in 1947, America was never again in danger of war. It was in danger of defense. "Use It or Lose It" is how superpowers regard military power, including the ancient Greeks, who, he points out, seemed always to be in conflict with everyone all over the world, prospering on tributes exacted with brawn and bronze from weaker cities. It is part of Heller's thesis that, much as Athens oppressed its neighbors—as much to coerce fealty as out of fear of losing its coercive leverage—so has the United States been oppressing its own.

Nothing illustrates this thesis better than the blood-spattered history of American interventions in Latin America. Agrarian and economic reforms in the 1950s Guatemala, including legitimizing trade unions, were perceived as a menace to US interests inasmuch as they threatened not only its capital but the very capitalist system. Something had to be done, lest the socialist disease spread through the region, and in 1954 the democratically elected Arbenz government was toppled and replaced by four decades of US-backed dictatorships.

Recently declassified White House files document the same hysteria about social reforms initiated in the 1970s in Chile. They document Nixon's panic about keeping the democratically elected Allende from taking office or, barring that, removing him by all means necessary, from black ops to outright coup d'état. A still legible handwritten note by the CIA director Richard Helms records his heat-of-the-moment orders from the president of the United States:

> 1 in 10 chance perhaps, but save Chile!; worth spending; not concerned; no involvement of embassy; $10,000,000 available, more if necessary; full-time job—best men we have; game plan; make the economy scream; 48 hours for plan of action.[21]

The rest, as they say, is history. In 1973 Nixon's wishes were granted as a CIA-driven coup replaced Socialist Allende with a military junta, which then metastasized into a quarter century of Pinochet dictatorship. At the time of the latter's death in 2006, hundreds of lawsuits were pending against him across Chile for gross violations of human rights ranging from political assassination to systematic torture to disappearing thousands of people.

On Reagan's watch, as a direct consequence of its socioeconomic reforms, Nicaragua was declared a threat to national security and had to be brought to heel, even at the cost of illegally selling arms to America's perennial enemy—Iran. In the 1990s, with the world distracted by the splendid little wars in the Persian Gulf and then the Balkans, under the mantle of the War on Drugs, leftwing Colombian guerillas were targeted by chemical warfare (disguised as crop fumigation) that ravaged agriculture and livestock, driving left-leaning peasantry from the land.

The 1970s Senate hearings on a century of American foreign policy in Latin America uncovered persistent torture, disappearances, and killings by police trained and equipped by the United States. In words taken directly from the US Army Special Forces training manual, the Green Berets trained dictators and their security apparatus in "guerrilla warfare, propaganda, subversion, intelligence and counter-intelligence, terrorist activities, civic action, and conventional combat operations."[22] All in a day's work for benevolent hegemonists.

Déjà Lu

Alarmed by the ambitions of Athens, Sparta and other Greek cities forged defensive alliances wherever they could. Alarmed by these defensive alliances, Athens began to forge defensive alliances of her own against these defensive alliances that had been forged to defend against Athens.

Joseph Heller, Picture This

Heller and Thucydides's joint diagnosis of the Athenian empire—the "cause of all these evils was the desire to rule which greed and ambition inspire" (168)—applies in equal degree to the American. There is no better explanation for George W.'s "fiction" that nonexistent Iraqi WMDs constituted an imminent danger to the United States. The story began to unravel from the moment the president evoked a fat dossier, "Iraq—Its Infrastructure of Concealment, Deception and Intimidation," which, he said, contained the smoking gun. That same dossier was used by Colin Powell during the buildup to the invasion to railroad the UN Security Council in a performance that should have earned him and his boss Academy Awards for Best Actor and Best Director.

Only on the eve of the invasion did the truth begin to flip the White House script. Glen Rangwala, a lecturer in politics at Cambridge, blew the whistle on the dossier when he realized that he had seen the allegedly top-classified information before. It turned out that Bush's top-secret smoking gun was plagiarized, in some places verbatim, from an intelligence dossier supplied by his sidekick Tony Blair. Blair's dossier—which was mostly "rumint" (CIA in-house for rumor-intelligence) anyway—was in turn plagiarized from old academic essays. "Apart from passing this off as the work of its intelligence services," wrote Rangwala in the postmortem to this smoke and mirrors, "it indicates that the UK really does not have any independent sources of information on Iraq's internal policies."[23]

The alleged link between the fundamentalist al-Qaeda and the secular regime of Saddam has never existed and could not exist, due to their incompatible ideologies and mutual mistrust. Ditto for the slam-dunk WMDs. But the Iraq war went ahead just because, like the entire War on Terror, it had been planned since the 1990s. Born of the historical constants in the US petro-military strategy, the plan had its roots in the 1992 "Defense Planning Guidance" (DPG). Drafted by then Secretary of Defense Cheney, Chairman of the Joint Chiefs of Staff Powell, and Undersecretary of Defense for Policy Wolfowitz, the DPG was to warrant continued growth of military spending after the collapse of the Soviet Union.[24]

The bottom line came in the form of two directives. First, the US military ought to be beefed up to prevent the emergence of any rival to its power. Second, perceived threats to the country's interests ought to be pre-emptively and, if need be, unilaterally neutralized. Fleshed out by a neoconservative think tank Project for the New American Century in a 2000 paper called "Rebuilding America's Defenses," the new doctrine became the bedrock of Bush II's national security strategy and foreign policy. In 2004, even as he began to retract his UN speech and the allegedly solid sources behind it, Colin Powell reiterated preemption as a doctrine for making the world a better and safer place:

> If you recognize a clear and present threat that is undeterrable by the means you have at hand, then you must deal with it. You do not wait for it to strike; you do not allow future attacks to happen before you take action.[25]

Compare this to the terrorist manifesto of Ayman al-Zawahiri, released that same year, and you might be forgiven for the feeling of *déjà lu*:

> We shouldn't wait for the Americans, English, French, Jewish, Hungarian, Polish and South Korean forces to invade Egypt, the Arabian Peninsula, Yemen, and Algeria and then start the resistance after the occupier had already invaded us. We should start now.[26]

Once the clouds of dust from the World Trade Center and the clouds of disinformation that mushroomed in its wake had dispersed, it became clear that, in spite of counterevidence or even long-term American interests, Team Bush had decided in advance to go after Iraqi oil. This is, however, only half of the truth. As every illusionist knows, the trick lies in misdirecting the audiences while you pull the rabbit out with the other hand. And so, while the world's attention was fixed on the Iraq offensive and the subsequent occupation, American troops were quietly pouring into oil-rich central Asia: four thousand into Afghanistan, two thousand into Uzbekistan, three thousand into a new base in Kyrgyzstan, more into another long-term base in Tajikistan—for starters.[27]

The invasion of Iraq, which was to touch off a wave of democratic reform in the Middle East, instead touched off a wave of antagonism toward the United States and the escalation of instability and violence. Already 9/11 was a backlash against its presence in the region, and while anti-American sentiments are by no means a new phenomenon, the occupation of Iraq in the name of sweet crude has elevated them to unprecedented heights. The past and the future were both spelled out back in 2003 by rapper Immortal Technique on his signature track "Cause of Death." From the military industry to the Wolfowitz Doctrine, the song puts it plainly to Rumsfeld—and to the listeners—that 9/11 was hijacked as a pretext for the invasion of Iraq and for bloating the defense budget to world-conquest proportions. It hammers on:

> And Dick Cheney, you fucking leech, tell them your plans
> About building your pipelines through Afghanistan
> And how Israeli troops trained the Taliban in Pakistan
> You might have some house niggas fooled, but I understand
> Colonialism is sponsored by corporations
> That's why Halliburton gets paid to rebuild nations.

Shrugging off the evidence to the contrary, some political analysts remain, however, hostile to the idea that America is, or could ever become, an empire. One of them contends, in fact, that the United States is not an imperial power and is not likely to become one, "because an empire is a system of formal, territorial control which carries prohibitive cost and is incompatible with basic American values."[28] Heller demolishes such naïveté, documenting that ancient Athens did rule an empire and disproving the contention that democratic values are somehow incompatible with formal, territorial control.

As for prohibitive costs, belying its vaunted military muscle, the United States does face a problem of imperial overstretch, corroborated in 2014 by the Pentagon's plans to reinvent itself as a leaner force for the good. The phrase itself gained currency with Paul Kennedy's 1987 classic, *The Rise and Fall of the Great Powers*, which argued that, due to vast strategic commitments, the United States ran the peril familiar from the rise and fall of all Great Powers—that of its mouth being bigger than its stomach. Composed at the same juncture of history, *Picture This* identifies imperial overstretch as the factor that sucked Periclean Athens into a vortex of political expediency which eventually paved the way for the war that brought the city to its knees.

Although the United States has not yet suffered a calamity of comparable proportions, it does not mean that it is impervious to the consequences of its imperial appetites. Never mind the American casualties in Iraq alone: nearly four and a half thousand dead and one hundred thousand maimed, many of them for life. It cost a cool million dollars a year to keep a soldier—any soldier and every soldier—in Iraq. During the entire period, war and homeland security outlays matched the level of the country's GNP from the time of the Vietnam War. There is no politically correct way to spin the fact that today, American military outlays make up almost half of the Earth's total, in absolute numbers approaching the GNP of Greece and the Netherlands combined.[29]

Einstein and Eisenhower were right. The Pentagon and the military industry are the closest thing to a government within the government. And the social and financial costs of their democratic coup d'état are incalculable: hospitals unbuilt, schools unrepaired, textbooks unpurchased, teachers not hired, policemen not trained, immigrants not integrated, schoolchildren without meals, forty million functionally illiterate, thirty million without basic medical coverage, infrastructure crumbling, production costs soaring, environmental pollution amok.

The Devil Shits Dutchmen

The American economic system was barbarous, resulting, naturally, in barbarism and entrenched imbecility on all levels of the culture.

Joseph Heller, Picture This

For a lesson in comparative economics, Heller goes to the fountainhead of modern corporate capitalism: the seventeenth-century Netherlands. As with the Greeks, the history of the Dutch republic exhibits uncanny parallels with the American, beginning with fighting the war of independence from a colonial superpower and ending with founding an empire of its own. Equally under control of its business oligarchy, the Dutch republic also turned its premier city into the nexus of world commerce and finance, only to see it eclipsed by New Amsterdam—New York.

Highly urbanized, prosperous, tolerant of diversity, the city of Amsterdam and the entire United Netherlands could have been mistaken for New York and the United States as they became ethnocultural melting pots for immigrants of all creeds and races who flooded in to make a guilder. The business of mercantile Holland was business, with politics, religion, and even art subsumed under that category. René Descartes, who himself had found political refuge in the Low Countries, wrote with a touch of scorn that could have come from Heller:

> In this great town where apart from myself there dwells no one who is not engaged in trade, everyone is so much out for his own advantage that I should be able to live my whole life here without ever meeting a mortal being.[30]

Like in America, riding an economic boom fueled by a virtual monopoly on commodities such as tulip bulbs, spices, refined textiles, and herring, Holland instigated a raft of civil liberties. By the time New Amsterdam became renamed New York, Dutch children could no longer legally work for more than fourteen hours a day. In some municipalities religious disputes were banned as being injurious to business. Even slavery was outlawed in the United Netherlands, although slave trading was not, so that capacious Dutch flutes continued the lucrative business of running blacks from West Africa to the Americas.

When it comes to making money, nothing can compare to the Dutch East India Company, a name synonymous with corporate capitalism. As Heller notes, founded in 1602, it promptly secured a monopoly charter for all the seas and lands east of the Cape of Good Hope, in no time controlling world trade in commodities from spices to textiles. In its time a major source of income for the entire country, the company remains legendary, as much for the invention of publicly held shares and perfection of a banking system as for the rapacity with which it administered its colonial fiefdoms.

Its New World-directed counterpart was the West India Company, which, among others, enjoyed a monopoly charter for commerce between Africa and the Americas, including notably shipments of up to fifteen thousand black slaves a year. Scrupulous as ever, Heller jots down that the East India Company's annual revenue averaged 300–500 percent, while the shareholders' dividends averaged 40 percent—forsooth, a business empire within an empire.

Although the Dutch were mainly pursuing commercial and not territorial gain, their methods could mislead one to think otherwise. Jan Pieterszoon Coen, governor general of the overseas territories of the East India Company, is only one example. A longtime national hero, in 1618—as

Heller dutifully records—this slash-and-burn capitalist massacred and burned the entire city of Jakarta. Chided by the bosses back home for his high-handed methods, he retorted that there was nothing in the world that gave one a better right to do whatever one wanted than power and might added to right. The Jakartans would probably concur with William Batten, as quoted by Samuel Pepys, as quoted by Heller in an epigram to *Picture This*: "I think the Devil shits Dutchmen."

Like the United States, this seemingly invulnerable empire, which at its economic peak stretched halfway around the world, also financed a Golden Age in culture. The burgeoning purses of the Dutch burghers patronized a procession of artists, among them Rembrandt van Rijn, whose life provides a perfect foil for Heller's satirical sniping. Paralleling his country's economy, the painter's career also traced a cycle of boom and bust indexed to his wife's dowry, inheritance, real estate holdings, ex-mistress's demands for maintenance payments, and not least compensation from his patrons. Indeed, writes Heller, the sole surviving samples of Rembrandt's handwriting are his letters to an agent of a prince, wheedling for money. Surviving only in translation is another missive to his patron in Sicily:

> In addition Your Lordship complains about both the price and the canvas, but if Your Lordship wishes to send the piece back, at your own expense and your own risk, I will make another Alexander. As regards the canvas, I found I had too little white while painting, so that it was necessary to add to its length, but if the painting is hung in the proper light, no one will notice this at all.
>
> Should Your Lordship be satisfied with the Alexander this way, everything is in order. Should Your Lordship not wish to keep the said Alexander, the lowest price for a new one is 600 guilders. And the Homer is 500 and the cost of the canvas. (239–240)

One may be forgiven for thinking that to Rembrandt his paintings are not so much art as commodities to be exchanged for credit or cash. No wonder, sneers Heller, that the figures in his pictures have sad faces. They worry about money.

And on he continues, tripping the light sarcastic. The chief consequence of the invention of money in the seventh century before Christ was servitude, so that people became free to borrow at interest and go into debt. Much as the Gilded Age in America, the Dutch Golden Age created two classes of citizenry: the privileged property owners and the vagrant poor whose numbers were in the millions. Rich is the country that has plenty of poor, is his Swiftian conclusion, for even though the Dutch had no slaves, "they always had enough poor to work like niggers and, for a living wage, to go to sea and to war" (178).

Nixon Made Me Do It

Playboy: But do you really *care* about politics? In 1972, you said you hadn't
voted for a President in 12 years.
Heller: Then I voted for McGovern.
Playboy: Why?
Heller: Nixon made me do it.

Joseph Heller, Playboy interview, 1975

A closer look at the United States through the lens fashioned by the Dutch
empire explains Heller's quip about *Picture This* being a book about money
and war. Just as in the Enlightenment-era Netherlands, American capitalism also is umbilically connected to war. Insofar as war production is
driven by federal appropriations, a permanent state of readiness for war
is engineered by the military-industrial-congressional complex—the very
syndrome Eisenhower diagnosed in his 1961 valedictory address as being
intrinsically harmful to democracy and liberty. Like Heller, he may have
cribbed his message from Plato, who cautioned in *Laws*, "Every individual,
because of his greed for gold and silver, is willing to toil at every art and
device, noble or ignoble, if he is likely to get rich by it."[31]

Once a country's economy becomes entwined with military production,
there is no easy way to reverse the course, simply because the current one
is too profitable for those who oversee it. Outsourcing companies tasked
with supplying weapons, munitions, fuel, clothing, meals, transportation,
accommodations, and provisions of any kind know that wars and lucrative
contracts go hand in hand. So do politicians who peddle wars as employment to their constituents. This secures their reelection, which means more
of the same politicians voting to maintain war production, which means
more wars, more reelections, and so forth. This is why half of the federal
discretionary budget goes to war while only 1 percent goes to International
Affairs, and only 0.6 percent of that 1 percent to peacekeeping operations.[32]

War has indeed been a historical boon to the American economy. During WWII more than two thousand of the largest firms in the country
reported a 40-plus percent rise in after-tax earnings.[33] All this was a fitting
prelude to the 1950s, during which investments in companies specializing
in Cold War defense work were nearly twice as profitable as in non-defense
firms. It is not an accident that the decades that experienced the biggest
economic booms in the United States followed the biggest wars. War is
good for business, not only while hostilities rage, but also for years after,
when the wrecked infrastructure needs to be rebuilt, when suppressed consumer spending rebounds with a vengeance, and when spikes in population
growth require housing, food production, and general consumer goods.

Figure 1.2   War is Business ". . . War production is, in short, a prerogative of an empire . . ."

Credit: Carlos Latuff

War production is, in short, a prerogative of an empire. The Congressional Research Service documents that, planetwide, the American share in arms exports shot up from more than one-third in 1990 to more than one-half in 2000 and only increased its share by 2010. Put differently, *before* the mammoth military buildup under Bush II and then Obama, America sold 2.5 times more arms to the world than the second and third largest weapons exporters (Britain and Russia), ten times more than France, and almost twenty times more than China.[34]

Subcontracting, which allows private businesses to provide services to the military—anything from peeling potatoes to manufacturing materiel to tactical training—creates quasi-monopolistic leviathans that harken back to the Dutch East India Company. With Halliburton's former CEO in the White House, was it really a coincidence that Halliburton's subsidiary Kellogg Brown & Root got a $2 billion-plus contract to rebuild Iraq's oil infrastructure? Protesting that his links were severed for good, Cheney must have plumb forgot his six-figure deferred salary and his massive stock options.

The result of such nepotism is an inundation of waste and abuse. In just one example, in 2003 the Department of Defense's audit revealed that Halliburton charged $2.27 a gallon for fifty-six million gallons of gas brought into Iraq since the invasion. That was more than a buck more than charged by another contractor. What's a dollar plus? A sixty-plus-million-dollar giveaway of tax dollars to Dick Cheney.[35] There was money to be made in Iraq—as John Dos Passos would put it, Big Money. The 2003 audit by the General Accounting Office found out that the Pentagon could not account for more than a *trillion* dollars. It disappeared without a trace. Paul Bremer, after replacing Jay Garner as the colonial governor of Iraq, ordered an airlift of thirty-six *tons* of federal cash for the country's reconstruction. It also disappeared without a trace.

Who needs thirty-six tons of cash, anyway? Even prior to the invasion of Iraq, Lockheed Martin's stocks rose by 36 percent.[36] Boeing made thirty-eight billion out of 2003 homeland defense contracts alone. In 2003 Bechtel won the bid to rebuild the Iraqi infrastructure. Official pricetag: three billion (real pricetag estimated to be at least double that). The post-invasion years of 2004 and 2005 were the most profitable in Chevron's 126-year history. It is a sobering thought that, while the 9/11 attacks cost about half a million dollars to launch, the cumulative costs of the Iraq war alone are estimated at two trillion. This is why, to every president who would seek refuge behind Lyndon Johnson's "we make war that we may live in peace," Heller offers this advice:

> Do not make war in a hostile distant land unless you intend to live there.
>   The people will outnumber you, your presence will be alarming, the government you install to keep order will not keep order, victory is impossible if the people keep fighting, there is only genocide to cope with determined local military resistance. (198)

Even the grey eminence of ultraconservative Christian fundamentalists, Tim LaHaye, was compelled to admit in his teaching booklet called *The Bible's Influence on American History*, "It would be futile for me as a Christian to deny the evils of capitalism in America" (44). Still, one must not generalize from the United States to capitalism at large. Not all countries let their military tail wag the socioeconomic dog. For one, democratic Sweden, whose economy consistently rates as one of the most competitive by the World Economic Forum, enjoys an enviable standard of living under mixed-market capitalism and statist welfare. Nor have they invaded anyone of late. The conclusion? Whatever is rotten in the American machinery of state is endemic to the United States, not to capitalism *sui generis*.

Mistah Kurtz

The death of no person is as important to the future as the literature about it.

Joseph Heller, Picture This

The truth is cruel, wrote George Santayana in "Ideal Immortality," but it can be loved, and it makes free those who have loved it. By this standard, Heller is a free spirit, having wrought a nonfiction novel out of imperial history at its most cruel. Not without reason did he describe *Picture This* as his most damning, critical, and pessimistic creation ever. And yet, in spite or perhaps because of this pessimism, it won the hearts of the readers for whom the release of every Heller novel used to be an event measured on the Richter scale.

Heller's pessimism about the professional managers of the United States' economy, foreign policy, and way of life finds an abiding artistic embodiment in *Picture This*. Its twin historical perspectives—the top-down panoramas of Greece and Holland at the heights of their imperial glory and the up-close-and-personal biographies of Socrates, Plato, Aristotle, and Rembrandt—help him reconstruct history from their seemingly endless trials and tribulations.

Of course, where there is pessimism, history cannot be far behind. Back in *Catch-22* Heller seamlessly interwove his surreal Second World War with all too real postwar red-baiting, starting with McCarthy's vilification of a US Army major who would not stoop to signing the loyalty oath. No less faction from page one to the last, his political novel *Good As Gold* reproduced a riot of current newspaper clippings and political commentary, including this ten-word anatomy of Henry Kissinger: "greasy, vulgar, petulant, obnoxious, contemptible, self-serving, social-climbing Jewish little shit" (274). No wonder that Gore Vidal picked *Good As Gold* as one of his five favorite post-World War II novels.

If Heller's *summa historiae* teaches anything, it is that the more human nature does not change, the more it remains the same. So does the frequently retold (although most likely apocryphal) anecdote of Rembrandt stooping to pick up coins painted on the floor by his apprentice, Govaert Flinck. Both remind us how easily we confuse appearances with reality, how quickly we are led astray by duplicity, how gullible we are when spin artists get to work on our bearings.

Perish the thought, however, that taking liberties with history and truth are confined to the United States, or to the modern era. We have been victims of spin and editorial caprice from the first moment somebody spotted an opportunity in the inevitable delay between the unfolding of a live event and its record for posterity. This simple truth, whose mother is always history, casts a shadow over any naïve notions of veracity, no matter how contemporary or ancient in the making.

How contemporary?

In 2011 a parliamentary committee of the growingly rightwing Canada issued a deadline to the national media regulator to repeal the ban on broadcasting false or misleading news. News standards, it announced, ought to be relaxed to allow falsehoods, insofar as the current ban might interfere with the right to free speech. Apparently nobody informed the ruling Reform Party—whose former top gun has recently launched Sun TV, aka Fox North—that there is a big difference between individuals spouting what they will, even when manifestly wrong, and public broadcasters licensed to use the airwaves on the premise of being held to a socially acceptable standard.

How ancient?

Cicero, one of the most famous Roman senators, was revered throughout the antiquity for his gift of oratory, which is said to have jump-started the Renaissance via Petrarch's rediscovery of his letters. Yet, as historians have gradually come to realize, Cicero's speeches as they have been written down for posterity differ vastly from what is known of them (or from what can reasonably be inferred) as they were delivered on the floor of the Senate or the Forum.

It is not just a matter of massaging their contents and style before being released in the authorized version, the results of which can range from merely vexing to Orwellian, as corroborated by anyone who ever sat in on a minuted department meeting. Some of Cicero's courtroom speeches are now known to be outright fabrications, which is to say, great historical fictions. Such is the case, for example, with his philippics against Verres, a corrupt governor of Sicily, whose well-documented flight at the opening of his trial would have left Cicero with no target for his finger-pointing denunciations.[37]

Keep this in mind when you access Wikipedia to take advantage of its crowdsourced, or just creatively edited, contents. Or when Google throws out millions of webpages at a click of a mouse, creating an illusion of mastery over trillions of crumbs of information scattered in cyberspace. The fact is that no one could ever check even a minuscule fraction of this embarrassment of riches, nor monitor the algorithm's search priorities. Blind subroutines demand blind faith from the end users, a quaint notion in view of the docketful of lawsuits against Google for fixing their search results.

Heller has no patience with the fictions spun by empire-builders through the ages, and *Picture This* is his literary and historical testament to hypocrisy that has not changed an iota in twenty-five centuries. Every word of this nonfiction novel asks, in effect, whether the sociopolitical system that produced the Patriot Act is really worth sustaining. At what point does the Statue of Liberty's torch of progress become a neocolonial flame-thrower by means of which today's avatars of Mistah Kurtz set alight the barrios and the kasbahs of the world? When did the world's liberator from the first and second world wars turn into the world's biggest weapons manufacturer and seller?

When did it sign over its soul to the devil by unilaterally breaking disarmament treaties, weaponizing space, developing "usable" nuclear warheads, invading sovereign countries in violation of international laws, using chemical WMDs, massacring civilian populations, sanctioning torture—in short, declaring overt and covert war on whatever does not please its eye? And, last but not least, if Saddam Hussein could be tried and hanged for his culpability in the killing of 148 Shiites, what about the culpability of George Walker Bush and Richard Bruce Cheney for the deaths of more than a million Iraqis of all denominations since March 2003?[38]

2

No Child Left Behind

Tim LaHaye and Jerry B. Jenkins, *Left Behind:*
A Novel of the Earth's Last Days

I Thessalonians

The next two hundred years, should Jesus tarry, could well depend on you!

Tim LaHaye, *The Bible's Influence on American History*

In 1995 two born-again evangelists sat down to pen what would turn out to be a phenomenally lucrative franchise. On paper, they were an odd couple behind a multi-platinum bestseller that from 1999 on would top the *New York Times* bestseller list with each new installment. One of them would never write a word of it. The other would ultimately dash off more than six thousand pages of earnest prose. Together they would become avatars of not being taken seriously by literary critics but being taken very seriously by the bankers.

Jerry B. Jenkins, the actual wordsmith but only the second name on the cover, is the author of more than a hundred and fifty books, including several bestselling sports biographies and the nationally syndicated comic strip *Gil Thorp*. He is also a former president for publishing at the Moody Bible Institute of Chicago, which runs the Moody Press, the port of call for biblical prophecy writers. Of late he has also cofounded the Christian Writers Guild, which helps born-again novelists with marketing and writing in the same meat-and-potatoes style that drives *Left Behind* and the entire Left Behind Series (LBS).[1]

Tim LaHaye, the prime mover behind the series, is himself the author of a long line of publications on Bible prophecy. Characteristically, in parallel to the LBS, he launched the PreTrib Research Center dedicated to promoting the dispensationalist spin on the Book of Revelation. Back in 1979 he persuaded Jerry Falwell to found the Moral Majority and sat on its board of directors. In the 1980s, forsaking the pulpit to make room for writing and politics, he locked arms not only with Reagan-era Republicans but also with the ultraconservative John Birch Society, whose agenda, from vilifying the UN to promoting an evangelical interpretation of the Constitution, gets a sympathetic airing throughout the LBS.

LaHaye also got involved in presidential politics as a co-chairman of Jack Kemp's 1988 campaign, only to be kicked off in the first week when his inflammatory anti-Catholicism became a public liability. In 2000 he played a major role in rallying the religious right to vote for Bush II, and in 2007 he publicly threw his weight behind Mike Huckabee in the Republican primaries. The would-be president returned the favor by endorsing *Left Behind* and its sequels as a "compelling story written for nontheologians."[2]

By then the entire series was winding down after fifteen years of commercial success, with *Left Behind* nominated for Novel of the Year by the Evangelical Christian Publishers Association, LaHaye and Jenkins making the cover of *Time* (July 2002) and then *Newsweek* (May 2004), and sales receipts proving Matthew's error when he pontificated that ye cannot serve God and mammon. In short, a mammoth triumph for a story that refurbishes the Old and the New Testament by cutting and pasting contemporary events into the dispensationalist catechism—"Nostradamus rewritten by Jeffrey Archer" in the wry summary of the London *Times*.[3]

Dispensationalism itself, an evangelical denomination with roots in the late 1820s Plymouth Brethren Movement, emigrated from the British Isles to America in the 1860s via the agency of an Anglican dissenter and itinerant preacher, John Nelson Darby. The centerpiece of his theology was the division of religious history into seven periods, or dispensations. In the beginning, preached Darby, was the Dispensation of Innocence (Adam and Eve in the garden east of Eden), succeeded by the Dispensation of Conscience (after the forbidden fruit). It was followed, in turn, by the Dispensation of Human Government (after God gave Noah the basic laws), of Promise (after the covenant with Abraham), of Law (after the Mosaic Law on Mount Sinai), and of Grace or Church (after Jesus's resurrection).[4]

The millennium-long kingdom to be established by Christ after the Second Coming is called the Dispensation of the Millennium. It will be inaugurated by the Rapture, during which all born-again Christians will be beamed up to heaven, and followed by the Tribulation, during which Earth will be scourged by plagues and calamities of apocalyptic proportions. The holy war between God and Satan will wipe out most of humankind before the glorious return of Jesus, who will smite the Antichrist on the plain of Armageddon. He will then establish a thousand-year kingdom, albeit not on Earth, which will itself be annihilated, but instead on a planet identical to ours, miraculously created in its place. All that, including the pogrom of several billion souls—atheists, Catholics, Muslims, Buddhists, Hindus, Jews, and others who do not subscribe to the dispensationalist creed—is part of God's master plan to bring all to the true faith.

For Darby, this theodicy was not a problem: his divine omelet clearly called for the breaking of a few billion eggs. The fact that God's retribution might rain indiscriminately on all people on Earth, born-again or not, was more disconcerting. In the end, Darby solved the problem by declaring that, rather than suffer the equivalent of Amalric's "Kill them all, for the Lord knows them that are His," true Christians would be spirited up to heaven just before the reign of terror began. Bailed out by the Rapture, they could then safely look down on God's carnage of those left behind. As to who qualifies as a true Christian, Darby's teachings were no different from those of the Calvinists, the Puritans, and the Separatists, whose dogma also revolved around typology and prefiguration: nobody knows except the Lord, and he keeps his cards close to his chest.

Darby's uncompromising stance deliberately distanced him from institutionalized churches like the Roman Catholic, which guarantee salvation to all who embrace it, and which historically allowed the wealthy to buy indulgences, pardons, benefices, dispensations, and other forms of simony. In contrast, in the born-again order, there would be no cutting corners. No church membership or pious works could put you among the regenerate. Only unquestioning obeisance to the doctrine as elucidated by the doctrinal elders would do.

Darby's doctrinal platform was founded on his interpretation of I Thessalonians 4:16–17:

> 16 For the Lord himself shall descend from heaven with a shout, with the voice of the archangel, and with the trump of God: and the dead in Christ shall rise first:
> 17 Then we which are alive and remain shall be caught up together with them in the clouds, to meet the Lord in the air: and so shall we ever be with the Lord.[5]

Although his evangelicalism remained largely ignored by other Christian denominations, his disciples spared no effort to popularize its bright side, insofar as the Rapture exempted prospective converts from the hell on earth that was to befall unregenerate humankind. In 1909 they received a major boost with the publication, by none other than Oxford University Press, of the *Scofield Reference Bible* by an apostle of Darby's, Cyrus I. Scofield.

Forging the illusion that these wildly eclectic texts all point toward the dispensationalist creed, Scofield cross-referenced the entire Old and New Testament, printing his glosses directly under the scriptures and in the same font. Despite his exegeses being superimposed on the biblical verses—or perhaps because of it—the book became a big hit with born-again readers (the revised 1966 edition is still in use). Institutionalized in the fundamentalist Bible schools founded across the United States in the early twentieth century, it sold well in excess of twenty million copies, paving the way for *Left Behind* and its version of Apocalypse Now.

Satan's Cause Is Coming to Town

> Even some of the works of non-Christian writers and painters in the United States contained Biblical principles. This is in marked contrast to the wild art that goes under the guise of "impressionism," the loud beat "music" with its desolate and often mournful laments, and the pornography that is so frequently dubbed "literature."
>
> *Tim LaHaye, The Bible's Influence on American History*

Left Behind opens aboard a transatlantic flight during which some passengers suddenly disappear from their seats, leaving nothing but bundles of clothing behind. Routed back to Chicago, the jetliner lands on the last open runway in the midst of pandemonium. Air-traffic controllers, dispatchers, motormen, drivers, surgeons—who could know there were so many born-again evangelicals in our midst?—were raptured while on duty, leaving a blaze of collateral death and chaos in their wake.

Against the terrors of the ensuing Tribulation, the book and the series follow a core group of characters: Rayford Steele, senior airline pilot from the opening pages, his spirited daughter Chloe, and her eventual husband, ace journalist "Buck" Williams. Rented out for the series from Madame Tussauds, by the end of the first book, all three become steadfast converts to dispensationalism. Tsion Ben-Judah, a Jewish rabbi who converts later in the series, becomes the theological spokesman for the group and for their real-life creators.

Together with Pastor Barnes, they form the so-called Tribulation Force that, over eleven sequels and four prequels, will evangelize the infidels and combat the Antichrist, Nicolae Carpathia, as he rises from obscurity to become president of Romania, secretary-general of the United Nations, and finally world dictator. Seven years and several billion corpses later, the Left Behind Series culminates in the glorious appearing of Christ at Armageddon, where Carpathia and the forces of evil get slain exactly as prophesied by Scofield. The end.

If all this Bible-meets-Tom-Clancy soap opera sounds vaguely familiar, it is because once you have read one dispensationalist tract disguised as a novel, you have read them all. Even the locations (the United Nations, Petra, Babylon, Armageddon) are recycled from the stock of previous paper apocalypses, as are the Antichrist's campaigns for One World Government, One World Currency, and One World Religion, together with their political insinuations: the EU, the World Bank, and the ecumenical movement are minions of Satan. This is not to say that returns to familiar faces and places cannot be a source of aesthetic pleasure and emotional gratification, as corroborated by die-hard fans of genre cycles like Ed McBain's 87th Precinct or television soaps like *The West Wing*. And genre and soap formulas come thick and fast right from page one of *Left Behind*.

The scenes of panic aboard the airliner hail straight from Arthur Hailey's *Flight into Danger* and the bedlam on the ground from his other disaster thriller *Airport*.[6] Brushes with death, including a car-bombing that rains a leg and part of a torso on the sidewalk, are all in a day's work for the born-again action hero Buck. Like all handsome, loaded, lone-wolf investigative reporters, he packs his MacGyver ingenuity next to his false passport. Like them, he also operates in a comic-book fairyland. Tossing the passport and ID at the site of the bombing, Buck feels safe since the police would now conclude that he was one of the casualties. Evidently Jerry B. Jenkins has never heard of forensic odontology or DNA.

On another level, the series also styles itself as a self-help book and a *vade mecum* for the millennial Everyman. Rayford Steele may be another generic action hero—his name clearly rings up 1980s TV and Remington Steele—but his quest for salvation becomes a handbook of instructions for every would-be spiritual pilgrim. "So how do we become true Christians?" demands Steele. "I'm going to walk you through that," replies Pastor Barnes, "and I'm going to send you home with the tape."[7]

The sequels to *Left Behind* pump up the bloodshed over global theaters of war, deploying the obligatory military hardware, battle tactics, weapons specs, and aide-de-camp mindset of a techno-thriller. The LBS also attempts to fashion itself into a geopolitical exposé. Buck penetrates the periphery of a Bilderberg-like cabal of politicians and high financiers who use their global leverage to elevate Carpathia to the status of world dictator. The Antichrist's acclamation as president of Romania is but the first in the succession of bloodless coups d'état, politically as surreal as "a freshman congressman becoming president of the United States in an off-election year, no vote, president steps down, and everybody's happy" (138).

As for the book's partisan colors, the title alone displays them in full. There is no love lost between the authors of the LBS and the liberal Left— or, for that matter, what's left of the liberal Right—so much so that, when in the inaugural novel the righteous are whisked up to heaven in advance of the Tribulation, the president of the United States and his family are left behind. The rightful occupant of the West Wing is manifestly not made of the right stuff. Bill Clinton, eat your heart out.

Generic plotline, stock characters, potboiler formulas, and fairy-tale miracles—at every turn *Left Behind* demands a suspension of disbelief. So does, of course, the *credo quia absurdum est* of the entire premillennialist belief system. Ironically, this literal and figurative affirmation of the power of fiction to imagine an alternative world while commenting on the affairs of this one could lie behind the appeal of the LBS. So could Jenkins's utilitarian style, which depicts the Apocalypse in the narrative analog to plain brown paper, with occasional hints to the confessional prosody of Edward Taylor and the confrontational one of Jonathan Edwards. At the end of the day, it may have been another selling point with the consumers: a book that tells it plainly like it is.

True enough, ignoring most cardinal rules of narration, LaHaye and Jenkins tell it all. They tell us that Buck is a writer's writer and a Pulitzer winner, although they never furnish a word of this scintillating prose. They tell us that Carpathia's oration to the UN General Assembly brims with incredible knowledge, but the two short paragraphs of it we get to see are banality itself. Nonstop editorializing, such as when they tell us that the Antichrist rose from his chair with "pseudodignity" (447), is on a par with third-grade theology, such as when Steele undergoes an epiphany that, "if *genesis* meant 'beginning,' maybe *revelation* had something to do with the end" (121).

Isaac Asimov's not unsympathetic quip that the Golden Age of science fiction is twelve also holds for premillennialist fiction. It is more than the matter of the faithful walking unscathed through A-bomb blasts or of lions becoming petting-zoo leaf-eaters. In what passes for the debate on abortion in *Left Behind*, the only pro-choice argument comes from Hattie, the whore of Babylon: abortions are good, or else abortion clinics could not make a living.[8] "Heckuva" is the limit of adult language in the White House, perhaps in deliberate contrast to the Nixon tapes, which shocked Americans as much with their dirty tricks as with four-letter expletives. But not to worry. In the tradition of Christian romances or holy rock music, Satan's henchmen will condemn billions to nuclear hell but will not say "hell" in the middle of the most heinous acts.

Torn between evangelizing and selling copy, LaHaye and Jenkins settle for an uneasy truce, with dispensationalist exhortations scrambled palimpsest-like into an action thriller. This helps explain why, when they profess that during the Rapture, "everything was left behind" (16), they do not stop to sort out the theological import of grafted skin, artificial limbs, transfusion plasma, and other miracles of modern medicine that also should have been left behind. The apocalyptic plotline has no room for such trifles, so long as *Left Behind XVI* is gorier than *Left Behind XV*. And on cue, battle forces in *Kingdom Come* (2007) are a millennial thousand times larger than in *Glorious Appearing* (2004), vindicating reviewers who see the series as a prime example of dispen-sensationalism.

Deus ex Machina

America is the human hope of the world, and Jesus Christ is the hope of America.

Tim LaHaye, The Bible's Influence on American History

In narrative terms, the LBS is a franchise made in heaven, with sequels built in by the premise of prefiguration. After all, the last sentence of *Left Behind* could well be the first sentence of the sequel, *Tribulation Force: The Continuing Drama of Those Left Behind*: "The task of the Tribulation Force was clear and their goals nothing less than to stand and fight the enemies of God during the seven most chaotic years the planet would ever see" (468). To be continued.

By their own admission, LaHaye and Jenkins were taken aback by the popularity of what began as a trilogy, written in the hope of reaching half a million readers, which morphed into a bestselling dodecalogue and finally a sixteen-novel franchise with a long line of merchandise (what's Apocalypse without a T-shirt?). Upsizing the narrative canvas meant recycling subplots and second-string characters at a rate that should earn them a hand from the environmentalists. This brings unintended comic effects, such as when one infiltrator of the Antichrist's computer banks falls by the wayside, only to be replaced by his narrative clone, different in name but little else.

The Tribulation Force is LaHaye and Jenkins's evangetainment hybrid of born-again Green Berets and "doomsday preppers" from the National Geographic Channel reality TV series. As befits an evangelical comic book, albeit one without frames, Christ's commandos are all top-gun graduates of the lantern-jawed school of *Dick Tracy* vintage. In the beginning, Buck actually confesses to have "always considered the 'born-again' label akin to 'ultraright-winger' or 'fundamentalist'" (396). Once he is elevated to the holy trinity of the Trib Force, he has a change of heart. Born-again ultraright-wingers are heroes.

Jesus Christ himself is little more than the quintessential *deus ex machina*. Alighting over the fields of Armageddon, he smites his enemies and blesses the dispensationalist creed in pages upon pages of rambling monologue excerpted verbatim from the scriptures. What should have been the series' most exalted sequence, evincing the true measure of its epic design, is nothing short of an epic anticlimax. Watching the Jewish messiah morph into a Bible-spouting action figure, Nikos Kazantzakis must be turning in his grave.

No less questionably, LaHaye and Jenkins replace the charitable turn-the-other-cheek Essene from the Gospels of Matthew and Luke with a death-sowing theocrat. In *A Planet for the President,* Alistair Beaton will also slay billions of innocents, but within the framework of an off-the-wall burlesque. In the name of Jesus, LaHaye and Jenkins wipe out three quarters of the Earth's population in earnest. Surveying these hecatombs, instead of towering larger than life, their Son of God looks more like a moral midget.[9]

The premillennial Savior is a brook-no-dissent autocrat who, on occasion, mimics the Antichrist in all but name. Carrying himself with vanity, stamping out all theological opposition, Jesus shrugs off what is known of human nature and human history. Even post-Casablanca FDR, who called for the Axis's unconditional surrender, did not call for obeisance.

Figure 2.1 If Jesus Were GOP . . . ". . . The premillennial Savior is a brook-no-dissent autocrat who, on occasion, mimics the Antichrist in all but name . . ."
Credit: Monte Wolverton

In contrast, the dispensationalist Messiah tolerates only faith that is not even blind so much as servile. In the dispensationalist disjunction *tertium non datur*: either you're with us, or you're against us. Either you embrace the light with Tim LaHaye, Pat Robertson, Jim Bakker, and Jimmy Swaggart, or you embrace Satan.

Even more incongruously, in *The Rising* (2005), young Carpathia encounters an unidentified character who leads him to a desolate wasteland, forsakes him for forty days, bids him turn stones into bread and to throw himself off a temple roof and be saved, and pledges to him all the kingdoms of the world "if you but kneel down and worship me" (379)—all in an outré recreation of the temptations of Christ. This incongruity carries even into the spinoffs, such as the violent *Left Behind: Eternal Forces* video game, in which players can hack away at Christians as troopers of the Horned One.

Even as the LBS pays homage to the wisdom of all men and women reading the Bible for themselves, the only interpretation that looms self-evident to everyone is LaHaye's.[10] Not one word about those who read the Bible differently, as all unbelievers and most believers do. Not one word about its prophecies being as lucid as those of Nostradamus. Not one word about the standard problems of textual scholarship rooted in the fact that the scriptures collate fragmentary and often contradictory accounts written by chroniclers with vested religious and sociopolitical agendas.

All of which highlights the fundamental quandary of appealing to the Bible as the ultimate religious or political authority. Which is *the* biblical text? Is it the synoptic gospels? And if so, in which transcription—Aramaic, Coptic, *koine* Greek, or Latin—and why? Or is it some synthetic reconstruction thereof? If so, does it include the apocrypha (and *whose* apocrypha)? The Dead Sea scrolls? The Nag Hammadi codices? The Codex Tchacos, including the recently discovered Gospel of Judas? If LaHaye is even aware of these and other hermeneutical conundrums, he dismisses them out of hand.[11]

Were the LBS *Paradise Lost*, its most interesting creation would be the ur-rebel with a cause: the Romanian-born Antichrist. And so he is, in the first half of *Left Behind*, before he plays his hand and becomes a cipher onto which LaHaye and Jenkins write all their religious and political evils. Subtlety being their strong suit, the name of the Beast is a portmanteau of Nicolae Ceausescu, the communist-era despot of Romania notorious for his personality cult, and the Carpathian range of Transylvania, home to the no less infamous Vlad Dracula.

In political terms, the Antichrist heads the organization that, in the eyes of LaHaye and his fellow dispensationalists, aims to emasculate the United States. Symbolically, the great deceiver, who is fluent in all six of the official

UN languages, removes its headquarters from New York to Babylon. Just like his social platform, which brims with global-village rhetoric straight from the mouths of American liberals, his campaigns to end Third World hunger, unify global currencies, and foster ecumenical coexistence of the world's religions prove to be satanic ruses. But it is Carpathia's call for global disarmament that marks him for what he is. Given that the Tribulation is said to be unavoidable, anyone who brings peace must be a false pretender, if not the devil incarnate.

In a grand slam at the American political mainstream, Carpathia is also at home with "millenarianism, eschatology, the Last Judgment, and the second coming of Christ" (255), a rather different agenda from that of most members of Congress. Still, when the members of the Tribulation Force are pressed to keep an eye on him, LaHaye's message is as plain as the Plains of Abraham: born-again Christians should keep an eye on American politics and politicians. His fiction only reinforces his nonfiction: throughout his career LaHaye has made it no secret that "leadership in America should be filled by Christian men and women."[12]

Carpathia is, of course, only a fictional president, but historically LaHaye already got his wish in Reagan, not to mention Reagan's Defense and Interior secretaries, Caspar Weinberger and James Watt. Known for their fundamentalist convictions, the three highest politicians in the land openly embraced the born-again exegesis of the Book of Revelation and, consequently, the inevitability of apocalyptic war on Earth in our time. Indeed, stumping for reelection, Governor Reagan went as far as to publically state his belief that "the day of Armageddon isn't far off."[13]

De Gustibus Non Est Disputandum

Have you ever tried to imagine what America would be like if all Christian and Bible influence were removed? What would we have left? The ugliest kind of twentieth-century barbarism, resembling the inhumanity perpetuated in Nazi Germany or Russia and China since the war.

Tim LaHaye, The Bible's Influence on American History

Shooting themselves in the foot while putting the other one in their mouths, LaHaye and Jenkins have hardly a leg left to stand on. Not that this has ever stopped premillennialists from hurling bolts of eschatological doom on humankind. God is Love, but it is tough love all the way, so much so that the entire planet Earth is earmarked for doomsday. And since the question is not *if* but *when*, fundamentalists have been rushing in to tip God's hand by prophesying when his patience with our wicked ways runs out and End Times begin.

Historically, even as the obsession with the end of the world peaks with every fin de siècle, it reaches maximum intensity at the end of every millennium, much as it did during the Dark Ages, when the entire Christendom quailed in terror on the eve of January 1, AD 1000. Never mind that the medieval theophanists failed to get their Judgment Day right, what with calendar reforms from Numa Pompilius on or the absence of zero in the Roman numerical system.

Proving that modern minds are no less susceptible to eschatological superstition, in 1809 the Reverend George Stanley Faber published *A General and Connected View of the Prophecies Relative to the Conversion, Restoration, Union, and Future Glory of the Houses of Judah and Israel; the Progress, and Final Overthrow, of the AntiChristian Confederacy in the Land of Palestine; and the Ultimate General Diffusion of Christianity*. With the help of numerology and similarly foolproof techniques, he divined that the Antichrist was Napoleon Bonaparte and that the world would end with the end of the latter's imperial rule.

Over the next two centuries, undeterred by the predictive successes of Faber and his league of successors, countdowns to Armageddon began to multiply at an accelerating rate, once more rising to a crescendo as the second millennium drew to a close. Increasingly cognizant, however, that they were swimming against the tide of modern science, apocalyptic prophets would preemptively voice their disdain for critical reasoning. Like LaHaye and Jenkins, time and time again they would exhort readers "to move beyond being a critic, an analyst" (214). Without batting an eyelid, on the other hand, they would appeal to reason in their divinations, as Edgar C. Whisenant did in *88 Reasons Why the Rapture Will Be in 1988*.

Reason dictates, of course, that, quite apart from their continuously revised timetables, the very proliferation of apocalyptic prophecies reduces their credibility to zero. But even as it pays lip service to reason, dogma is immune to it. It is for no other reason that, armed with convoluted charts, Marilyn J. Agee could announce in *The End of the Age* that the End Times were due on May 31, 1998, and when things did not quite work out that way, calmly sit down to write *Revelations 2000*.

In *Planet Earth—2000 A.D.*, Hal Lindsey counseled all Christians not to plan to be on planet Earth by the year 2000. This was the same Lindsey who back in 1970 predicted Armageddon for the 1980s in the bestselling nonfiction of the decade, *The Late Great Planet Earth* (ghostwritten by Carole C. Carlson). In between, Lester Sumrall waved goodbye to Earth in *I Predict 2000 A.D.*, Charles Berlitz and J. Manson Valentine obliterated it in *Doomsday 1999 A.D.*, Kirk Nelson prophesied the Second Coming for 1998 in *The Second Coming 1998*, Harold Camping foretold the end of the world for 1994 in *1994?* and then for 2011 in *Time Has an End: A Biblical History of the World 11,013 B.C.—2011 A.D.*, and so on, and so forth.

Pinpointing the end of the world is even more popular in fiction, which allows authors to reach a wider audience without losing credibility over falsifiable predictions. Dispensationalist fiction is, it must be said, distinguishable from nonfiction primarily by the authors incestuously citing one another as evidence of scholastic respectability. Paradoxically, the same evangelists who profess their disdain for critical thinking never fail to shore up their eschatology with exegetical "proofs" cited thereafter in the stream of "scholarly" publications as evidence of their accuracy.

In recent years, the line between premillennialist fiction and nonfiction has blurred even further, owing to the burgeoning practice of releasing novels in parallel with ancillary pseudo-scholarly apparatus. In study guides, digests, and workbooks such as *The Authorized Left Behind Handbook* (2005), dispensationalists neglect no opportunity to spell out their nonfictional exegeses of their fictional exegeses of the Bible. But it was *The Late Great Planet Earth* and its mammoth triumph at the box office that spawned a whole school of "have Scofield Bible, will novelize."

Lindsey himself was nearly beaten to the punch by Joe Musser—later a co-author of a long line of thrillers with Irangate's Oliver North—and the apocalyptic *Behold a Pale Horse* (1970). Also in 1970 appeared *666* by the founder of the Second Coming Ministries, Salem Kirban. Three years later it was followed by his premillennial sequel, titled simply *1000*. Kirban's associate, Gary Cohen, rolled out his version of the Armageddon in *Civilization's Last Hurrah* (1974). He was followed by Frank Allnutt of New Heart Ministries, whose *The Peacemaker* (1978) featured a Henry Kissinger look-alike as the Antichrist.

In 1979 Carol Balizet of Home in Zion Ministries released *The Seven Last Years*. Pastor Dan Betzer of First Assembly of God finished off the Earth in *The Beast: A Novel of the Coming World Dictator* (1985). Frank Peretti, assistant pastor with the Assemblies of God, followed suit with *This Present Darkness* (1986) and *Piercing the Darkness* (1989), in which, among other evils, demon-seized professors corrupt university curricula and students. Erstwhile professor of politics and NSA analyst James BeauSeigneur contributed *Christ Clone Trilogy*, to this day the most literary specimen of the dispensationalist genre (republished by Warner in 2003–2004).

He was followed by evangelist and part-time exorcist Bob Larson with *Abaddon* (1993), himself followed by evangelist and candidate for president of the United States Pat Robertson with *The End of an Age* (1995), himself followed by former Moody radio affiliate David Dolan with *The End of Days* (1997), followed by Peter and Paul Lalonde's *Apocalypse* (1998), followed by Mel Odom's *Apocalypse Dawn* (2003), and so on, and so forth, in a long and growing line of paper apocalypses.[14]

Subject to the same commodifying pressures as other pulp genres, dispensationalist fiction recycles the same plotline based on the premise that the history and the calamitous future of our civilization are described in the scriptures. At the same time, through the process known in ecology as adaptive radiation, it produces an endless number of variations on this basic template. With the lion's share of every novel devoted to the terrors visited upon the Earth, first by God and then by Satan, the seven-year Tribulation looks every inch like the seven-year itch that has to be scratched over and over again—albeit to no avail, since the compulsion to foretell the day when the Antichrist rides into Babylon on a pale mount shows no signs of tapering off.

Facing these anachronistic prophecies, a skeptical inquirer may be excused for asking where fiction ends and reality begins. The standard concept of "reality" does not, of course, allow for much in-betweenness. Its semantic bivalence is simple: something is either real like a pen or unreal like a unicorn. But what about the reality of centers of gravity? You can never hold the latter in your hand like you hold a pen, yet civil engineers and acrobats stake their lives on them. Interestingly, psychoanalytic talk-cures or psychosomatic placebos work to the extent that people believe them to be real.

In 2002 a Time/CNN poll reported that nearly 60 percent of Americans believe that the apocalyptic prophecies intimated in the Book of Revelation will come to pass.[15] No matter that this belief flies in the face of scientific knowledge, not to mention the Bible itself, which puts the End Times at the end of the first century AD. No matter that we have by now survived hundreds of these premillennial and postmillennial apocalypses, always to wake up the morning after and go to work.

Any rational enterprise that got all of its deductions and predictions wrong might be tempted to take a step back and reassess the theory on which they are based—in this case the theory of Rapture, Tribulation, and Apocalypse. But not premillennialism, which, espousing intelligent design while making intelligent thinking look like a sin, reveals itself to be less a rational enterprise than a sectarian psychopathology. The rapture, insist LaHaye and Jenkins, "could not be dissected and evaluated scientifically from a detached Ivy League perspective" (394), demanding a suspension of disbelief instead.[16] So did David Koresh.

At the end of the day, much like in art, in religion *de gustibus non est disputandum*. All the same, as a literary critic with a mandate to think critically, I prefer to throw my lot in with Paul Tillich, who, in his existential sermons collected in *The Shaking of the Foundations*, cautioned that the command "to sacrifice one's intellect is more demonic than divine. For a man ceases to be man if he ceases to be an intellect" (62).

Apocalypse Now

It is no exaggeration to say that the most powerful single influence on the founding of America was the Bible. Had there been no Bible, there would be no America as we know it today.

Tim LaHaye, The Bible's Influence on American History

For American Christianity these may be the worst of times and the best of times. Many congregations are in decline, sex and child-abuse scandals are driving pewsitters away, and in some areas of life, from gene therapy and contraception to abortion and gay marriage, the church looks antiquated, perhaps even reactionary. Not much seems to have changed, in short, since 1966, when *Time* magazine baited Americans from its first-ever pictureless cover with "Is God Dead?"

Naturally, rumors of God's demise have been greatly exaggerated. In April 2005, for example, *Marie Claire* ran a special feature on Christian iconography that left little doubt that the divine brand identification could be the envy of every marketing whiz. Crosses are ubiquitous, splashed on billboards, dangling from necks and ears, tattooed on raw skin. God speaks from T-shirts, bumper stickers, and coffee mugs. Jesus sells a diversified portfolio of products, from diets (kosher) to hobbies (carpentry) to footwear (sandals). This is not to even mention a backlist of bestsellers such as *What Would Jesus Eat?* or, for those who do their penance in the gym, *Body By God.*

In 2007 *USA Today* published a Gallup poll according to which two out of three American adults believe that the Almighty created human beings in their present form during the last ten thousand years. This dramatic evidence of born-again fervor is even more impressive in light of the fact that over the last half a century, membership in mainstream denominations has nosedived. Presbyterian and Methodist congregations, for example, are only half of what they were when *Time* needled believers from newsstands. The registered number of Episcopalians is down by almost 60 percent. Ditto for the United Church of Christ.[17]

One can spin these numbers in a number of ways, but there is no denying that born-again Christianity is no longer playing catch-up to the American religious and cultural mainstream. These days it *is* part of the mainstream, lending some credence to Pat Robertson and Jerry Falwell's claims of commanding a television audience of one hundred million.[18] Its religious and political clout helps, in turn, to explain the number and commercial success of story cycles like *Left Behind*.

Yet, instead of celebrating their social and cultural penetration, many evangelical leaders bemoan society's decline among accusations of moral turpitude and political decay. Neither is this spirit of doomsday anything new. Back during America's bicentennial, Tim LaHaye himself made no bones about the evil rampant in the fifty states. In parallel with his efforts to counter the work of the American Civil Liberties Union, the National Organization for Women, and the National Education Association, he thundered, under the imprint of Christian Heritage College,

> Today we face our greatest enemy, atheistic humanism, which seeks to destroy our moral character and divert us from the principles that have produced the greatest nation in the history of the world.[19]

Forget global warming, with the fate of the planet hanging in the balance. Forget the menace of militant fundamentalism at home and abroad. Forget street violence, drug culture, systemic poverty, political disfranchisement, and education limping on a wing and a prayer. None of them pose as much threat as America's Enemy Number One: humanists who have wrested the helm of the ship of state from the hands of those who would train it on the Star of Bethlehem. And the results of their machinations? Nothing short of Apocalypse now:

> Government induced socialism in the guise of liberalism is raping the American free enterprise system, human initiative is being sapped by welfarism, the morals of our nation have dropped to an all time low, crime threatens our personal safety, and the liberal media is seeking to control the thinking of our people. (73)

Oddly, not once do LaHaye and other doomsayers pause to reflect on the fundamental, not to say fundamentalist, self-contradiction in their theologic. On the one hand, they squander no opportunity to affirm that the Almighty is in absolute control of everything there is. In *Left Behind* LaHaye and Jenkins could not be more categorical that all that happens happens as decreed by a celestial master plan: "Bible prophecy is history written in advance" (214). They reprise their message in *The Remnant*: "God has given us in the Bible an accurate history of the world . . . It is the only truly accurate history ever written" (228).

This belief in predestination goes so far that Tsion Ben Judah, the authors' ill-concealed mouthpiece, enunciates in *Soul Harvest*, "the outcome has already been determined. We win!"[20] Then, pray, what is the point of rallying people to the cause? Why not break open the champagne and sit the Apocalypse out while Satan gets his comeuppance—as he must, if the Bible is right? Why worry about not doing your part or, for that matter, about being prideful, or lustful, or avaricious, or covetous, or otherwise sinful in your daily life? None of it could ever be your fault, seeing as your actions and inactions have been predetermined from time immemorial by the Master Planner.

This is why, taken at face value, evangelical fulminations against atheism, humanism, liberalism, socialism, or other *isms* are inherently blasphemous. If history unfolds in accordance with what is in the Bible, twentieth-century liberalism and humanism are also agents of the divine will. Opposing them amounts to opposing God's decree, which is not only sacrilegious but, in fundamentalist terms, impossible. In sum, LaHaye advocates rebellion against divine providence while maintaining that it cannot be done—a logical and theological suicide.

Undoubtedly, a devil's advocate might object at this point that this *reductio ad absurdum* is predicated on taking *Left Behind* and its exegetical maneuvers at face value. Is it not, however, a category error to read fiction as if it weren't? Is it not wrongheaded to emulate Madame Bovary and take LaHaye's novels to be the gospel truth? Has not Sir Philip Sidney already apologized on behalf of every writer that he nothing affirmeth, and therefore never lieth?

He has—while holding his fingers crossed behind his back. As Sidney knew too well, literary fiction can have profound consequences in the real world. Even those novels that do not make national history, like *Uncle Tom's Cabin* or *The Jungle* did, remake readers in their image by affirming or challenging their ideas about the world. But it is when they expressly call on readers to stand up for these ideas that they expressly cross from fiction into political activism and mass propaganda.

Such is the case when LaHaye and Jenkins demonize their partisan adversary, Molly Ivins, known for her libertarian broadsides at bornagain Republicans from Pat Buchanan to Dubya (whom she liked to dub Dubdub). In the *Left Behind* series, she is incarnated as Viv Ivins, a woman who raises the Antichrist and whose very name in Roman numerals spells VI VI VI—the number of the Beast. Importing their fundamentalist and Republican commitments so expressly into their fiction, LaHaye and Jenkins expressly absolve their readers from the sin of Bovarism. In the end, the *Left Behind* novels more than licence being read in the light of their authors' real-life religious and partisan convictions. They demand it, precisely because they represent a mass-market popularization of their apocalyptic eschatology and their arch-conservative politics.

Dehistoricizing History

Merely *personal* Christianity is not *Biblical* Christianity at all. A personal Spirit-filled life followed by dynamic service and action in all areas of life, including education, politics, etc. is *Biblical* Christianity . . . Christians, including ministers, should become politically active.

Tim LaHaye, *The Bible's Influence on American History*

One should not judge a book by its cover, but in the case of *Left Behind*, the original hardcover from Tyndale House gives credence to *The New York Times'* dismissal of the LBS as an "exercise in brand management."[21] Bible-black monochrome with a stenciled title serves as an emblem of the Good Book—and, as such, a good book. Between the covers, unjustified margins reinforce the symbolism. No justification is needed in a book premised on transcribing God's moves for the Endgame. No matter that Matthew 24:34 identifies End Times with the end of the first century AD, leaving its modern exponents behind by nearly two thousand years.

In a tacit admission of this flagrant anachronism, in the preface to the final book in the series, LaHaye forswears his core premise of reading the Bible literally. In a dramatic U-turn, God is now to be taken at his word only "wherever possible."[22] In one fell swoop, the purportedly true history of humankind is reduced to a hermeneutist's paradise. The problem is, of course, that there is little in the Old Testament to justify LaHaye's hermeneutics in the name of the New. The alleged prophecies of the Second Coming of Christ in our time are taken out of context and hammered onto gospels that by and large have little to say about them.

The real guiding light in all such free-for-all exegeses, documents James Barr in *Fundamentalism*, is not the gospel truth but the impulse to show the Bible to be inerrant. Cherry-picking the scriptures for "evidence," often by means of free association and wordplay, premillennialists forsake "the literal sense as soon as it would be an embarrassment" (46).[23] Worse, LaHaye's gospel *à la carte* is grounded in deliberate misrepresentation. It is more than the awkward fact that there is not one word in the scriptures about dispensations, and even less about the Rapture or the Tribulation. In *Tribulation Force* and then in *Soul Harvest*, LaHaye and Jenkins claim that the Tribulation Force is named after "what the Bible calls 'tribulation saints'" (236). Except "tribulation saints" does not appear anywhere in the scriptures.

At the end of the day, all this narrative and theological skulduggery makes it difficult to see the LBS as anything else but a species of juvenile adventure. Whatever its artistic demerits, on the other hand, it has more than proven its staying power with the American audiences (significantly, translations were almost uniformly flops), providing a rightwing pulpit for evangelizing fidel and infidel alike. So what if, as weapons in the fight for the minds of the American public, the *Left Behind* novels are artless and crude? Much as in politics, in religion a bludgeon is sometimes more effective than a lancet.

Moreover, even if forgettable as an aesthetic experience, the LBS is invaluable as a social seismograph for getting a reading of the influence of Christian fundamentalism in American public life. This is largely because apocalyptic fiction never strays far from politics *tout court*. As a matter of fact, many tenets of evangelical Christianity, such as the absolutist view of the scriptures, the belief in divine agency, or the desegregation of state and religion, are mirrored in its political platform—such as an apocalyptic view of history, the displacement of democracy by charismatic leadership, and the advocacy of behavioral control.[24]

The end results of the apocalyptic notion of history are particularly insidious. The Judgment Day perspective on the course of human affairs in effect dehistoricizes world history, replacing self-realization and material causation with the divine finger in the name of a teleological fulfillment of wildly anachronistic divinations. More perniciously still, it transmutes the workaday political process—premised as it is on vigorous debate, hard-nosed negotiations, and bipartisan horse-trading—into an apocalyptic standoff between the forces of good and evil.

Apocalyptic politics in the United States goes beyond evocations of doomsday, branding of sundry axes of evil, appeals to "What Would Jesus Do?," or agitprop about America's divine election. Crucially, it eliminates the political middle ground between the Left and the Right and the presumption of vectoring a collective impulse, and with them the culture of collaboration and compromise. In their place it cultivates a politics of hardline disjunctions, block refusals, and wedge issues contrived to polarize the electorate and turn partisan politics into a zero-sum showdown of Manichean proportions. In short, to borrow a word from Jon Stewart, it turns American politics into a daily cliffpocalypsemageddonacaust.

Seen in this light, apocalyptic fiction and apocalyptic evangelism are clearly not just about religion. Krishna Kumar's analysis of modern-era fundamentalism in India is particularly useful in this context. His insights into communalism—whereby a community of adherents shares not only religious affiliation but also social, economic, and not least political objectives—open a window onto the engagé variety of fundamentalism ascendant nowadays in the United States. Personified by the authors of *Left Behind*, it stands in sharp contrast to the traditional Christian suspicion of striving for reward in this world as opposed to the next.

Like all other fundamentalist denominations, dispensationalism has traditionally viewed human history as inherently corrupt, with the

RIGHT WINGERS AND LEFT WINGERS GOING NOWHERE

Figure 2.2 **Rightwingers and Leftwingers Going Nowhere** ". . . It eliminates the political middle ground between the Left and the Right and the presumption of vectoring a collective impulse, and with them the culture of collaboration and compromise . . ."

Credit: Grea

contemporary times as the best case in point. Such a perspective is not conducive to active engagement in society's affairs, seen as they are as a source of degeneracy and vice. Indeed, the dimensions of the political revolution in evangelical circles are apparent when one considers that in the first half of the twentieth century, several denominations questioned whether it was even moral to vote.[25]

The apparent clash with science, reason, and liberal social values has led many to see in fundamentalism a rejection of modernity and even an epitome of antimodernity.[26] It is at least as plausible, however, to see it as a quintessential expression of modernity and its fragmented, unstable nature that produces a cultural antithesis for every thesis. Ironically, with dispensationalism ambivalent about so much of the contemporary world, dispensationalist fiction exploits this anxiety even as it recruits rank and file for its political goals.

Today millennialism and meliorism go hand in hand with an active, even proactive, attitude to social engineering and political engagement. Historian Michael Standaert makes this point in the context of LaHaye and the LBS by showing how the grafting of dispensationalist theology on the American myths of exceptionalism and rightwing conspiracy fantasies made for resurgent political activism.[27] Johann Pautz documents how *Left Behind* belongs to a far-right social landscape that runs from the militia movement to the John Birch Society, exerting "considerable influence in American politics" (283). And Melani McAlister completes the picture of evangelism engagé by detailing how evangelical fiction and nonfiction articulate a clear and present "political agenda" (775).

Ironically, among this sea of analysis, the LBS has remained largely ignored by literary scholarship, perhaps not surprisingly given its double handicap as a popular and political blockbuster.[28] Literary paucity aside, however, the series hit home with an estimated eighty million American readers, including ten million in the Kid's Edition (starring Judd, Vicki, Lionel, and the Young Trib Force). Factor in the *Left Behind* film viewers, video players, and spinoff readers, and you begin to grasp the scale of the educational and political forum commanded by men for whom the direst perils are non-evangelical politics and non-evangelical education.

There are, of course, reasons to believe that apocalyptic fiction may be little more than an exotic form of entertainment for the majority of its readers, and that evangelical adventure thrillers, even those as long as the *Left Behind* series, may be no more than a short-lived experience for thrill-seeking consumers. On the other hand, LaHaye and Jenkins never miss a chance to proselytize, perhaps on the assumption that those who come for the adventure may stay for the evangel. And, in case that does not work, they found Bible schools where their version of messianic prophecies is taught as history.

Idiot Nation

Christian schools that offer a thorough but Biblically-oriented education comprise the fastest growing movement in the country.

Tim LaHaye, The Bible's Influence on American History

Pat Robertson's TV show, *The 700 Club*, is the flagship of the Christian Broadcasting Network syndicated to more than a third of a billion viewers around the world. Launched in the 1960s, it had gone through a few lean years before it proved televangelism to be a viable commercial enterprise. In parallel with the ascendancy of the Moral Majority during Reagan's first term, the program began to expand its coverage to include local and federal politics, steadfastly lining up behind the Republican and Christian right wing. Eventually, it even served as a launching pad for Pat's own run for president in 1988.

Overwhelmingly repudiated by the voters, Robertson channeled the campaign publicity into the launch of the Christian Coalition (now

Christian Coalition of America), arguably the most political nonpolitical organization in the country. Diehard pro-GOP as it is, however, it is unfair to use it as a partisan piñata. Historically, it was not the Republicans but the Democrats who instigated the tactics later perfected by the Coalition: using chartered nonpartisan organizations to run more or less covert partisan campaigns.[29]

It was in March 2006 on *The 700 Club*, while plugging a new book by liberal-basher David Horowitz, that Robertson made a sensational accusation. With *The Professors: The 101 Most Dangerous Academics in America* already steeped in controversy, he poured gasoline onto the fire by claiming that the individuals tarred in it were only a mere fraction of thirty to forty thousand leftwing faculty members in the United States, all of them "racists, murderers, sexual deviants and supporters of Al-Qaeda—and they could be teaching your kids!"[30]

Robertson clearly borrowed a page from Horowitz's dust jacket, which agitated that the eponymous 101

> teach our young people—who also happen to be alleged ex-terrorists, racists, murderers, sexual deviants, anti-Semites, and al-Qaeda supporters. Horowitz blows the cover on academics who:—Say they want to kill white people.—Promote the views of the Iranian mullahs.—Support Osama bin Laden.—Lament the demise of the Soviet Union.—Defend pedophilia.— Advocate the killing of ordinary Americans.

Anti-intellectualism boasts, of course, a long history in American culture and politics. The twice-told case of Adlai Stevenson, perhaps the most intellectually gifted presidential contender ever, is exemplary in this respect. Tagged by Eisenhower's spin doctors as an egghead, he never fully recovered from this damning epithet, losing to the self-styled Man of the Hour both in 1950 and 1954. More recently, Bush's spin machine heaped abuse on Gore's "fuzzy" math and "phony" numbers and walked away with a victory. In 2004 they slapped Kerry so hard for being a Francophile—the ultimate *faux pas* of an intellectual—that he balks at speaking French even as Obama's secretary of state. Meanwhile, the multimillionaire governor of Texas was packaged as a man of the people, a lowbrow, barbecue-loving George Schmo.

Nevertheless, if Robertson is right, American academia must be in a sorry state. So what if American universities are spearheading a wave of expansion into the lucrative Asian and Arab markets, franchising their names for hefty tuitions and tax exemptions? Even as some parts of the world buy into the American tertiary system, with students lining up from Shanghai to Dubai, the evangelical Right does not. Instead, with LaHaye and Falwell in the lead, they establish their own schools and colleges to counter what they see as the closing of the American mind.[31]

LaHaye has founded a number of institutions that disseminate his religious and political tenets, starting in the early 1970s with the Christian Heritage College (now San Diego Christian College) and the Institute for Creation Research. In a continuation of politics by other means, he also opened a number of high schools, part of an entire born-again Christian education system. He also co-founded the Council for National Policy, an exclusive (invitation-only) lobby of some five hundred influential evangelicals and rightwingers ranging from former senator Jesse Helms to congressman Tom DeLay, Pat Robertson, John Ashcroft, Oliver North, and Larry Pratt (leader of Gun Owners of America). Tellingly, it is listed as an educational foundation.

This type of marriage of religion, politics, and education is far from unusual. Having founded the Moral Majority and its successor, the Liberty Foundation, Jerry Falwell himself went on to establish Liberty University (formerly Liberty Baptist College). Among the partisan bickering and academic obfuscation, it is not always easy to tell how closed the American mind is in the first place. Into the breach stepped Michael Moore with *Stupid White Men . . . and Other Sorry Excuses for the State of the Nation!*, one of the publishing events of the last decade. Selling an estimated nine million copies, Moore's trademark display of guerrilla journalism touched a nerve with Americans—those who can read, that is. After all, his entire chapter 5, "Idiot Nation," is devoted to showing that, with George W. Bush in the lead, the United States is a nation of idiots.[32]

Lobbing example upon example of education standards falling to the bottom of the bottomless pit, Moore caps his Georgic with a stunner: "There are forty-four million Americans who cannot read and write above a fourth-grade level—in other words, who are functional illiterates" (88). How could the United States, home of the Ivy League, the highest number of Nobel Prizes, and the smartest bombs, be taxed with being an Idiot Nation? How could the president destined to go down in history with a book in his hand (never mind it was only *The Pet Goat*) be shortchanging education?

Alas, far from being another gimmicky montage, Moore's data is right on the money. National adult literacy rates compiled by the Department of Education reveal that almost a quarter of all American adults perform at the lowest of five skill levels on literacy tasks related to daily life. Equally shockingly, the next fifty million score at the second lowest level. Like father, like son: 15 percent of high school graduates cannot read above sixth-grade level. Like son, like father: nearly half of American grownups cannot follow a bus schedule, and one in five cannot follow the front page of a newspaper.[33]

No Child Left Behind

Today's schools are so godless, immoral, drug-ridden, unsafe, and in many cases sub-par educationally that they are no longer acceptable to many parents.

Tim LaHaye, The Bible's Influence on American History

A man of the people, Bush II also only scanned news headlines, relying on his staffers' digests instead. And while he paid lip service to education, his promises were like New Year resolutions, made with little expectation of being kept. A case in point: the No Child Left Behind Education Act, signed with fanfare in 2001 with the goal of salvaging ailing primary and secondary schools. No sooner, however, had the last flash flashed and the last shutter clicked shut than the administration took to treating it like Cinderella.

To take just one example, in the same year that Robertson made his wild denunciation, strapped by the escalating costs of two fullscale wars in Asia, Bush requested only a little more than half of the already authorized budget for the Act. The consequences of these cuts, publicly deplored by the American Federation of Teachers, were predictable: critical shortages in manpower and teaching materials in local schools. Bush's 2007 extension of his first-term tax cuts made things even worse. Favoring the upper rungs of society, they made the class division between private and public schools more entrenched than ever. As if that were not enough, his $3.5 billion cutbacks in education put dozens of programs for schoolchildren—almost a third of all so targeted—up for elimination.[34]

Nature, of course, abhors a vacuum, and where the government makes itself scarce, business interests can be counted on to take up the slack. Welcome to the world of corporate education, where profits step right from the boardroom to the classroom. BOOK IT! campaign masterminded by Pizza Hut—Dental Health Classroom Project sponsored by Colgate-Palmolive— corporate history lessons for future patty-flippers supported by Burger King—scholastic-sounding Edison Project by Whittle Communications, which supplies schools with TV displays and, as a *quid pro quo*, requires schoolchildren to watch "news" shows littered with commercials—scientific curricula designed or only "enriched" by Amoco, Ford, and Chevron—all show how pervasive the commodification and commercialization of education has become.[35]

With financially strapped school districts targeted by fast-food chains, soft-drink bottlers, computer and software companies, and other corporations keen to diversify into the education market, students are increasingly vulnerable to such "partnerships." Learning aids that are little more than corporate logo-carriers, tax deductions that deplete public coffers, or Taylorization of the underage workforce are, however, only the tip of the iceberg. The long-term effects run deeper than anyone is prepared to admit. The growing fixation with assessing academic standards in cash-value terms is the clearest sign of how the corporate mindset has reset the scholastic and the moral compass for young Americans.

So much for the reforms instigated in the wake of a scathing 1983 report by the National Commission on Excellence in Education. Entitled "A Nation at Risk," it attacked—albeit for different reasons than LaHaye—the tide of mediocrity eroding American education. The sense of alarm it instilled triggered a large-scale reorganization of the national system: state standards, charter schools, alternative teacher certification programs, and more test-based accountability. Later came two massive federal programs, Bush II's No Child Left Behind and Obama's Race to the Top.

Today, notwithstanding isolated pockets of improvement, scores remain as mediocre as they were under Reagan. A year after the United States led the world in the number of medals at the Beijing Olympics, American high schoolers placed fourteenth in reading, seventeenth in science, and twenty-fifth in math among industrialized nations.[36] Not only did they trail students from Estonia to Poland, but one-third of college entrants needed remedial education. In the race to the top of the world in Olympic hardware, to say nothing of military hardware, American schoolchildren got left behind.

Come to think of it, education used to be the favorite talking point of that spectacularly underachieving reformist, Barack Obama. In *The Audacity of Hope*, the political nonfiction that made him a household name after Oprah's thumbs-up transformed it into a chart-topper, the senator gave much play to his visit a year earlier to Thornton Township High School. A townhall-style meeting with youth and teachers from a poor, mostly black suburb south of Chicago, and a politician who talks policy and not politics—*Primary Colors* writes itself all over again.

In his prescient analysis of the young senator as just another racehorse from the Chicago stables, David Freddoso documented, however, how the future president elected not to support even basic reforms of classroom discipline, an eternal problem in urban schools. When the state legislature debated such reforms in 2001, Obama twice voted "No" on a bill that required teenagers to complete their suspensions before they could be shunted to new schools. Needless to say, his own children—like those of his former chief of staff, Rahm Emanuel, now the mayor of Chicago hell-bent on reforming public education—attend private schools. Perfect fodder for *The West Wing*'s Sam Seaborn when he rails in "Six Meetings Before Lunch" against rich liberals who patronize private schools while defending public education that handicaps the less privileged.

The Texas Textbook Massacre

Modern educators inundate the minds of our youth with the false notion that our freedom had its roots in the "enlightenment movement" of the French Revolution, but nothing could be further from the truth.

Tim LaHaye, The Bible's Influence on American History

In January 2011, a Minnesota congresswoman and Tea Party stalwart, Michele Bachmann, took it upon herself to teach the Iowans for Tax Relief rally something about the Constitution and slavery. Bondage of the black population was a blight, conceded the politician, but "we also know that the very founders that wrote those documents worked tirelessly until slavery was no more in the United States."[37] This was only one of a number of historical blunders perpetrated by an elected member of Congress who made a point of toting a pocket edition of the American Constitution in her pocket.

Just like *Left Behind*, Bachmann's crowd-pleasing account was an American fiction. In fact, the Emancipation Proclamation was signed in 1863, by which time all the Founding Fathers were dead. Moreover, the proclamation did not set American slaves free. It outlawed bondage only in the confederate South, while saying nothing about the victorious North. It was not until the Thirteenth Amendment, passed on December 6, 1865, that slavery and involuntary servitude were finally abolished nationwide. In 2013 Daniel Day-Lewis received an unprecedented third Best Actor Oscar for his portrayal of the politician who revised the Constitution by hook and by crook to achieve this goal.

If Bachmann is anything to go by, American citizens all too readily forget their history, or maybe they have never learned it in the first place. And if the Texas Board of Education has anything to say about it, they never will. Controlled by fundamentalist conservatives, the board voted in 2010 in favor of a new curriculum for primary and secondary schools. As the second most populous state in the nation, with more than five million children enrolled in the system, the Lone Star wields disproportionate sway over other states that, loath to invest scarce resources to develop their own teaching materials, often find it expedient to teach Texas-style.

The result is that the national heritage is getting a facelift more thoroughgoing than any of Michael Jackson's. Among numerous other changes, it deletes references to the late Senator Kennedy, adopts a uniformly laudatory stance toward Reagan, requires students to follow conservative organizations such as the Moral Majority or the NRA, reduces the coverage of minority leaders such as Cesar Chavez and liberal Supreme Court justices such as Thurgood Marshall, teaches that taxation harms economic progress in contrast to free-market economics, and questions the separation of church and state.

Symbolically, the new curriculum also drops Thomas Jefferson from the list of Enlightenment thinkers. This may have as much to do with the third president's deep-seated sympathy for direct democracy as with his deistic (not to call it enlightened) stance on the separation of church and state, expressed in his thoroughgoing suspicion of the Old Testament and a principled rejection of what he branded as "so much absurdity, so much untruth, charlatanism and imposture" in the New.[38]

The arch-conservative agenda of what has been dubbed the Texas Textbook Massacre is even more salient in comparison with the textbook wars of the previous generation. The most consequential of those was the 1974 clash in West Virginia that pitted reformists against evangelical Christians, who rose up in opposition to the new multicultural (i.e., liberal) curriculum. With the national media fanning the flames from the firebombing of several schools, with firearms fired and open threats of escalation from both sides, the Christian conservatives won the battle but lost the war. They forced a review of the new textbooks that in the end substantially upheld the revamped curriculum.

Texas also leads America in the criminalization of education. Hundreds of schools have armed police patrolling the playgrounds and corridors to keep order. Pupils are sent to the courts of law for infractions as trifling as cutting classes or writing one's name on a desk, with both the children and their parents receiving Class C misdemeanors and felony convictions. Using the courts to fix student behavior is big business, with the annual budget for surveillance and security in Dallas alone exceeding $20 million. Meanwhile, Texas criminalizes more than three hundred thousand "felons" a year—mostly for truancy.[39]

Among culture wars fought left and right, it is not easy to give the final grade to American education. Is it as underperforming as religious fundamentalists and global comparative indices suggest? Or as first-rate as the Third World takes it to be? Judge for yourself. From the truckloads of undergraduate bloopers that crossed my desk in a quarter century, here are only a few highlights from the lowlights from only one course in only one term. On the menu were Hammett's *Red Harvest* and *The Maltese Falcon*, Cain's *The Postman Always Rings Twice* and *Double Indemnity*, and Chandler's *Playback*. See if you can recognize them in this hilarious cryptobabble from North American sophomores.

Frank's complete reliance on bodily reaction also tints his individualism with the absurd.

He got involved with Iva, his partner's wife, when he was still alive, but when he died he did not want anything to do with her.

The three never use guns, but if they do they usually use not their own.

Her character's autonomy and self-control are limited by the function of its role.

Thus the hero finds himself smacked right into the mean stream of the city life of American culture.

The use of realism veers directly into the proverbial on-coming traffic.

Spade and Huff differ in elements.

The detective business of the op frees the character from the homogenized space-time of the majority of capitalist labour.

She uses language as a mode of transport.

It is she alone who commits the possible murders.

Huff has an inner adrenalin pumping inside of him not only at the site of Phyllis.

Frank differs from the typical model is in his being far too human.

Like Brigid, she missiles her protector with her sexual intrigue.

When Marlowe meats Miss Vermilyea for the first time he does not describe her proportions.

Betty pawns men for her own ends.

The quality of the nation was prone to poverty, filthy streets, and a rise in crime.

The essential personas of the protagonists, the op, Frank Chambers, and Philip Marlowe, mark the development of the anima of the community.

Marlowe uses his position as a spectator who moves in private spaces unmarked.

The women are attributed with provocative looks and bodies to match, which they can turn on or off at their will.

But there must be some greater explanation behind these women. They all have different endings and so must be different in some ways.

Californians are not real people; they do not have problems; shreds of morality creep up with them.

Team America

> If given enough time, the rapidly growing Christian school movement, I believe, will someday replace the atheistic education system as the primary source of future American leadership.
>
> *Tim LaHaye, The Bible's Influence on American History*

Historically, the granddaddy of apocalyptic bestsellers was not *Left Behind* or *The Late Great Planet Earth* but Michael Wigglesworth's 1662 narrative poem *The Day of Doom*. His literary terrors of Judgment Day, especially the part in which God damns unbaptized children to hell, proved so scandalizing to his contemporaries that today not one copy of the first two editions survives. They were all thumbed to shreds.

Although end-of-the-world fantasy has lost none of its fascination for today's readers, it was smart marketing rather than smart writing that turned *Left Behind* and its sequels into crossover sellouts. While popular with born-again buyers, the books did not get legs with the mainstream until the publisher began to stack them at the checkout counters of mass retailers like Costco, Kmart, and Walmart. In the middle of the 2000s, just as Beaton was waging satire on political and religious fundamentalism in *A Planet for the President*, LaHaye and his next hired pen secured a forty-million-dollar advance from Warner Books for a "new" doomsday cycle.[40]

Viewed in one light, the LBS is no more than a commercial spinoff from the bestselling and arguably the most important book in the history of the Western civilization. Viewed in another, however, it is a continuation of a time-honored tradition of modernizing the Christian gospel for its contemporaries. Going back to the ancient corpus of Vetus Latina, via the now canonical Vulgate, it extends right up to the beehive of twenty-first-century Bibles tailored to the eclectic tastes of American consumers.

For the tree-huggers, there is *The Green Bible,* printed on recycled paper with soy ink, with all references to the environment highlighted in green. For the yuppies, there is Bible Illuminated in a GQ-style glossy, oversized format and adorned by photos of celebrities from Che Guevara to Angelina Jolie. There is the Power of a Praying Woman's Bible, Spiritual Warfare Bible, Spirit-filled Life Bible, Livin' Out Your Faith Bible, Duct Tape Bible, Backpack Bible, Extreme Teen Bible, American Patriot Bible, and—rounding up a catalog of hundreds of other niche offerings—the Veggie Tales Bible.

The evangelical United States may not be ready, however, for the findings documented in 2009 in *Evolutionary Psychology*. Countries with low levels of social dysfunction—as measured by the rates of homelessness, unemployment, teen pregnancies, abortion, divorce, imprisonment, homicide, STDs, and others—are invariably the most secular. In contrast, countries afflicted by social problems, such as the United States, are the most religious (as reflected by belief in God, religious service attendance, frequency of prayer, and so on). Behind the correlation lies causality. The easing of social and economic problems dims religiosity, while social ills turn it back on.[41]

The apparent ease with which populations shrug off God when conditions improve bucks the view popular in American evangelical and political circles that religious observance is the bedrock of existence. Instead, it appears to be an adaptable coping mechanism. When socioeconomic dysfunction reaches critical levels, people deal with the trauma by turning their eyes toward heavens. This is an awkward truth in a country in which, if Tim LaHaye and Jerry B. Jenkins are anything to go by, "atheist" and "humanist" are four-letter words—a culture in which coordinated political action from groups such as the Moral Majority and Christian Coalition of America aims to keep godless liberals from forging a nation in their own image.

This is the country that in 1955 legislated "In God We Trust" on all currency and in 1956 made it the United States' official motto. A country in which "God bless America" is stapled to every politician's lips, so much so that—George Clooney's recent film *The Ides of March* notwithstanding—a card-carrying atheist stands as much chance of being anointed by either wing of the Demublican party as a Satanist does. A country whose elected representatives apparently aim to convert it into a theocracy, with the Bible in the place of the Constitution.

The rallying cry of the religious Right is, after all, that the Constitution was written to promote a Christian order. So what that this contradicts the historical record? "If you're not electing Christians, then in essence you're going to legislate sin," maintains Florida congresswoman Katherine Harris, co-chair of Bush II's 2000 election campaign and a would-be senator.[42] Some senators even vow not to confirm atheists to the Supreme Court, thus violating the very Constitution—which mandates that no religious test shall ever be required as a qualification to any office or public trust—on which they took an oath.

We no longer live in the relatively enlightened era when Jefferson could win the presidency while being denounced not merely as an atheist but a *French* atheist. More representative of America today is the fact that writings by and about Jefferson had been banned from the Philadelphia public library until 1830 because of his supposed atheism. Mitt Romney's eleventh-hour ploy to boost his sagging 2012 campaign by accusing Obama of plotting to drop "In God We Trust" from the legal tender is just a recent chapter of the same story.

With cheap stunts like these, the Republican Party only dilutes the legacy of one of its greatest stalwarts and publicists, who happened to be a bestselling novelist as well. It would be an exaggeration to say that William F. Buckley Jr. made conservatism respectable and even attractive in the postwar decades dominated by the statist legacy of the FDR/Truman era. But he certainly played a major hand in it as the founder of *National Review*, host of *Firing Line*, syndicated columnist, and author of political thrillers starring the American James Bond, Blackford Oakes.

With his legendary erudition, Buckley dramatized his conservative vision for postwar America in novels spanning Eisenhower's first term and Reagan's second. Known for adroit plotting, crisp dialogue, and political savvy, he proved himself as adept at espionage adventure as John le Carré, even if without the latter's moral ambiguity and liberal leanings. Not that Buckley *was* le Carré, from whom he set himself apart throughout his career. For every gem of political espionage worthy of Eric Ambler, such as his alternative history of the downing of the U2 spy plane in *Marco Polo, If You Can*, there is a spy-fi turkey like *Mongoose R.I.P.*, in which Oakes plots to overthrow Castro after the Bay of Pigs.

For that matter, even *Marco Polo, If You Can* is not exempt from clichés, such as when Buckley's hero falls a-praying in a dig at the godless, easily-led-by-the-nose Soviets. With Allen Dulles as the director of the CIA and Hoover at the helm of the FBI, everybody on his Team America is on the side of the angels. If the real America of the period—the Red paranoia, the witch-hunts, the McCarthys, and the Nixons—makes an appearance at all, it is not even as warts but as harmless moles on the body politic.

For all this, Buckley's Republicanism was decidedly more tolerant, not to say centrist, than the give-no-quarter partisanship that reigns in Washington these days. Much of the latter can be laid at the doorstep of the Bible-and-Constitution-toting Tea Party, which is forcing the GOP and the country to take a turn to the right, after the neocon turn to the right in the 2000s, after the Gingrich-led turn to the right in the 1990s, and after the Reagan-era turn to the right in the 1980s. Four right turns later, the country is right back where it started, with politicians swearing that the promised land lies just around the bend.

Had Buckley lived into the new millennium, he would be dismayed at the central message of rightwing, born-again Christianity, which appears to be that the only change necessary to secure salvation is to change one's mind on a few theological issues. Changes in lifestyle or in relationships to other people are less important. Such a dissociated theology downplays the duty to care for social justice that most strains of Christianity endorse, enabling guiltless egoism, not to mention overexploitation of national and world resources.

In 1999, on the pages of their premillennial book of prophecies *Are We Living in the End Times?*, LaHaye and Jenkins warned that "Deception will continue to increase as the end times approach" (34). Taking their words at face value, we may indeed be approaching Judgment Day.

3

A Planet for the Taking

Alistair Beaton, *A Planet for the President*

All in the Family

I realised belatedly that the name "Ritchie" might awaken *The West Wing* echoes.

Alistair Beaton to Peter Swirski

He was a cowboy first and last, even after he had traded the governor's office for the White House at the beginning of the first of two terms. Once he was in power, the Oval Office became an extension of his ego. Narcissistically, he enjoyed being in charge even as he evinced little interest in the nitty-gritty of day-to-day governance. His staff pre-chewed for him daily news digests, which he skimmed or ignored altogether, preferring to play with his dog. Scant knowledge of the world did not stop him, however, from riding it like a herd of beeves: stampeding it when it pleased him, branding America's name on all that moved, and culling heads in the name of defending freedom and all that is good and just in the world.

Emotionally insecure, he could be affable in a backslapping, locker-room kind of way. He preferred joshing with the grunts and photo-ops featuring badass military hardware to diplomatic protocol, and cheeseburgers to state dinners. His folksy, proud-to-be-an-American style was underlined, he felt, by cracking with a four-letter word when there was no press around. Telling somebody to go be fruitful and multiply, especially when they started to rant about eco-nut issues, was part of his ranchero style. Hey, why worry about the planet? Does the planet worry about the president? Besides, once you're out of the office, the ball is in someone else's court.

After the terrorist attacks on New York's Twin Towers, he fomented an outburst of anti-French sentiment when the Élysée Palace refused to support him and the British prime minister in the illegitimate invasion of a tiresome small country. The whole cheese-eating-surrender-monkeys episode proved a godsend, diverting attention from the hijacking of color-coded terrorist alerts for political purposes. With America isolated in the War on Terror, he went it alone, doubling defense budgets even as photos of Iraqi prisoners tortured by the good guys emerged in the media.

Anti-intellectual and anti-liberal, in many ways he was a throwback to the days of *All in the Family*: an all-American bigot given to seeing the world in black and white. More Manichean than Machiavellian, he reduced politics to homespun axioms: terrorists were bad, tax cuts were good, budget deficits didn't matter. His earth-costing campaigns were bankrolled by backrooms of incorporated friends and well-wishers who never asked for anything in return save a spot of grease on the skids of friendly legislation.

He was a former alcoholic who cultivated the image of sobriety to please his conservative voters. He opened cabinet powwows with a prayer and justified political expediencies by invoking God, regardless of whether they were actually in keeping with the Christian ethic he affected to embrace. Deeply homophobic, he spouted off on family values and donated to teen abstinence programs. Liable to mangling the American language, he was an all-American with an all-American attitude to foreigners: they rubbed him the wrong way.

He was unpopular in Europe but found a devoted—many said fawning—sidekick in the British prime minister. His administration swarmed with crooked opportunists and his inner circle with born-again fundamentalists who believed in the Rapture. Fixed only on boosting their own power and influence in the White House, they milked his flat-out incompetence, passing a raft of legislation that benefited their corporate puppet-masters while turning a deaf ear to the conservationists.

When it came to environmental issues, he was shamelessly ignorant of, if not downright hostile to, the science behind global warming. He refused to acknowledge that man-made climate change was a fact—the approved White House soundbite was that the jury was still out—even as torrential floods, arctic winters, and unprecedented heat waves lay siege across the country from Washington State to Washington, DC.

With the president and the administration in denial, one of the deadliest and costliest natural catastrophes in American history flattened New Orleans. A freak hurricane dumped trillions of tons of rainwater on Louisiana, flooded Lake Pontchartrain, breached the ill-engineered levees, and overran the ill-maintained dyke and drainage system. It killed thousands, displaced millions, and inflicted billions of dollars of damage while the president and his team dallied with a response.

Also on his watch, government-operated agencies funded a profusion of studies directed at undermining scientific data on global warming. The same agencies lobbied for nature protection laws that allowed them to plunder the nation's natural resources, pollute its air and waters, and open the Alaskan wilderness to mining, drilling, and logging. Meanwhile, the president hung back on his ranch, hobnobbed with a procession of Hollywood celebs, and stood resolute in the War on Terror.

His name? Fletcher J. Fletcher, president of the United States in Alistair Beaton's bestselling novel *A Planet for the President*—the 2005 paperback edition, that is. Readers familiar with the original 2004 hardback would notice a major discrepancy: the president's name here is Ritchie J. Ritchie. Either way the satirical overtones are unmistakable, harking back to Major Major and the black comedy of Heller's *Catch-22* and, via E. Abbott Abbott, to the political dystopia of *Flatland*. Nor is it difficult to decode the symbolism of the double moniker: Fletcher J. Fletcher doubles for George W. Bush. But whence the change?

The culprit was *The West Wing*. On the show, three-time Governor Ritchie of Florida was the Republican presidential nominee running against "the Education President" Jed Bartlet. Ritchie's ultrarightwing politics and limited intellectual capacity were, naturally, telltale pointers to then Florida governor Jeb Bush, brother to the president. To escape these metafictional and nonfictional entanglements, not to mention imputations of ripping off the best political drama on television, with a heavy heart (he preferred the old name), Beaton decided to redact a winner.

With the hardback basking in kudos from *The Mail on Sunday* ("Dr Strangelove for the eco generation") to *Church Times* ("Tom Sharpe's burlesque and the didactic thrust of Ben Elton") to *The Scotsman* ("those in power should be very afraid of Alistair Beaton"), Ritchie squared became Fletcher squared in the paperback edition.[1] It may have been a paranoid and unnecessary change, conceded the author to me with ten years' hindsight. But then, being paranoid does not mean that you are not right, especially when it comes to politics.

With Fletcher a clear stand-in for Bush II, Beaton's satirical game of "name this villain" is far from over. Fletcher's right-hand man is the oldest member of his entourage, Defense Secretary Joe Skidelski: thin lips, mafia tactics, king-size leverage owing to the king-size budgets under his control, and a bottomless hunger for power. Altogether a spot-on thumbnail of Donald "The Don" Rumsfeld, the oldest defense secretary under Bush II who made a name for himself as the youngest defense secretary under Ford when—as Bob Woodward notes in *Bush at War* (2003)—many Republicans, "including Rumsfeld himself, thought he might be headed for the presidency."[2]

There is also the striking, educated, non-Caucasian, exotically named bigwig in Homeland Security. The token female among the president's senior staff, she is a ringer for Condoleezza Rice, Bush's first-term national security adviser. This is not to say, on the other hand, that everyone in the novel is intended to be a facsimile of a Bush crony. Vince Lennox, special adviser to the president and the other major focalizer in the story, is merely a generic yuppie whose sporadic bursts of moral pique are neutralized by the rush of power he gets from having Fletcher's ear.

In the same manner, the surgically youthful Hollywood leading man Cheech Lingaard is just a one-size-fits-all Malibu highflier. He picks up checks worth millions of dollars for being what every American wants to be: rich, envied, and a celebrity. Like the underpaid salesgirl who works nights in an exclusive supermarket on Dupont Circle, selling shaved black winter Périgord truffles to White House staffers and dreaming of one day being able to buy them, he only personifies the American Dream.

Planet America

My aim is not really to change people's minds—I am not that arrogant. My aim is to entertain, stir a few thoughts and—above all—bring a little comfort and vindication to those who believe our leaders can be bastards. This is often attacked as "preaching to the converted." But what's wrong with that?

Alistair Beaton to Peter Swirski

This farce writes itself. The carbon footprint of a statistical American is more than four times the global norm. What with the rest of the world playing catch-up in terms of economic development, not to mention standard of living, this is unsustainable. Drastic times call for drastic measures, and Al Boyd, a fat, nerdy, socially inept—in short, Karl Rove-ish—thinktanker floats a solution that will solve once and for all the problem of too many people sapping the Earth's finite resources. Can't accommodate them on a shrinking planet? Wipe them out.

Skittishly at first, soon with mounting enthusiasm, the president and his entourage begin to think the unthinkable. To solve both the environmental and the population crises at a stroke is pure genius. Granted, exterminating most of the people in the world might seem a little cruel at first, but not when weighed against the chance to save the planet (to be renamed planet America) from the multitudes who are only dying to start living and consuming like Americans do.

But killing more than six billion people without harming US citizens is a big and tricky job. The solution? A biological weapon of mass destruction. The pathogen is Flaxil-4, a virus extracted from the lung tissues of the victims of the 1918 influenza pandemic that is estimated to have left fifty million dead in its wake. The plan is to immunize all Americans prior to releasing the Satan bug, now 100 percent lethal after being weaponized by the US Army labs, under the cover of scientific overflights on the International Day of the Planet.

Meanwhile, as if sensing the hell to be unleashed upon it, the planet rears up. Freak natural disasters pummel the United States, from brush-fires that engulf California to a hurricane that dumps a biblical deluge on New Orleans. Reeling from the discovery that global warming is for real and that his son is gay, Fletcher looks deep inside his soul and a bottle of Wild Turkey and greenlights Operation Deliverance. His allergies mean, however, that he cannot be injected with a mass-manufactured American vaccine, so in the end, he alone gets a foreign-made one.

With preparations for Op Del under way, jockeying for power among the White House mandarins begins in earnest. As they begin to carve the planet into private fiefdoms amid clandestine arrangements to smuggle their friends and retinues onto the vaccine-borne ark, the secret begins to leak. Even Vince finds what is left of his conscience and rats out the plot to the British prime minister. Instead of going public, however, the PM flies in for a tête-à-tête in the White House, during which he lines up behind Fletcher's plan, asking only to put the Brits on the vaccination list. The special relationship being what it is, he is assured of all-around support. Meeting concluded, shortly after takeoff the PM's jet is shot down by terrorist-piloted F-22s, which then return safely to the Langley Air Force Base.

On D-Day folks all over the world begin to drop like flies. The only hitch is, so do the Americans. Deregulation of industry production standards permitted biotech and pharmaceutical companies to cut corners, with the net result that the American serum is worthless. Only Fletcher's, cultured in a German lab, works as prescribed. On the last page, the president strolls around the ghostly White House and the overgrown Rose Garden, lighting a candle to the return of the bald eagle whose survival he had unwittingly ensured. The planet is his and his alone.

Who is the man who penned this political satire to end all political satires? Who predicted Hurricane Katrina and its deadly devastation a year before it even became a blip on USCG, NHC, NWS, and FEMA's radar? Who warned of the danger of the genetic reconstruction of the Spanish flu virus even as it was being accomplished by US Army scientists? Who employed two fulltime research assistants to nail these and other scientific and political facts right?

To say that Beaton is no stranger to politics and political journalism is like saying that Obama is no stranger to politics and political pragmatism.

Kicking off his career in television and current affairs, for years he reported on British party conferences for BBC Radio and even notched a stretch as an activist in his union and in the Labour Party. At the end of the day, however, he decided that his true allegiance was to his satirical muse.

This may have been the unspoken reason for his falling out with Gordon Brown, whose speeches he used to buff up back when the prime minister was still in opposition. After zesting Brown's policy doublespeak with humor, the two would then rehearse these jokes late into the night, albeit always on the phone, since the standoffish Brown avoided face time, even sending in his drafts by fax. Be that as it may, shrugged Beaton, "any of my lingering support for the Labour Party was finished when Blair took us into the Iraq war."[3]

One of the most popular satirists across all media, from theater to books to radio to television, Beaton may be best known for his political-satirical play *Feelgood* (2001). Winning the Evening Standard Award for Best Comedy, a Best New Comedy Award, and an Olivier nomination, it enjoyed a rash of translations and stage runs all over Europe and North America. He is also ubiquitous as a writer and/or presenter on BBC Radio, with *The Beaton Generation, Dome Alone with Alistair Beaton, Not the Nine O'Clock News, A Question of Fact, Little England Big World, Fourth Column, The Way, The Truth, The Video, Electric Ink, The World Tonight,* and not least *The Trial of Tony Blair* (the erstwhile PM faces charges of war crimes in the International Criminal Court) to his credit.

As a novelist, he regaled his fans with the 1980 mock exposé *The Thatcher Papers*—one hundred-plus pages of political and farcical collage—followed by the 1994 millennial political farce *Drop the Dead Donkey 2000.*[4] The same year produced an uncompleted literary nod to Byron, entitled *Don Juan on the Rocks,* set in Spain and starring a teenage heartthrob, a winsome barmaid, and an East End gangster husband. The turn of the millennium saw a troika of pocket-size *Little Books* of *Complete Bollocks, New Labour Bollocks,* and *Management Bollocks,* respectively. And then, in anticipation of Bush II's reelection, the environmental *tour de farce* to end all *tours de farce.*

Beaton may be that rare species of political animal who is as good as his word. Peace marcher against Bush II and Blair's incursions in the Middle East, he sold his beat-up Volvo 240 at the time he started writing *A Planet for the President.* He also no longer flies short-haul. "How many miles did *you* rack up last year?" he stabbed his email finger in my chest when pressed on whether environmental issues are political ("You bet they are!").

Notwithstanding some talk around Hollywood about filming *A Planet for the President,* Beaton's name may not be as familiar in America as that of Michael Moore or Tom Lehrer. The same cannot be said, however, of his take-no-prisoner variety of political humor, which made the cult satirical program *Spitting Image* such a ringing success. Alongside a posse of equally irreverent pen-slingers, Beaton skewered the politicians and newsmakers from the mid-1980s into the mid-1990s, with the hot seat reserved for Ronald Reagan and Margaret Thatcher.

As for American politics, his savvy is kindled by reading and frequent visits to Washington, where, thanks to a network of political contacts, he meets with people with inside knowledge of the congressional and federal scene. As much as anything else, this might account for why *A Planet for the President* exemplifies the maxim that if you are looking for a friend in DC, you should domesticate a rat.

L'état, c'est moi

When I wrote *Planet* I was of course fully aware that I was caricaturing the Bush presidency and the rise of the Neo-Cons.

Alistair Beaton to Peter Swirski

A Planet for the President hit bookstores in 2004, when most of the world was still reeling from the fall of the Twin Towers and the fall of Saddam's statue in Baghdad. The timing was not coincidental. As Amber Day remarked in *Satire and Dissent* (2011), "much of the exponential growth in satiric offerings in the United States in particular roughly coincided with the eight years of George W. Bush's tenure as president" (4).

At the top of this exponential curve sat Michael Moore, who delivered a flurry of body blows to the American body politic in *Stupid White Men*. His rightwing detractors notwithstanding, Moore's bestseller was, of course, bona fide nonfiction, whereas Beaton's plot could hardly be more fantastic. All the same, the differences only underscore the similarities. President Fletcher, his supporting cast, and the mindset they epitomize were lifted lock, stock, and two smoking barrels from the administration of the forty-third CEO of the United States.

Yet, even as he gave Fletcher a gay son in an instantly recognizable allusion to Dick Cheney's gay daughter, in interview after interview, Beaton demurred at drawing a straight line between Fletcher's gang and Bush's. Authorial coyness about tying one's satirical salvos to an unmoving target is, of course, as time-honored as satire itself. Who wants to risk becoming obsolete the moment the USSR or the PRC undergoes a regime change, or the day the Obamas replace the Bushes in the West Wing?

Some do. Christopher (son of William F. Jr.) Buckley's 2012 *They Eat Puppies, Don't They?* owed a big measure of its success to the current geopolitical climate in which China is seen as an emergent threat to American hegemony. A generation back this role was foisted on another Asian super-power, making long-term prospects for Buckley's satire as bright as those of a string of Japan-bashing bestsellers from the 1990s, starting with Michael Crichton's *Rising Sun*. It is for no other reason that, even as the surreal goings-on in Mikhail Bulgakov's *Heart of a Dog* remain funny to this day, his political satire about a talking dog equipped with a man's testicles no longer packs the punch it did in the early days of Soviet *nomenklatura* and citizens' committees.

There is only one thing that fades faster than the politics of yore, and that's the satire that feeds on it. In his time, Aristophanes' powers of ridicule were so fabled as to be hailed even by his sworn enemies. Plato himself denounced *The Clouds* as slander that paved the way for the kangaroo trial of Socrates. Aristophanes' second play, *The Babylonians* (now lost), was publicly condemned by the Athenian democratic tyrant Cleon as slanderous against the polis. Cleon himself found himself on the receiving end of the playwright's satire in *The Knights*, where he was panned as a protean form of evil clinging to power like a hungry leech to a hippopotamus's behind. But who, except classics professors, gets in a lather about *The Knights* nowadays?

The premise and the lifeline of topical satire is being recognizable to its contemporaries. This is both the source of its immediate appeal and, at the end of the day, its Achilles heel. Headline news on Tuesday is seldom more than a distant memory on Wednesday, and nowhere more so than in politics, where 24 hours last a week. Be that as it may, topicality and universality are not necessarily antagonistic toward each other, permitting satire to bloom into art when it manages to escape the exigencies of its historical time.

Seeing how deeply Beaton has reflected over the years on his calling as a burr in the saddle of the powers that be, it can hardly be a coincidence that *A Planet for the President* frames the Bush regime in terms of another historical system and another political time. With the planning for Op Del in full swing, Skidelski's state visit to Versailles intimates thoroughgoing parallels between Fletcher I, Bush II, and Louis XIV, the absolute monarch who went down in history as much for his extravagant remake of the Palace as for his egotistic *l'état, c'est moi*.

While the no less megalomaniacal Skidelski identifies with the Sun King, enraged demonstrators boo him from outside the gold-leafed portals of the palace, just like *les misérables* did during the French Revolution. Know thy history, warns Beaton. Louis XIV may have lived out his reign in full, but it was not long after when the desperate French commoners revolted, overhauled their political system, and took their royals' heads on a guillotine.

Ripping up one of the most reviled presidencies in history, Beaton does not pass on a chance to sink his teeth into more "universal" themes: abuse of power, economic inequity, geopolitical hypocrisy, the degree to which Big Money is in bed with the political-military establishment, the culture of spin, and the almost total lack of accountability in today's democracies. Even so, he could ask on behalf of all satirists: Why should universality trump topicality? Does not one-size-fits-all wit risk becoming too diffuse to get traction even in the present?

Topical satire may not be timeless by default. But does it mean that it is doomed to being, or at least being regarded as, mere journalism tainted with propaganda? But then, what could differentiate historical fiction or historical faction from history narrated from the point of view of someone who believes that you can't be neutral on a moving train? History that is unapologetically personal—as Howard Zinn's iconic *You Can't be Neutral on a Moving Train: A Personal History of Our Times* is? History that does not necessarily seek to distance itself from a *roman à clef* steeped in historical fact?

Satirist and songwriter Tom Lehrer famously quipped that satire died the day Kissinger got the Nobel Peace Prize in 1973. Like Philip Roth in the 1950s, he implied that American politics increasingly defies the power of fiction to bring it to justice, let alone to its senses. Artists with a contrary bent of mind, however, may have taken his words as a challenge to go where even politics did not dare to go. One of them was Beaton, who in 1973 ditched the idea of getting his doctorate, sold his first satirical sketch to the BBC, and never looked back. More than three decades later, the mature artist—according to *The Independent*, perhaps Britain's greatest living satirist—reflected on this tightrope balance between the true and the outré:

> Anger and outrage are at the heart of all good satire, but it has to be coupled with a desire to entertain and a desire to laugh. Can you change things as a satirist? You never know, but at least you are giving heart to people who share your outrage.[5]

But the question of topicality will not be sidestepped so easily. If all *A Planet for the President* does is hold a mirror to its historical time, how much point is there in rereading it ten years after the original publication? How relevant can Beaton's *roman à clef* be today, when the miscreants it takes a scalpel to have all left the White House? How can a Molotov cocktail that draws its incendiary punch from the crimes and excesses under Bush II ignite the fire in the belly under Obama?

When Michael Moore touted Clinton as a great Republican president, it was to underline the *plus ça change, plus c'est la même chose* under the

Demublicans in the White House. Likewise, the question of how topical Beaton's satire is is really a question of the degree to which Obama is only a reincarnation of Bush. "Reincarnation?" someone will ask. "What reincarnation? Obama is a liberal Democrat, Bush a neoconservative Republican. Obama is a Nobel Peace Prize winner, Bush a warmonger. Obama is intellectual and eloquent, Bush anything but. Obama admits the perils of human-made climate change, Bush blew them off on principle."

Historically, in fact, Obama's popularity and eventual success in 2008 owed to the simple fact that he was not W. Not for nothing did the Democratic candidate distance himself earlier that summer from his predecessor's "failed presidency."[6] How, then, could *A Planet for the President* satirize his time in office, when in 2004 Obama was not even a glint in the Democratic wing of the Demublican party bosses' eyes? Piece of cake, Beaton will say. So little ever changes in Washington that topical satire becomes universal by default.

Osawatomie High School

The Obama presidency? Disappointing, of course. Partly caused by his own failings, partly caused by the partisan ferocity of Congress and a very dumb GOP. So many lost opportunities, notable among them climate change.

Alistair Beaton to Peter Swirski

Late in 2011 Obama flew into Kansas to deliver an address on the economy to students at the local Osawatomie High School. The choice of venue may have been baffling, except for the fact that it was the same school at which Teddy Roosevelt stumped on his own campaign trail a century earlier. Under the vague but stirring banner of New Nationalism, Roosevelt tried to own the mantle of Progressivism contested by the incumbent Taft, the eventual winner Wilson, and the Socialist Debs, who fought his party's best campaign ever (6 percent of the national vote).

Roosevelt's calls for a stronger and more activist executive certainly rang familiar during Obama's photo-op. Indeed, the doggedly contested 1912 election demarcated a milestone in the redrawing of federal powers. From the establishment of the national income tax and the Federal Reserve, all the way to the universal enfranchisement of the electorate, the birth of labor rights, and economic regulation, the American presidency was poised to become far more proactive and controlling than ever before, even prior to the founding of national social programs and welfare state.

A century after his unsuccessful comeback, Roosevelt would hardly recognize his own party, not to say his own country. The 2012 Republican primaries were dominated by anti-progressive rhetoric, meshing with anti-Obama attacks precisely to the extent that the incumbent president sought to reclaim the high ground of the social reformists from a century before. Clothing his Democratic rhetoric in Teddy's Republican tweeds, Obama preemptively raided his rivals' ideological headquarters even before the formal declaration of electoral hostilities.

The flip side of this partisan cross-dressing is that, much as it made sense for Obama to position his reelection campaign via Roosevelt's, it makes sense to contextualize his presidency in terms of Roosevelt's incomplete two terms. After all, just like Barack, Teddy was a natural crowd-pleaser whose executive bite fell distinctly short of his election-trail bark. Notwithstanding the popular image of Roosevelt as a steam engine in trousers, his legislative record was paltry even in comparison to his low-profile successor, Taft.

For that matter, Obama shares as much, if not more, with another popular centrist Republican: Eisenhower. Admittedly, the sitting president's work ethic is at variance with the general's two-term pursuit to perfect his approach shot. But the domestic and foreign challenges that bedeviled Ike were uncannily similar to those facing Barack: running war, runaway military expenditures, bloated budgets, stagnant economy, partisan bickering, urgently needed tax reform, bogged down social legislation.

Oddly enough, however, Obama's as yet incomplete two terms display the greatest affinity with the policies of yet another Republican president, one to whom he is almost automatically contrasted rather than compared: George Walker Bush. On a closer look, however, outside of partisan propaganda and the handful of policy nips and tucks that followed the Democrats stepping into the wingtips of the Republicans, the differences between the two leaderships run only skin-deep. Obama may look nothing like Bush in person, but his policies are cloned off his predecessor's just because the Demublican party competes with itself for political power, regardless of ideology.

Not to look too far, Bush's recession became Obama's, together with the dread of calling it by name. So did Bush-era trade deficits, lax regulation, falling productivity, and the budgetary fiscapocalypse. Just as the outgoing president's stimulus package and too-big-to-fail financial sector bailouts became synonymous with the incoming one, so did Bush's game plan on education—lots of smoke, little fire. Lobbying and election finance reforms, from which candidate Obama wrung so much election-day mileage, were also duly scrapped in favor of the status quo.

Both proved to be legislative underachievers blaming an unfriendly Congress, despite the fact that both were inaugurated with super majorities. Both headed a den of thieves, with Bush's appointment of Halliburton's our-man-in-the-White-House Dick Cheney mirrored by Obama's appointment of Tim Geithner. That's right—the same president who promised to sweep the White House clean handpicked a tax-cheater caught with his hand in the federal cookie jar to run the federal treasury. Obama also kept Ben Bernanke as the chairman of the Federal Reserve despite the latter's

Mr. Bush...Tear down this wall!

Figure 3.1   Mr. Bush . . . Tear Down This Wall! ". . . Obama's as yet incomplete two terms display the greatest affinity with the policies of yet another Republican president, one to whom he is almost automatically contrasted rather than compared: George Walker Bush . . ."

Credit: Brian Narelle

complicity in the banking meltdown, putting to rest any idea of being the vehicle for change Americans thought they voted for.[7]

After infuriating the Democratic liberal caucus by extending Bush's tax cuts for the rich, Obama began to copycat the Republican administration on environmental issues. His stance on offshore drilling, nature conservation, and the Keystone pipeline, to name only three, has earned him the wrath of the green lobby, with Al Gore in the lead. Tweedledee in Durban to Bush's Tweedledum in Kyoto, the United States under Obama stonewalled key parts of the climate deal, such as funding for developing economies to tackle global warming.

Bush's record-setting military budgets ballooned under Obama (no surprises there: Senator Obama voted in favor of Dubya's). Symbolically, the Democratic president retained Bush's defense secretary, Robert Gates together with his predecessor's priorities. Ditching his election-trail word of honor, he did not close Guantanamo, did not stop indefinitely detaining and otherwise stripping the rights of anyone tagged as an enemy combatant, and did not terminate Bush's warrantless wiretapping program plus all the other unconstitutional provisions of the Patriot Act. Barely months into Obama's first term, that perennial gadfly on the American body politic Noam Chomsky had seen enough: "The rhetoric is different. On substance, there is little that is new."[8] His appraisal was echoed by none other than Donald Rumsfeld, who, on the tenth anniversary of the Twin Tower attacks, could scarcely contain his glee:

> They ended up keeping Guantanamo open not because they like it. We didn't like it either. But they couldn't think of a better solution. The same is true with the Patriot Act and military commissions and indefinite detention. All of those things were criticized but today are still in place.

Most of all, Bush's wars segued into Obama's. The incoming president oversaw the surges, deployments, and massive military infrastructure buildups in Afghanistan and Iraq, not to mention muzzling the media at home, lest they print photos of Stars-and-Stripes-draped coffins returning on military flights from Asia. He emulated Bush's foreign policy toward Iran (stalemate), North Korea (saber-rattling), Israel and Palestine (status quo), and China and Russia (walk softly and carry a small stick). And he continued to govern as if the United States were divinely empowered to decide who gets to live or die in the world—which, albeit on a different scale, is what Fletcher does when he thumbs up Operation Deliverance.

Barack Bushama

I hate to put Obama in the same paragraph as George W., for whom there are no obscenities adequately filthy to describe him and the Neo-Con project for which he was the front man. But let's face it, in terms of foreign policy, Obama has failed utterly. Climate change? Ditto. Rich v. Poor? Close to ditto.

Alistair Beaton to Peter Swirski

With his mediocre first term behind and the reelection safely in his pocket, it is Obama's time to aim for his place in the history books. Will his second term, much like that of the fictional Fletcher, be remembered as more than another electoral IOU? More than another remix of W's signature policies? More than a blank check on which the Chamber of Commerce can write its price? The evidence so far is far from reassuring.

Three core provisions of the Patriot Act, all of which violate the Bill of Rights, were set to expire in May 2011. These were the right to conduct roving wiretaps without court warrants, the right to secretly access business records—anything from financial statements to medical files to library and Internet data—and the so-called Lone Wolf provision, which permits surveillance of foreign nationals with no known affiliation to terrorist organizations. In a rare show of solidarity, both major parties reached across the aisles of both chambers of Congress and reauthorized all of these unconstitutional provisions, which the president signed into law for another four years.[9]

After signing off on Bush's unconstitutional legislation, Obama signed off on his own. Section 1032 of the 2012 National Defense Authorization Act allows for the first time the indefinite detention of US citizens, violating as such the Sixth Amendment, which grants the right to a fair trial. Although the president made noises about vetoing it, his main concern proved to be whether suspects should be tried in military tribunals or civilian courts, and not that the NDAA turned the Constitution into toilet paper.[10]

While in office, Bush personally approved the torture of Guantanamo terrorist suspects through techniques such as waterboarding, flaunting this in his 2010 autobiography *Decision Points*.[11] This despite waterboarding being a direct violation of federal laws, international treaties such as the Convention Against Torture, and the Geneva Convention to which the United States is a signatory. The obscenity of a president publicly endorsing torture prompted even former congresswoman Elizabeth Holtzman to call for the prosecution of the country's top criminal.

Faced with the forty-third president's unequivocal admission to violating federal and international law, Obama—who is bound by oath to uphold and faithfully execute the laws of the land—declined to launch any investigation of his predecessor or, for that matter, anyone else involved in torture at the Guantanamo facility. Tracking these developments, or rather lack thereof, even the liberal *Los Angeles Times* slammed him in terms formerly reserved for his predecessor: "A Disaster for Civil Liberties."[12]

Worse still, after Obama's election a number of military and political officials reported that the president-elect promised in private that no one from the Bush administration or the CIA would be prosecuted or even investigated for torture. Halfway into his second term, Obama made good on that promise. In spite of repeated petitions from the ACLU, the attorney general refused to prosecute any of the Bush officeholders responsible for ordering torture. His grounds? They were only following orders: the very defense that was resolutely spurned by the United States at the Nuremberg trials.

In *Taking Liberties* (2011), the president of the ACLU herself voiced her misgivings about Obama being at best Bush lite, at worst Bush reloaded.

Meanwhile, Team Obama has been fighting to block dozens of public-interest lawsuits filed against the government's violations of privacy and presidential abuses of power—all this before anyone had even heard of Edward Snowden. All this from the man who, much like Fletcher J. Fletcher, promised to return America to the moral high ground in the War on Terror.

Speaking of war, candidate Obama staked his reputation on pulling out of Iraq within sixteen months of being elected. Far from being out of Iraq even today, the United States is officially going to keep military units in Afghanistan beyond 2024.[13] As for the war Obama launched on his own, in his March 2011 address he emphasized that it was to prevent the massacre of Libyan insurgents by pro-Gaddafi forces. A praiseworthy goal by any standard, except that Obama kept American troops in Libya beyond sixty days without seeking congressional approval as demanded by the War Powers Act of 1973 (enacted over Nixon's veto) for any military operation in which there is a strong likelihood of armed conflict.

The president's disregard for congressional authority incensed many lawmakers on either side of the aisle. Be that as it may, in spite of a palpable combat-weariness among the recession-ravaged public, the limited rules of engagement for American forces in conjunction with the eventual overthrow of Gaddafi meant that Obama's indifference to the rule of law became glossed over among praise for his handling of the regime change. Once again, history was scripted by the victors.

In the speech delivered to Congress in September 2001, Bush II tried to legitimize his invasion of Afghanistan by claiming that freedom itself was under attack. Right there was a gross simplification from a Sunday morning children's show, to be displayed next to the War on Terror. When it comes to debasing language into PR pap, however, Obama stands shoulder to shoulder with his predecessor. Arm-twisting the Defense Department speechwriters to describe Obama's military operations employing the Newspeak of "overseas contingency operations," his administration argued that the War on Terror was . . . too vague.[14]

In the end, Obama is a sham even in the eyes of his own senior military officials, who concede that the Nobel Peace Prize-winning president allows "things that the previous administration did not." Beaton's topical satire has just become more universal.

General Sherman

The environment is the biggest issue of them all. It's also so overwhelming that it's hard to write about. I felt, though, that with *Planet* I had a plot that sustained an eco-satire without drifting into the didactic.

Alistair Beaton to Peter Swirski

Named in 1879 by naturalist James Wolverton in honor of Lincoln's general of "forty acres and a mule" fame, the General Sherman is a giant sequoia located in the Sequoia National Park in California. How giant? At almost two thousand tons in mass, it is the largest living tree on Earth. As such, it is also a symbol of America's nature and conservation. Its fictional death in flash fires that scythe across California rattles even Fletcher, whose green credentials are confined to knowing the color of the legal tender.

The immolation of the General Sherman haunts *A Planet for the President* in an emotional chord that stands apart from its laugh-a-minute pacing. These *ubi sunt* undertones are resolved only on the very last page with the return of the bald eagle to the world where humankind is no longer. Having disarmed the ecological time bomb for all eternity, Fletcher would be a lock-in for the Green Man of the Year, if only there were anyone left on Earth to award it.

This is quite a turnaround for the president who, as Beaton puts it, had previously "signed the Alaskan Wilderness (Stage Two) Protection Act which opened up most of the remaining Alaskan wilderness to mining and logging" (24). If this sounds like satirical hyperbole, a quick fact-check reveals it to be anything but fiction. Bush's 2002 Clear Skies Initiative relaxed restrictions on air pollution, toxins and all, and cut the budget for enforcement. A year later, his Healthy Forests Initiative, also known as the No Tree Left Behind Act, opened public forests to high-intensity logging.[15]

A long-standing admirer of Teddy, Dubya did his best to undermine his Republican forerunner's conservationist legacy. No sooner did he move into the Oval Office than he slashed funding for renewable energy sources while stepping up oil, gas, and coal mining. Environmental tripwires such as Swiss-cheesing ozone, off-the-charts air pollution, rising global temperatures and sea levels, shrinking polar ice caps, increasingly erratic ocean currents, and mounting incidence of extreme weather at home and abroad were laughed off as fairy tales for the industrial age.

With Gore looking over his shoulder, Clinton had at least endorsed the Kyoto Protocol before it stalled in the Senate. Bush pulled out of the Protocol in a move that his own head of the Environmental Protection Agency vividly summed up as "'flipping the bird,' frankly, to the rest of the world."[16] As the world's biggest emitter of CO_2 and other greenhouse gases and as the biggest consumer of fossil fuels and energy, America's participation in Kyoto was and is essential. Yet, to this day the United States remains the only one of the 192 signatories to the Protocol that refuses to ratify it.

Adding insult to injury, Bush's chief negotiator went around dissing Kyoto as a "political agreement . . . not based on science," while his boss was busy stifling the scientific evidence to keep the public uninformed, over the protests of his top NASA scientist.[17] Political interference with and outright censorship of scientific research, especially when it came to climate change and conservation, became so bad that in 2006, led by 52 Nobel Prize winners, ten thousand American scientists went public demanding restoration of scientific integrity in federal policy. That same year, the president slashed the EPA budget while floating a $4,000,000,000 earmark for drilling in the Arctic National Wildlife Refuge. To his credit, Bush has been nothing but consistent. In 2001, baited over whether his boss would urge Americans to modify their energy consumption habits, his spokesman, Ari Fleisher, shot back:

> That's a big "no." The president believes that it's an American way of life, that it should be the goal of policy-makers to protect the American way of life. The American way of life is a blessed one . . . The president considers American's heavy use of energy a reflection of the strength of our economy, of the way of life that the American people have come to enjoy.[18]

Given how toxic Bush had been for the environment, it was always going to be an uphill struggle for Obama to be seen as anything other than a spectacular improvement. And Obama *is* doing more than Bush II. In his first term he pumped $90 billion of stimulus money into green energy and passed tougher rules on drinking water and on emissions from cars

Figure 3.2 Dnal-sdrawkcab ". . . Given how toxic Bush had been for the environment, it was always going to be an uphill struggle for Obama to be seen as anything other than a spectacular improvement . . ."

Credit: John Jonik

and new power plants. But this is as good as it gets. By and large, his green policy has been a spectacular no-show underscored by a string of high-profile PR disasters, starting with his 2009 Earth Day flight to preach conservation, which burned nearly three hundred tons of jet fuel and united the entire political spectrum, red, blue, and green, against him.[19]

Also in 2009, brushing aside warnings that it was high up the financial creek, Obama rushed a half-a-billion dollar loan to solar-panel manufacturer Solyndra, which may have had nothing to do with Solyndra's contributions to him and other Democrats in Congress. Before anyone could say "Icarus," this showcase for how the stimulus bill would stimulate employment went belly up, putting eleven hundred employees on the street. Instead of hotfooting it to the Gulf in the wake of the Deepwater Horizon oil rig explosion, Obama chose to host U2's Bono. After the spill, he put a moratorium on new off-shore drilling, but just a year later, he opened huge swaths of coastal waters to oil and natural gas exploration—from the Atlantic to the Gulf of Mexico to Alaska to the Arctic Ocean—even before the investigation into the Deepwater spill had been completed.

Failing to live up to his election-trail promise to pass cap-and-trade legislation as a way of reducing industrial carbon emissions, in 2009 Obama borrowed another page from Bush by torpedoing the Copenhagen Climate Change Conference. Then he overruled his own EPA officials in order to block stronger anti-smog standards. Even the British press has taken note, with the normally Obamista *Guardian* flogging him for being "just as zealous as George Bush in stripping away environmental, health and safety protection at the behest of industry."[20]

On cue, Obama has been lobbying for the Keystone XL oil pipeline, the proposed link between the environmentally disastrous tar sands of Alberta and the Gulf Coast refineries. Howls of outrage from both sides of the border forced the White House to tactically delay the decision until after the second-term midterms, but the writing, you could say, is on the well. Little wonder that, for all his Kermit rhetoric, Obama has been trashed even by his fellow Democrat Al Gore for being "no real change from the era of George W. Bush."[21]

Today the country's environmental record is just as appalling as that of the hyperbolically corrupt Fletcher administration. With 5 percent of global population, Americans consume a quarter of the world's resources. Candidate Obama promised that one-tenth of American energy production would come from renewable sources by 2012, and a quarter by 2025. At the rate things are going, he could have said 2125 and still fail to keep his word.

Exactly halfway through Dubya's first term, Clinton's chief strategist—the same who got his boss elected by putting Bush I on the defensive with

"It's the economy, stupid"—reprised his political wisdom in a widely popular book *It's* Still *the Economy, Stupid.* Politically speaking, every word that
Paul Begala—a prototype for Josh Lyman on *The West Wing*—wrote was
very true. Except that the economy won't matter on a dead planet. And
dead it will be, if not tomorrow, then by the time we are done playing
Rodney King with it.

The Poodle Factor

> There's maybe something universal in the way in which our leaders can be
> sucked into doing terrible things for apparently high-minded reasons.
>
> *Alistair Beaton to Peter Swirski*

We live in an era of political doctrines and indoctrinations. The historical
time when state power could do without them—the time of divine incarnations and absolute monarchies—has gone by, never to return. And since
power without justification is no longer possible, even in a dictatorship,
evil must be spun as good. The cravenness of the deceit is transparent, but
even this is a part of the public-relations game as it is played in the realm
of political communiqués.

This is also the reason why *A Planet for the President* is so much fun to
read. There are no good guys in the White House, in the Pentagon, or at
10 Downing Street. Beaton's satire is isotropic, with everyone at one point
or another coming into his line of fire. Yet, exemplifying Hanna Arendt's
point on the banality of evil, most of his villains are not even that sinister.
They are only doing their jobs the best way they can. Compounding
the irony, the most honest person in the novel is Al Boyd, the architect
of Operation Deliverance, who feels no compulsion to spin his heinous
actions as noble causes.

Writing from across the Atlantic, Beaton is attuned to the imbalance
of power between the United States and the United Kingdom. When on
February 15, 2003, coordinated worldwide protests delivered a deafening
NO to Bush's impending invasion of Iraq, American citizens also took their
anger to the streets, from Los Angeles to New York. But it was Europe that
saw the largest antiwar rallies in history, including the Million March in
London that belied Blair's dogged support of his American counterpart.
A Planet for the President lampoons the special relationship between the
British and American heads of state by having the obsequious PM nonstop
call Fletcher on his private line, while the president rolls his eyes at the staffers.

Fletcher's problem is that his British sidekick keeps phoning, thinking
he can influence policy in Washington. In reality, most Britons felt it was

the other way round—that George W. Bush was setting policy in London. Indeed, in the run-up to the invasion of Iraq, almost half of the British public saw Blair as no more than Bush's lapdog (and almost a quarter saw Bush as a greater threat to world peace than Saddam).[22] Beaton was far from alone, of course, in dismissing Blair as Bush's lackey. The perception was so widespread, in fact, that it raised serious concerns in Washington about Blair's political credibility (the White House term for it was "the poodle factor").

Fletcher in his way honors the British PM by not calling him in the dead of night, a prank he loves to play on other European leaders, feigning to have forgotten the time difference. Bush also honored Blair by grandstanding in 2003 that "America is fortunate to call this country our closest friend in the world."[23] Of course, in 2001 he also claimed that the United States had no greater friend than Mexico, and a year later he voiced the same sentiment about Canada. As if to dispel any doubt, in 2006 his senior State Department official went public: "There never really has been a special relationship . . . We typically ignore them and take no notice."

As with almost everything else, attitudes under Obama are difficult to distinguish from those under Bush. Shortly after moving into the West Wing, the president returned to Britain the bust of Winston Churchill, loaned to his predecessor in the aftermath of 9/11 in a gesture of transatlantic support. To add injury to the insult, Wikileaks cables revealed that Obama's administration had been steadily feeding Britain's nuclear secrets to Russia.[24] Of course, the White House may simply have reckoned that nuclear secrets are passé in the day when, as Beaton's novel is at pains to point out, bioweapons are literally lying around.

Mirroring Beaton's eerily accurate prediction of Hurricane Katrina, his scenario of the weaponization of the 1918 flu virus is no less prescient. But as it ratchets up the stakes, painting a picture of a White House clique armed with a biological agent with which they exterminate six billion people, it mixes the preposterous and the plausible so cunningly that it is difficult at times to tell which is which. Fiction aside, however, bioterror has a long history in the Americas. By far the worst outbreaks date to the two and a half centuries after Columbus, so much so that by the mid-eighteenth century the hemisphere was literally decimated, losing about 90 percent of the aboriginal population of at least fifty to sixty million (at the very least four million in North America).

The etiology of this cataclysmic carnage was microbiotic immigrants from Europe, with smallpox in the lead, to which indigenous inhabitants had scant immunological resistance. Perish, in other words, the abiding American fiction of a pristine paradise awaiting European settlers. The New World was both heavily populated and heavily developed before Old World bio-invaders won the war of the worlds. The myth of uninhabited virgin land dates, in fact, not to the seventeenth but to the *eighteenth* century, when the replacement of Amerindian tribes by Europeans and Africans was only just beginning on any notable scale. By the middle of the seventeenth century, there were, after all, less than fifty thousand colonists in all of North America, and by the middle of the eighteenth still only about 1.3 million, including slaves.[25]

More bioterror swept through the United States during the 1830s and 1840s when Asiatic cholera, carried by bacteria teeming in unsanitary water, landed on its shores. It was to the immigrants and migrants of the mid-nineteenth century United States what the bubonic plague was to mid-fourteenth century Europe. Crossing the country along the Oregon Trail, it did not discriminate between city dwellings, rural abodes, and wigwams and tepees of the again most vulnerable prairie tribes, killing every second person it encountered.

When Fletcher's gang weaponize the 1918 flu virus, they justify it with an argument rooted in the Prisoner's Dilemma: if we don't do it, they might. Their only error is that, given the symmetrical structure of the payoffs, they more than "might"—they ought to. But Fletcher's reasoning breaks down as soon as one considers the large picture by factoring more than the individual payoffs. The ostensibly cutthroat competition between would-be antagonists in the Prisoner's Dilemma masks the fact that their *joint* payoffs are always higher than what they can get by going it alone.

On the face of it, Beaton's premise looks, of course, ridiculous. How could politicians go into a huddle and emerge with a plan for slaughtering billions? But even if you ignore the Greeks and the Romans voting to put entire city-states to the sword, there are numerous precedents in the modern era, beginning with the 1942 Wannsee Conference on the outskirts of Berlin that papered the way for the final solution to the Jewish problem. As for Beaton's seemingly over-the-top Flaxil-4, it is only because the first newspaper reports came out of Spain that the 1918 pandemic was called the Spanish Flu (or the Spanish Lady). Its country of origin was most likely the United States.

The superbug spread super fast. Even with traffic levels nowhere near today's, it circled the globe in just four months, slaying some fifty million people in its wake. The death toll in the United States alone was 675,000, more than the First World War, the Second World War, the Korean War, the Vietnam War, and the two Iraq wars combined. The 1914–1918 trench warfare was, of course, a major factor. Vast assemblies of soldiers allowed for easy transmission and then re-transmission when the infected individuals mixed with civilians on frequent furloughs.

A virus so lethal would be of interest to every virologist—not least, as Beaton stresses, to every Pentagon virologist. Efforts to reconstruct it date to the mid-1990s, when the US Armed Forces Institute of Pathology succeeded in sequencing fragments of the virus's RNA from tissue preserved in Alaskan victims' metal caskets—preserved because the permafrost and the untypically durable coffins worked against rapid degradation of organic matter. But it was not until 2003 that they succeeded in engineering "a live virus containing two 1918 genes that proved to be very lethal in animal experiments."[26]

The Pentagon's hunt for biological agents that would allow the White House—be it Fletcher's, Bush's, or Obama's—to wage politics by other means is nothing new. Biosoldiers are every general's and politician's dream. They are not given to running for cover, disobeying orders, or thinking for themselves. They are immune to shellshock and physical fatigue, not to mention the need for food, sex, hospitals, danger pay, or pension plans. They are as invulnerable to biochemical hazards as to enemy propaganda. Most of all, they are utterly expandable at no political cost.

Year after year, US military budgets—excluding the costs of running wars, veteran benefits, weapons research, et al.—exceed half a trillion dollars. Concealed behind these mind-numbing numbers is the fact that, for the people America attacks, war is a national calamity consecrated with hecatombs of civilian blood, hunger, and disease. It is a disaster that affects everyone on the visceral level. For the White House, on the other hand, war frequently seems no more than an extra-tough game of American football, the ultimate real-life Superbowl where the good guys kick ass while kibitzers at home slurp sodas, chomp hot dogs, and blame the other side for cheating.

Saueramerican

I admire *It Can't Happen Here* for its boldness, its insight into the dangers of populism. And though it may now feel far-fetched in places, it reminds us never to take democracy for granted.

Alistair Beaton to Peter Swirski

War writers go to great lengths to represent the inability of people back home to grasp the fighting units' experience of physical trauma and moral nausea. This is as true of such classic portrayals of returning soldiers as Hemingway's "Soldier's Home," Salinger's "For Esmé—With Love and Squalor," or Tim O'Brien's "Speaking of Courage," as of the recent crop of war memoirs from Iraq duty jarheads-turned-writers. Long on indiscriminate slaughter and short on heroism that sells tickets to Hollywood action blockbusters, none of them has much use for flag waving.[27]

Even though *A Planet for the President* is a war novel chiefly in the sense that the White House wages a covert war on the rest of humankind, it rings up the recent history when the jingoism of the "coalition of the willing" boiled over into open xenophobia.[28] Early on in the story, as is his custom, Vince drives to the gourmet paradise on Dupont Circle to do his late-night food shopping. The special adviser to the president is already uneasy about driving a non-American car. Now he skulks around the supermarket, looking around to make sure he is not seen with a basketful of French comestibles:

> The cheese-eating surrender monkeys thing had more or less gone, but many people hadn't entirely forgiven France for refusing to support America's military incursions in the Middle East. If it wasn't any longer a hanging offence to be seen buying French wine, it wasn't exactly a career boost either. Not that Spanish wine was much better these days. Buying foreign wine had become a nightmare. (55)

In real life, even as they officially shunned French produce as a means of expressing discontent with the Frogs for not stampeding into Bush's phony war, Americans found it hard to walk away from their favorite munchies: French fries. Instead, the cafeterias in the House of Representatives relabeled them Freedom fries in a "symbolic effort to show the strong displeasure of many on Capitol Hill with the actions of our so-called ally, France."[29]

At the end of the day, Tom Lehrer was dead wrong. Politics does not kill satire. On the contrary: it gives it a kiss of life every time life imitates art. And much as it did when frankfurters became rebranded hot dogs in the run-up to the First World War, it does again and again. "Remember our war hysteria, when we called sauerkraut 'Liberty cabbage' and somebody actually proposed calling German measles 'Liberty measles'?" (21). The author of these words was not one of the Democrats, Republicans, and Independents who in 2002 voted against the Iraq War Resolution but the author of the best-known anti-totalitarian satire in American history.

Sinclair Lewis, the first American writer to make the cover of *Time* in 1927, was also the first American to be awarded the Nobel Prize in Literature, in 1930—evidently, in the eyes of the Swedish Academy, the first American to capture and express the essence of the United States. In its announcement, the Nobel Committee gave, in fact, special recognition to an earlier one of Lewis's satires, which gave the American language a catchphrase for its homegrown *petit bourgeoisie*: Babbitry.

Babbitt (1922) attracted praise from all corners of the world, including none other than Leon Trotsky, who jotted down in his private correspondence, "I find *Babbitt* curiously interesting and instructive although it is too bourgeois in character. In the last analysis, however, Babbitt, the man, is no more bourgeois than your John D. Rockefeller, J. P. Morgan and Henry Ford."[30] But America's infatuation with Lewis would not last long. It turned almost overnight to shock and derision in the wake of the publication of *It Can't Happen Here* (1935), a book that few wanted to read and fewer still to talk about.

By the time when Lewis accepted the Nobel Prize in Stockholm, Stalin had already massacred millions in the Soviet Union in the name of purging the country of subversive elements. Hitler's rampaging Nazis had secured almost 20 percent of the popular vote in the swiftly crumbling Weimar Germany. Mussolini and his blackshirts turned Italy into a police state. Still, few pundits in the United States took totalitarianism seriously, if they thought about it at all. When they did, more often than not they dismissed it as a modern phase of the nationalistic settling of old scores endemic to the decaying European autocracies.

In hindsight, Lewis's foresight cannot but seem remarkably acute. Just as Beaton's *A Planet for the President* and Roth's *The Plot Against America* seventy years later, *It Can't Happen Here* satirizes the triumph of home-grown fascism grounded in the erosion of free speech and other constitutional rights, institutionalization of federal surveillance programs, and not least Orwellian propaganda. It does not speak any less of Lewis or, for that matter, Beaton or Roth, that they did not have to invent their material. History was their teacher, with the United States joining the league of other nations in a systematic suppression of civil rights and freedoms.[31]

In 1917, for example, young Lewis witnessed how, on the excuse that the country was honeycombed by German agents bent on sedition and agitation of the American workforce, Congress passed the Espionage Act and in 1918 the Sedition Act. The former mandated twenty years' imprisonment for anybody found guilty of encouraging disloyalty to the United States. The latter extended the penalty to anyone who employed disloyal language about the government, the Constitution, the flag, or the uniform. No sooner had the Act been passed than more than two thousand people were thrown in jail for disloyalty. Very few among them had ties with Germany; most of them were labor leaders and leftist activists.

It is true that on that occasion German sausages and sauerkraut were not renamed "Freedom sausages" and "saueramerican." But state laws were enacted that banned teaching German in schools, books by German authors were thrown out of public libraries, and German-speaking musicians were barred from playing in public. There were forced deportations, kangaroo courts, media-fanned accusations of disloyalty against those who tried to shield themselves with the Constitution, mass hysteria about mass infiltration and subversive menace, and outcries for 100-percent Americanism. In short, an orgy of xenophobia fanned and manipulated by Hoover's FBI.

That Sonofabitch Lied to Us

Spitting Image and *South Park* are both outrageous, but so is the truth.

Alistair Beaton to Peter Swirski

Most Americans could not care less about politics. Too tired from scratching out a living without a paycheck or from juggling two and a half McJobs, they have no time to pay mind to what the Man says. Many ignore politics on principle, fed up as much with congressional reenactment of the Hatfields and McCoys as with the endless reruns of government-by-crisis. Many don't read books on politics at all, many don't read period, and tens of millions just don't know how to read.

In contrast, those who would stay abreast of politics are drowning in a cacophony of news feeds, video clips, broadcasts, podcasts, talk shows, shock jocks, and not least the blogosphere groaning under the weight of partisan invective and the latest conspiracy theories (Obama is *really* a Democrat!). Deafened and defeated by the noise, few Americans repair to bookstores to browse for enlightenment about what P. J. O'Rourke so colorfully labeled "Our Government: What the Fuck Do They Do All Day, and Why Does It Cost So Goddamned Much Money?"[32]

If they are going to spend money on political books at all, more often than not it will be on historical tours-de-force like *Picture This* or hysterical tours-de-farce like *A Planet for the President*, and for good reason. Politics, as testified to by daily broadcasts on reality TV known as C-SPAN, is dead boring. Political satire is dead funny. A member of the Michael Moore school of never-use-a-sidearm-when-a-cannon-will-do, Beaton is known for shooting from the hip, and not from a Beretta, either. His satirical weapon of choice is the bazooka.

As might be expected, there are critics who object that Beaton is self-serving in gunning after the worst of moral degeneracy in today's politics. His fans would retort that these are the very prerequisites for being a satirist in the first place. The reasons for going to war with high-caliber satirical weaponry may have, however, as much to do with the evolution of media technology as with the downward spiral of contemporary political discourse. The advent of information-age communication turned out, after all, to be far from the universal boon it was predicted to be. For the artists who live and die by the satirical sword, it has indeed proven a double-edged sword.

It is true that the World Wide Web magnifies potential outreach, freeing creators from local censors or vetters. On the other hand, that same numerical proliferation diminishes the impact of any one burlesque or cartoon, goading humorists to ratchet up the shock value in what is by now a runaway arms race. Its inflationary tendencies are all too apparent. Subtlety is out, and crudity is in, ironically depleting the power of any satirical broadside, to say nothing of the entire genre.

To be fair, at times reality seems almost too much like fiction, if only the lampoonists had the imagination to come up with pork-barrel bridges to nowhere, Democrats emailing snapshots of their naughty bits, Republicans bedding underage interns, or presidents empowering the NSA to spy on phone and Internet communications of everybody in the country (save, presumably, themselves). How can a satirist resist sticking his hand into this cookie jar? You can imagine Beaton sliding limp in his writing chair, muttering, "These guys make it too easy. Where do they come up with this stuff?"

But just as it might seem that it is no sweat being a political satirist, at times it is no joke being one, either. As Rudolph Herzog describes in his *Dead Funny: Humor in Hitler's Germany* (2011), when during the 1930s "Heil Hitler" became a formal and mandatory greeting in all public offices, one satirically minded entertainer trained his performing chimps to raise their arms in a Nazi salute whenever they spotted someone in uniform. Rapidly a decree was issued prohibiting "Heil Hitler" salutes by apes—on penalty of death.

Not long thereafter Berlin cabarets, the wellsprings of satire and anti-Nazi farce, were shut down. Harsh, then brutal penalties were leveled at even the mildest forms of political nonconformism. At one point in 1942, among claims that she was undermining the defensive strength of the country, the widow of a German soldier was thrown in jail for telling this lame joke: "Atop the Berlin Radio Tower, Hitler says to Göring that he wants to put a smile on the Berliners' faces. Göring replies: Why don't you jump?" Found by the court to be guilty of defeatism, she was guillotined.

Face to face, a sharpshooter's bullets will always win against satirical bulletins. This is why proponents of direct social action will always complain that a novel like *A Planet for the President* may convince some readers to get German-made flu vaccinations but little more besides. Why write it in the first place, considering that its subject, from the wrongdoings of the Bushidos to the groans of strain from the environment, is a no-brainer, at least to those book buyers who would pay for it in the first place?

A political writer might answer that a novel is released into the world in the hope of making readers feel and think, and if even one does, the writer has achieved his purpose. A satirist might answer that even though humor and opprobrium might not directly change society and its circumstances, for ages now they have excelled in whipping up outrage against evildoers and in turning public opinion against them. A historian might answer that, in the long run, the pen is often mightier than the sword.

But even as he recognizes the legitimacy of all these arguments, the artist has no need to hide behind any of them. Instead, he can merely point out that the populist leftwing policies of Huey Long and the untrammeled rot of Louisiana politics also were no-brainers when Robert Penn Warren sat down to compose *All the King's Men*. So why write it? Because that's what writers do, hoping to win the Pulitzer and a place among the Modern Library's novels of the century, and thus transcend the contingencies of its historical time.

It remains to be seen whether *A Planet for the President* will find a place on the cultural shelf next to Petronius's *Satyricon*, Swift's "A Modest Proposal," Twain and Warner's *The Gilded Age*, and Lewis's *It Can't Happen Here*. Like every artist, Beaton has his detractors. For every reviewer boosting him as "one of television's most powerful political satirists," there is another who, not unkindly, is quick to observe that "occasionally his characters are caught clumsily preaching the writer's own philosophy."[33]

It is true that some things are so big that they call for a big mallet. All the same, isn't naming the director of the CIA Hickie Langshite overdoing things a little? "I was just looking for names that were a little colourful, a little exaggerated, to add to the satiric sparkle," smiled the writer. Still, he conceded, "maybe Langshite was a shite too far."[34] In a similar vein, the transformation of Fletcher's health secretary, Harriet Knibbs, from a co-conspirator of killing most of humankind to an elderly grandmother who quits Op Del on principle (only to be assassinated by CIA goons) is too abrupt to be driven by anything else but plot artifice.

A Planet for the President may be an imperfect masterpiece in other ways as well. Beaton's masterful command of political detail hides a curious glitch in chronology. Fletcher/Bush is said to have been in the White House for six years, making it early 2007, but midterm congressional elections are still to come, backtracking the time of the novel as prior to November 2006. Such a continuity error is, naturally, open to interpretation. Beaton could well be deliberately distancing himself and the reader from the historical topicality of his *roman à clef*. The same holds for his slang. Pitch-perfect through most of the novel, on just a couple of occasions it acquires a distinctly British flavor (Americans don't rubbish people or ideas—they trash them).

At the end of the day, the best reason for celebrating Beaton's novel on the tenth anniversary of its release is the timelessness of its satire, reprised four years later on American television on the occasion of presidential elections. *South Park* episode 12 from the twelfth season, entitled "About Last Night," was broadcast on November 5, 2008, less than 24 hours after Obama's victory. Adding to its immediacy, excerpts from the victory and concession speeches made by the candidates were included in the show.

In the episode, the Democrats carry the presidency, sparking off a riot of partying by the Obamistas and driving the McCain supporters to despair and suicide. All these goings-on, however, serve as misdirection for the presidential candidates to go about their true plot: a jewel heist. When Obama and McCain meet behind closed doors after the former's victory speech, they first greet each other cordially, then burst out laughing and go high-fiving. As quickly becomes apparent, both were playing for the same team all along, shamming partisan rivalry in order to steal the Hope Diamond (get it? Steal hope?). At the end of the episode, Randy undergoes a political epiphany:

Goddamit! Obama said things would be different! That sonofabitch lied to us!

4

(R)hyming (A)merican (P)oetry

Various Artists

The Harlem Renaissance

History repeats itself.

David Shabazz, Preface to The United States v. Hip-Hop

"American Slavery Was Not A Sergio Leone Spaghetti Western," spluttered Spike Lee on Twitter in December 2012, vowing not to see Tarantino's latest pulp fiction *Django Unchained*. Historically speaking, he had a point. Westerns do not usually depict blacks holding other blacks slave, and even less fighting in courts for their right to do so. But American slavery was not a spaghetti western, and, in one of the first freedom lawsuits recorded in the New World, a free black, Anthony Johnson, did file for his right to the life of black John Casor.

Johnson himself was one of the original "20 and odd Negroes" shipped to Jamestown in 1619. Industrious and frugal, in four years he worked off his forced indenture and over the next four decades became prosperous enough to acquire indentured servants of his own. One of them, John Casor, after putting in what he thought was *his* due number of years, began to protest his rights. In the lawsuit brought by Johnson to safeguard his investment, the county court sanctioned his right to hold Casor in perpetual service—in effect, ownership.

If Johnson's freedom suit set the course for race relations right until the mid-nineteenth century, another legal landmark set it until the middle of the twentieth. In the 1896 case of *Plessy v. Ferguson*, the United States Supreme Court upheld an 1890 Louisiana law that mandated segregation on state rail cars. The ruling was prompted by the arrest of Homer Plessy, a conscientious objector who boarded a car reserved for whites. Although white-looking, he was found to be legally black just because his great-grandmother was.

With the law turning a blind eye on racial repression, the last black congressman of the post-emancipation era, George White, was voted out in 1900. But other socioeconomic forces were already at work. In just a single generation between 1890 and the end of World War I, a million Southern blacks migrated to the cities on the other side of Dixie. The push factor was a succession of crop failures, abetted by social terrorism from the resurgent Ku Klux Klan. The pull came from the seemingly unquenchable thirst for cheap labor, only intensified by the Great War. At the bottom of this exodus, however, rested the simple desire to make something of the opportunities rural blacks sensed in the industrialized North.

The blues people were on the move, transforming the sociocultural geography of American cities as the people of urban jazz. Already groaning under the weight of millions of Southern European immigrants, northern urban centers were unprepared for this influx. Even as nationwide the black population dipped slightly, between 1910 and 1930 the ghettos of New York, Chicago, and Detroit tripled in size. They now included cohorts of demobbed black soldiers who had fought with distinction in France (in segregated units). Angry, jobless, inured to killing whitey, they formed a volatile mix. When it ignited in 1919, race riots swept through Eastern and Southern cities, with the worst in Chicago claiming more than twenty lives.

The two races collided head on and quickly retreated, each into its version of Jazz Age prosperity. Whites speculated, Taylorized, and imbibed Prohibition hooch. Harlem and its sister ghettos bootstrapped themselves out of extreme poverty, coalescing into something unthinkable even a generation earlier: the black middle class and a nationwide black consumer market. Its nexus became the Buying Power movement, with urban Negroes boycotting and even picketing businesses that discriminated against them.

On the cultural front, they patronized an unapologetically separatist art tasked with expressing their aspirations as citizens and Americans. Epitomized by Harlem, civic halls and storefront churches, performing centers and poetry lounges, cabarets and dance halls began to thrum with the words and music of the New Negro. Alain Leroy Locke, the quickly dubbed father of this Harlem Renaissance, rhapsodized, "Negro life is seizing upon its first chances for group expression and self-determination."[1]

Even as it splintered what had until a generation earlier still remained a relatively homogeneous black culture, the Harlem Renaissance propelled more black artists into the mainstream. Led by operatic singers and conservatory-trained composers like Roland Hayes, Marian Anderson, Paul

Robeson, and J. Rosamond Johnson, they began to smash—or, in any case, dent—previously sacrosanct racial and cultural taboos. But just as with rap half a century later, the heart and soul of the movement was popular music and popular poetry.

Jazz, with its "dirty" way of playing and "sloppy" arrangements, had been nurtured into existence by Buddy Bolden, King Oliver, and Jelly Roll Morton and mediated by a generation of boogie-woogie and stride pianists. Now it spread through ghetto nightclubs and speakeasies faster than the 1918 flu pandemic, replacing the country-blues cadences of Bessie Smith with the swinging scat of Ella Fitzgerald and turning Louis Armstrong, Duke Ellington, and Fletcher Henderson into stars.

Ironically, barring Langston Hughes, whose ardent populism was more attuned to the mass culture of his day, black intellectuals gave short shrift to jazz, which fell short of their yearning to see black symphonies on Broadway. It is not that it was not part of their intense deliberations about the image and self-image of the New Negro. But, just like rap fifty years later, it was frowned upon as instinctive and unrefined, lacking the intellectual thrust of highbrow art. Even Locke, who reveled in the ferment of black creativity, expected jazz to evolve into a more respectable art form.

As in rap, arm in arm with music went poetry. They may have tried their hands at novels, essays, or criticism, but the biggest names of the Harlem Renaissance—Langston Hughes, Sterling Brown, Arna Bontemps, Countee Cullen, Claude McKay, Georgia Douglas Johnson, James Weldon Johnson, Jean Toomer—all expressed themselves in verse largely insulated from the high modernism of Pound and Eliot. All strove to find a distinct, not to say separatist, idiom true to their skin color and their Americanness. All dreamt of the day when they would be freed from the ghetto consciousness to engage in purely lyrical struggles. All envied the success of a proto-blaxploitation bestseller *Nigger Heaven* (1926), whose author— literary executor of Gertrude Stein and celebrity photographer, Carl Van Vechten—stole the spotlight with a gangster-era love story pilloried for tawdriness and racial stereotyping.

Even as tenement crime and penury surged on the eve of the Great Depression, Claude McKay's *Home to Harlem* (1928) became the first black novel to make the *New York Times* bestseller list. Only four years later, the black satirist Wallace Thurman eviscerated the Harlem Renaissance in *Infants of the Spring* as little more than a citywide bootleg extravaganza and a confidence game. In doing so, however, he only reified this cultural awakening that would not see its equal until the 1970s, when another black renaissance caught fire in the streets of New York.

By then, with a wave of up-and-coming black Demublicans on the Hill and in gubernatorial and mayoral offices around the country, with *The Bill*

Cosby Show and black studies programs on campuses, it was easy to over-look the streetside goings-on in the South Bronx. Much as with blaxploita-tion movies, no one gave hip-hop any staying power, far less the power to break out of the ghetto. But break out it did, in 1982 taking the airwaves by storm with the ur-rap "The Message." Fronted by Grandmaster Flash and the Furious Five—featuring Grandmaster Melle Mel, the principal lyricist—and by the first rap video shot on location in the South Bronx, the single went platinum in under a month.

Repeatedly voted by critics and fans as the greatest hip-hop track ever, it was the first to be added to the US National Archive of Historic Record-ings. Its lyrical revolt from rap's block-party roots is writ large from the first stanza, full of broken glass, people pissing on the stairs, rats and roaches running loose at home, and baseball bat-wielding junkies crowding the back alley, punctuated by the iconic break:

> Don't push me cos I'm close to the edge
> I'm tryin not to lose mah head, ha ha ha ha
> It's like a jungle sometimes, makes me wonder
> How I keep from going under.

Ironically, Flash and most of the crew did not want anything to do with what would become their signature hit. They thought it was preachy, didn't fit their style, and was destined to be a commercial dud.[2] Instead, their archetypal rap of inner-city blues got them into the history books, almost single-handedly launching the subgenre of political (or message) rap. From then on, it was cultural milestone after milestone as rap chased after the pop mainstream, assimilated into it, and finally became its marquee face:

- 1986: Run-DMC rap album *Raising Hell* goes multiplatinum
- 1988: First MTV program devoted to hip-hop (*Yo! MTV Raps*)
- 1988: First magazine devoted to hip-hop (*The Source*)
- 1989: National Academy of Recording Arts and Sciences recognizes a new category: Best Rap Performance (won by DJ Jazzy Jeff and Will Smith)
- 1989: Black Entertainment Television launches *Rap City*
- 1991: NWA tops *Billboard's* Pop Album chart with ur-gangsta *Efil-4ZaggiN* (*Niggas4Life*)[3]
- 1996: First year rap nets a billion dollars
- 1998: Rap albums occupy more than half of R&B charts
- 1999: Grammy for Album of the Year, *The Miseducation of Lauryn Hill*
- 2001: Dr. Dre becomes the industry's second-highest earner ($62 million)

- 2001: Master P and P. Diddy make *Fortune*'s "Forty Richest Under Forty"
- 2002: Sales of urban music overtake rock
- 2004: Rap approaches 30 percent of all music sold in the country

The Black Panthers of Rap

Hip-hop is a culture or way of life.

> Julian L. D. Shabazz, *The United States v. Hip-Hop*

The roots of rap appear to be as many as musicologists and ethnographers care to enumerate, starting with the speech-chanted histories of West African *griots* and black folk church sermons.[4] In both, the metric fluidity allows skittering and cadencing lines of varying length within a time signature. With the pitch relatively stable, the singsong effect can sound a lot like rapping. Something akin is at work in traditional toast tales, street corner jive (jibe) that Chicago jazz cats made hep in the 1920s, adroitly insult-trading games of dozens, and live or radio emceeing. In each case, colloquial tonal inflections and periodic rhymes carry the verbal melody.

During the Harlem Renaissance, Sterling Brown experimented with the speech rhythms of jive, even performing (not to call it rapping) his poem "Long Track Blues" over live piano blues chops in a vintage Smithsonian-Folkways recording. Following his lead, in 1970 a troupe of black Harlem poets released their first of many albums of political rhymes rapped against a musical backdrop. The Last Poets became a national sensation with hardcore tracks like "Niggers Are Scared of Revolution" and "When the Revolution Comes," sampled by virtually everybody in the "bidness."

When the revolution came, however, it was not in national politics but in the national economy. The devolution of power from the industrial sector to the financial, coupled with the expansion of the service and information economy, wrought irreversible changes in post-Nixon America. Deindustrialization and market deregulation, accompanied by a Wall Street-friendly administration and a sharp turn to the right in social policies, left urban cores hollow. Meanwhile, crack sold faster than tickets to an Ali-Frazier fight: economic engine to some, deadly dalliance to many, urban blight to all.

New York became ground zero in the 1970s as acute poverty, chronic unemployment, gang warfare, police brutality, and an anything but color-blind justice system struck like the Mosaic plagues. Changing racial demographics and thinning capital investment ripped the heart out of the city. White flight reached its zenith, the taxable base plummeted, Tammany

Figure 4.1 My Turf "... Graffitists, b-boys and b-girls (breakdancers), deejays and emcees began to stake out their territory and rock the nascent hip-hop scene ..."
Credit: Grea

Hall went bankrupt, and the Big Apple hit rock bottom on October 30, 1975, heralded by the *Daily News* headline "Ford to City: Drop Dead."

Meanwhile, oil-crisis-era cuts in federal and state funding decimated arts and music programs for inner-city youth. Without the benefit of formal education and institutional patronage, in the poorest sections of the poorest borough of the bankrupt metropolis it was back to basics, with the spray can, the turntable, and the vocal chords spearheading the *risorgimento*. Graffitists, b-boys and b-girls (breakdancers), deejays and emcees began to stake out their territory and rock the nascent hip-hop scene, many of them Latino, many boasting more than one skill set under one hat.

If the heart of scene was the block party, the soul of the party was the deejay equipped with a souped-up sound system coming alive in the hands of a virtuoso performer. Scratching, riding gain, phasing, backspinning, and beat breaking were only some of the techniques of spinning records creatively—in effect, remixing them. With their hands full, deejays hired crews of emcees and apprentices to rap initially simple riffs ("Let's jam, y'all") on the mike. As the vocalists gained ground, they began to pair up with master deejays in a groundswell of homemade recordings of "old-school" rap. In parallel to this power shift from turntablers to rappers and then to studio producers, the music whose original identity was formed by sequencing and sampling (flipping, looping, chopping) began to move away from it and from potential lawsuits to rely on drum machines, synthesizers, and the rest of the technopop/electro-funk arsenal pioneered by deejay and high priest of the Zulu Nation, Afrika Bambaataa.

Just as early deejays improvised their equipment, emcees improvised their lines at open-mic poetry jams booming from the NYC's South Bronx to LA's South Central. Like in Eminem's 2002 movie *8 Mile*, participants would often form a cipher (circle), freestyling off one another's rhymes. Built, like jazz, on structured improvisation, these verbal jams reincarnated the spirit of the medieval lists, with lyricists rocking the mic in stylized taunts and duels.

All took note of the blistering sales of the 1979 hit "Rapper's Delight" cooked up on the fly by Sugar Hill Records. Inevitably, with the pot of gold came imputations of biting (stealing lines and rhymes), proving that hip-hop was far from immune to the copyright mentality it strove to disown. The pun in the title of Ice-T's proto-gangsta *Rhyme Pays* openly advertised this hot commodity, echoed by Dre's boast on "Niggaz 4 Life" about "gettin paid to say this shit here / makin more in a week than a doctor makes in a year."

In 1981 rap got its first taste of the big time when Blondie scorched the charts with "Rapture" (read: Rap-ture). With old-school booming from every boom box and ghetto blaster, it soon wormed its way into the club scene and even a smattering of mainly white radio stations—those, that is, that did not flinch from progressively hardcore rap, which, exemplified by Public Enemy, surveyed weedy ghetto lots and incited its denizens to fight the power. After all, as LL Cool J pointed out back in the day, rappers always

> reveal their environment in the music and poetry they create. The Bronx kids are always rappin about the street, being bums and stuff like that because that's their life. Brooklyn boys rap about sticking up places, robbing things. And us, we just rock this shit.[5]

Public Enemy rewrote the rules of the genre, in the process becoming the definitive hardcore of all time. Musically, Chuck D's brass-balls baritone was mixed by the production team, aka the Bomb Squad, into a sonic collage of political speeches, chanted slogans, news soundbites, assorted street static, and brain-hemorrhaging beats. Lyrically, the group exemplified the Black Power consciousness that would remain hip-hop's calling card until the early 1990s. Rapping revolutionary tactics and political activism, Public Enemy marketed themselves, as Chuck D put it in his book manifesto, *Fight the Power*, as "the Black Panthers of rap" (82).

By the early 1990s, the East Coast and hardcore became eclipsed by the West Coast and gangsta rap. Exemplified a few years hence by thugged-out Tupac's *All Eyes On Me*, gangsta relished more downtempo, fat bass lines topped by minor synth loops and funk samples from Parliament-Funkadelic to Isaac Hayes.[6] Lyrically it was aggressive, vulgar, insulting—the antithesis of what commercially viable music was thought to be like. Turf vendettas, drive-by wettings, and other takes on dope slanging and macking (pimping) became the hallmarks of gangsta, whose first-person storytelling lent it immediacy and authenticity that contrasted with Public Enemy's third-person incantations.

Even as it ushered in the boom years, gangsta became the ultimate polarizer. Proponents waxed lyrical about its gritty naturalism, thug-eat-thug mentality, and James Dickey-type survivalist ethic. Opponents hated it for precisely the same reasons, especially as whale-sized profits began to fuel a runaway inflation in imagery. The more outré gangsta became, the better it sold, feeding a frenzy of one-upmanship in dope-running, cop-icing fiction. Meanwhile, real-life gang members like Tweedy Bird Loc sounded more like community workers when they dissed these vinyl outlaws: "I'm fed up with busters like NWA . . . what the niggas did was market our life and our image . . . They never give back to the neighborhood!"[7]

Long divorced from political hell-raising, by the mid-nineties gangsta lost more of its in-your-face abrasiveness. Presaged by Dre's landmark *The Chronic*, it morphed into G-funk, a corporate-controlled mass product of the rap music industry whose ghettocentric sensibility was marked mainly by its absence. Among crass attitudes to violence, women, and life in general, by the century's end, the genre that spilled from the inner city had washed up on a suburban lawn, with white teenagers accounting for two-thirds of rap sales, together with its increasingly anemic politics and anomic poetics.[8]

By 2000 rap's share of the music business was second only to rock, and gaining—that is, if it still made sense to approach it as a single genre. Fragmented into a myriad of subdivisions, schools, and individual accents, it ranged over techno-funk (bounce), rap R&B, dirty South, Don rap, and neo-soul right down to nostalgia-powered old-school, complete with retro-style dookie chains and other accessories. Expanding and diversifying, it testified to the vitality of the art form that, like the novel or the concerto, could assume an almost infinite variety of incarnations while remaining identifiable at its core.

Jazzmatazz

> Politicians and wannabe politicians are not only trying to destroy the music, but the artist as well.
>
> Julian L. D. Shabazz, *The United States v. Hip-Hop*

In his classic *Blues People* (1963), LeRoi Jones set out to interpret black history by means of black music. He theorized, "If the music of the Negro in America, in all its permutations, is subjected to a socio-anthropological as well as musical scrutiny, something about the essential nature of the Negro's existence in this country ought to be revealed, as well as something about the essential nature of this country" (ix–x).

The best reason to speak of the nature of the music and the country in the same breath is that, like America, rap is an oxymoron. It is multiethnic yet defined by the binary of black and white. It is individualistic yet community-directed. It is capitalist and socialist, materialist and idealist, pro-laissez-faire and pro-social fairness. It is political and apolitical, moralistic and immoral, militant and peacenik, local-rooted and global-minded, egalitarian and racist, narcissistic and altruistic, doggy dog and amityville, radical and conformist, high-minded and opportunistic, populist and idolatrous, united and disunited. It is, in short, an objective correlative of the United States.

It is also ubiquitous, representing all folks and walks of life. There are women rappers, Asian rappers, child rappers, redneck rappers like Bubba Sparxxx, Christian rappers like Flame, and even born-again rappers led by "abstinence education" crusader Michael Peace, the first to tap rap back in 1980 as a medium for evangelical proselytizing.[9] Rap commercials sell everything on behalf of everybody, from the biggest corporations like McDonalds and Disney to the major sports leagues, with the NBA in the front court. These days if you wanna be hip, you gotta be down with hip-hop.

Having won in terms of consumer appeal does not mean, however, that rap enjoys universal appreciation for its aesthetics. Throughout Ken Burns' epic documentary *Jazz*, Pulitzer-winning trumpeter Wynton Marsalis lavished praise on the early Creole and black jazzmen who broke the rules on the way to a musical revolution. But in 1989 he gutted rap for *its* version of a musical revolution. Sampling, he sneered, was no substitute for composition. Lack of music theory and musical skill doomed the genre to looping simple breaks. Rappers broke the rules, all right, but for Marsalis they manifestly broke the wrong ones.[10]

There is no denying that much of rap is repetitive and as such eminently forgettable, but the same is true of every music genre, every art form, and every field of human activity. Yet we do not trash classical music en masse just because not every composer is a Bach or a Mozart, just as we do not automatically trash Eric Clapton's and David Bowie's albums because of their creators' racist and fascist leanings (virulent enough to have helped galvanize the late-1970s Rock Against Racism movement).

Yes, rap riffs and hooks are typically pared down to essentials—but so is *Kind of Blue*. This is not to mention that it takes ability, not to say artistry, to come up with catchy breaks or thigh-slapping grooves. And if rap is often compositionally straightforward, it is because it is often driven by heavy-duty lyrics. Tracks such as Nas's "Memory Lane" almost stupefy with the dexterity and velocity with which rhymes and concepts rain on listeners.

Some rappers, at least, work hard at defying pat assimilation, just like artists are said to do.

Marsalis's elitism is really the flip side of the bourgeoisie turning their noses up at Duchamp's nude at the 1913 Armory Exhibition, to say nothing of his urinal four years later. Crucially, however, conservatives who flog rap as the evidence or even the cause of decline in cultural standards tendentiously contrast the best of the past with the mediocre of the present. Naturally, with the benefit of historical hindsight, everyone is smart, including jazz experts at *Downbeat* who, a generation after the birth of bebop, had to re-review classic records by Bird, Monk, Diz, and others, which they had originally trashed as worthless.[11]

Refuting Marsalis in an elemental fashion, some of the great names in jazz have aligned themselves with rap, from Miles Davis (in posthumously released recordings), Herbie Hancock, and Greg Osby to Branford Marsalis, brother of Wynton. Also working with deejays and rappers is R&B legend Quincy Jones. There is even the classically trained dAKAH Symphonic Hip Hop Orchestra, which features turntables and an electronic rhythm section, as well as rappers and conservatory singers. Led by composer Double G, it uniquely fuses rap, funk grooves, jazz arrangements, and symphonic orchestration.

The musical traffic also runs the other way. For decades, starting with Grandmaster Flash, rap musicians have heavily sampled jazz for breaks and grooves. In parallel to their hardcore rap career as Gang Starr, DJ Premier and Guru produced a series of ambitious *Jazzmatazz* albums, fusing acid jazz with hip-hop. In 1990 their tellingly titled rap "Jazz Thing"— coproduced with the younger Marsalis—rocked the soundtrack of Spike Lee's *Mo' Better Blues*.

This abiding kinship between jazz and rap was symbolically captured in a media event staged in Harlem in 1998. Back in 1958, *Esquire* assembled a panoply of jazz legends for a historical photograph called "A Great Day in Harlem." Forty years later, the photo and the tribute were reprised by the hip-hop magazine *XXL*. Called "A Great Day in Harlem '98," its Kodak moment featured rappers, jazzmen, and assorted hip-hop heads in a salute to ghetto art that conquered the world in its own idiom.

Marsalis's diatribe turned out to be only the opening salvo in the war on rap launched in the 1990s from both sides of the political aisle. In contrast to the trumpeter, however, members of the 1994 congressional subcommittee— seconded by presidential candidate Bob Dole; Education Secretary William Bennett; Supreme Court nominee Robert Bork; chairwoman of the National Political Congress of Black Women, Delores Tucker; plus conservative groups ranging from the Parents' Music Resource Center (mostly wives of powerful Demublicans) to the Anti-Defamation League—ganged up on the lyrics.

After three months of recriminations, the hearings established what every-one knew beforehand: some tracks were violent, some were demeaning to women and men, and some were both. The solution? The FCC began slapping warning labels on the worst offenders, sending their sales through the roof and teaching those who did *not* rate a parental advisory that rapping clean was a commercial liability. The FCC also ordered partly sanitized versions of hit tracks for radio. While violence remained pretty much as before, "hos" was overdubbed as "girls" and "pussy" as "lovin," and morality was saved.

These palliatives never played well with those who took rap fictions at their word. In 1993 Reverend Calvin Butts III of Harlem made the national news when he proceeded to crush gangsta tapes and CDs with a steam-roller to condemn their attitudes to sex and violence. In his zeal he forgot to crush Hollywood mafia flicks that glorify the gangster lifestyle, big-screen westerns that lionize *pistoleros* and other "shoot first, ask questions later" renegades, the soft porn that sells every other commercial on TV, and other parts of mainstream American culture.

Butts's righteous rage obscured the fact that if gangsta rap thrives on vio-lence, so does the society that keeps buying it. America sanctions violence with every illegitimate war it foments, every international and domestic law it violates, every trillion dollars it sinks into the bottomless military pit, every "if it bleeds, it leads" news story it airs, every schoolground shootout it suffers, every gun-control bill it scuppers. Lyrical fiction, protested its defenders to the subcommittee, is just a convenient scapegoat.

It did not help their cause that a few hard-up criminal defendants tried to make gangsta take the rap for real-life murders, with claims that it dead-ened their sensibilities and incited violence.[12] Although these pleas of diminished responsibility met with zero success, they did nothing to per-suade crusaders like Bork that rap does not seed degeneracy in America. Census facts, however, belie his opportunistic fiction. In the last genera-tion—the hip-hop generation—murder rates, violent crime, and teenage births declined across the nation. Black high school graduations, university enrollments, and graduate degrees went up. Where the degeneracy?

Poetic License

Rap has always been socio-political from the artistic side since the beginning.

Julian L. D. Shabazz, The United States v. Hip-Hop

Hip-hop was embraced early on by pop-culture and music journalists, on the way to the academe where ethnomusicologists and social anthro-pologists have had a field day with an original urban formation. Together with cultural studies scholars, their pioneering studies in the 1990s laid the groundwork for understanding rap as a cultural movement and socio-political force. Among this flurry of interest, however, literary studies has been mostly content to take a back seat, even though a study of lyrics and other forms of poetry is part and parcel of its professional portfolio.

This is all the more unfortunate in that listeners at large evince a great deal of interest in rap poetry. Back in 1998 MTV commissioned a trendsetters survey to determine what fired up young music lovers. Not surprisingly, respondents craved more emotional engagement—that much has not changed from the days of Frankie Avalon. But, with rap sales hitting the stratosphere and the genre about to become the biggest player in the industry, they also reported "more of an interest in lyrics."[13]

While philosophers and lawyers from Richard Schusterman to Imani Perry champion inquiries into literary aspects of rap such as storytelling and lyrical expression, literary scholars seem content to sit on the sidelines. What might be the reasons for this complacency? The answer looms from Susan Jacoby's *The Age of American Unreason* (2008). Taking a dim view of the dumbing down of American cultural life, she makes a point of the "always vulgar lyrics of most rap and hip-hop" (164). Alas, the most striking aspect of this indictment is its illogic: rap cannot be *always* vulgar and only mostly so.

Naturally, Jacoby was only remixing critiques of rap—as nasty, brutish, and short on art—that had bedeviled it from day one. "Rap is all anger," spat one critic back in 1986, "and the so-called background music or scratching is so intense that it beckons you to act violent."[14] Unquestionably, many lyrics do truck in violence or misogyny. Punking rival rappers and producers in "I Smell Pussy," 50 Cent actually commits both sins at once. So what? Because brutality or hatred can serve as a lyrical means to an end, in and of itself their presence yet signifies nothing.[15]

Content attribution—the critical practice of inferring effects and attitudes—is a demonstrably unreliable method that, if applied with an unjaundiced eye, would find plenty amiss with the canon. After all, violence and sociopathy have been powering literature since long before *Oedipus Rex*, and the multitude of lascivious, thuggish, and otherwise politically incorrect material culled from the world's greatest playwright for Michael MacRone's *Naughty Shakespeare* (1997) easily upstages any badass in the rap business. In short, without defending rap lyrics across the board, one must not discount them as literature, either, as even well-meaning scholars do unintentionally.

Towards the end of his superb *Hip Hop Matters* (2005), S. Craig Watkins sketches a picture of hip-hop literature, by which, at it soon becomes apparent, he means exclusively prose fiction. Nary a word about the poetry that pulses at the heart of every rap. It is true that a growing number of (mostly women) hip-hop writers churn out street-life romances, crime stories, action thrillers, and even *Bildungsromane*. They have their stars, such as the former rapper Sister Souljah, and specialty publishers, such as 50 Cent's G-Unit Books, launched in 2005 to tap this lucrative market. Unfortunately, as even sympathetic black reviewers and black booksellers acknowledge, "street life" and "street vernacular" are largely euphemisms for thuggery and profanity that sell books despite solecisms and lack of almost any prosocial ethos.

Even so, the majority of cultural historians are too focused on rap as a racial and/or commercial phenomenon to approach its lyrics as literature—American literature. Predictably enough, this preoccupation with historical and cultural determinants has undersold the genre as an aesthetic force. In spite of Michael Eric Dyson's and bell hooks's dismay at reducing art to socioeconomics, claims such as that "gangsta rap . . . is the direct by-product of the crack explosion" remain the rule rather than the exception.[16]

Yet this kind of teleology makes little sense, socioeconomic or artistic. Just as not all instantiations of Fordism and Reaganomics give rise to hip-hop—or Thatcherism would have done so—not all crack epidemics give rise to gangsta, or it would have sprung in the barrios and favelas as surely as in the ghettos. Worse, historical determinism denies the very basis of social and artistic critique. If rap is merely an outgrowth of its street roots, it makes as much sense to fault it for lyrical vices or musical minimalism as to fault trees for growing from their roots. To be in a position to take rappers to task for what they profess presupposes approaching lyrics as the product of deliberate art-creative decisions and not only socioeconomic conditions.

And yet, while popular songwriters like Bob Dylan or Leonard Cohen are celebrated for their poetic touch, rappers await literary-critical acclaim for the virtues of the verses that made their music an American icon and a global bestseller. In a 1926 essay, "The Negro Renaissance," Walter White—journalist, novelist, and longtime leader of the NAACP (he drafted Truman's executive order to desegregate the military)—observed that poetry was "the most natural mode of expression next to song that the Negro possesses."[17] Today he could cite the Hip-Hop Renaissance as a proof of his thesis, echoed by Eazy-E, who, on the eponymous track from *Niggaz4Life,* calls himself "an underground poet."

As in other varieties of poetry, rappers select words for their rhyme and reason. When LL Cool J swaggers on "I'm Bad" that he "got concrete rhymes," he draws attention to the hard, concrete imagery of the elaborate metaphorical construction that likens rhyming to, among others, a prize fight. Intricate conceits of this nature illustrate concepts through complex figuration, arresting attention with parallels between apparently dissimilar or incongruous objects or situations. An almost metaphysical conceit controls the structure of the Geto Boys classic "My Mind Is Playin Tricks on Me," which gestalt-shifts a series of paranoid delusions that trick drug kingpins into committing horrible errors of judgment.

Like all performance poets, rappers use stress, intonation, and inflection to cadence words to the music. The rhythm track synchronizes the overall time signature with the rhymes, which ride the beat while syncopating in and out of it. This is occasionally enabled by shifting stresses within poetic feet, such as substituting a trochee (*po*lice) for a canonical iamb or an anapest (Washing*ton*) for a dactyl. Skittered in lockstep with the time, the semantic and rhythmic flow is also punctuated by enjambment—carrying rhyme over to the next line, as opposed to end-stopping.

Formal control is, of course, most apparent in rap's signature device: rhyme. Both an ornamental and a mnemonic device for stitching phrases together, it is grounded in the human adaptive predisposition to symmetry that aids in grouping and organizing imagery. Just like alliteration, refrain, chorus, or periphrasis, a rhyme scheme is a form of repetition or translational symmetry, in rap most often falling out into rhyming couplets, with frequent internal rhymes within the line on either side of a caesura. Generally speaking, standard rhymes run the gamut from masculine and feminine (or monosyllabic and bisyllabic) to, more creatively, an almost infinite variety of "off" rhymes, also known as eye rhymes, half rhymes, or slant rhymes.

When Nas assonates *ghetto* with *devil* in "Doo Rags," the pairing tells its own story, as does Killah Priest's consonant off-rhyme of *Sodom* and *Harlem* in "One Step." Another common variety is anaphora—technically, initial identical rhyme. The favorite rhetorical tool of a stumping politician, it is essentially amped-up alliteration (repetition of the initial sound or letter) that links verses by repeating the lead parts. Lyrics can also take the form of dramatic monologue or even shade into confessional poetry, self-directed and unstinting in self-revelation. Tuned into their internal logic and meaning, some may even ditch the artifice of rhyme altogether to flow in free (unrhymed) verse.

Heavy Mental

The 2 Live Crew said "We Want Some Pu**y." George Michael said "I Want Your Sex." Is there a difference? Certainly, one is a popular white man with a beard and blue jeans, and the other is a group of young men with gold chains and an attitude.

Julian L. D. Shabazz, The United States v. Hip-Hop

In July 2007 the leading black American magazine *Ebony* published a special issue decrying hip-hop diction. Even as it drew the bead on the rampant use of the N-word, it failed, however, to publicize a salient racial asymmetry. Although black rappers show few qualms about calling one another "nigga," white rappers do, beginning with Eminem, who publicly balked, saying, "There's just some things that I just don't do."[18] By implication, at least, "hoing" and "bitching" are okay, as is featuring black rappers who "nigga" on his albums left and right.

This is not to single out Eminem: Bubba Sparxxx and Paul Wall also pussyfoot around the N-word. Other white rappers, like Necro or White Dawg, who exhibit no such inhibitions, may have paid the price for keeping it real insofar as they never broke out from the underground. Perfectly defensible in terms of decorum (fitness of language to subject matter), racial epithets in the mouths of white rappers remain, incongruously, a commercial misstep in the milieu that made "nigga" a household term. Defused by in-group assimilation, the term remains explosive outside its ethnic boundaries.

As Henry Louis Gates has pointed out on more than one occasion, the debate over artistic responsibility is one of the hoariest in black literature. Its modern history dates back to 1926, the year of *Nigger Heaven*, when W. E. B. Du Bois marshaled a symposium called "The Negro in Art: How Shall He Be Portrayed?" Placing the problem of the representation of blacks by both blacks and whites at center stage, it anticipated today's handwringing over rap, whose descent from revolutionary to confectionary paralleled its ascent from the underground to the establishment.[19]

Rap in general is no stranger to what George Carlin used to satirize as Seven Words You Can Never Say on Television. Outside the teenage age bracket, however, their transgressive effect wears off rather quickly. The first rap about nappy dugouts was fresh, but with each successive repetition it became more insulting—not morally but artistically (ironically, it is the status of art that lets rap stave off charges of obscenity under the First Amendment). Easy as it is to blame the genre, you could as easily, of course, blame the *OED*. Resolutely fuckless and cuntless until 1972, it now prints virtually every expletive under the sun.

If hip-hop slang is the ultimate public art with feedback, its lexicon is a living expression of Walt Whitman's quest for raw authenticity in American speech. Indeed, rap lyrics mine the ghetto sometimes to the point where their spectacular vernacular is hard to distinguish from found poetry. At the same time, even as they make a fetish of expressing themselves in black vulgate idiolect, many rappers are perfectly articulate in standard English (and as such, "bilingual").[20]

Syntax and syncopation aside, the iconic trait of hip-hop has always been its diction. Novel usage and neologisms are prized for the same reasons that linguistic freshness is prized the world over. "Def," as even the *OED* knows, means excellent (so do "dope" and "phat"). "Stupid" means "very," as in "stupid short." "Bus" means to pay attention. "Skeeze" is to have sex. "Wack" is corny. "Jiggy": stylish. "Dead prez": greenback. "Rock star": junkie. "Chronic": joint laced with coke. "Dog": male buddy. "Props": recognition or respect. And so on, and so forth. The only thing is, hip-hop slang comes with a stupid short shelf life. "Def" is now beyond wack. Say word.

On their 1998 album, *Still Standing*, a member of Goodie Mob went so far as to append a "slumtionary" that glosses ghetto slang from Atlanta, where the group hails from. After all, not even native black listeners down with hip-hop are immune to being tripped by fleet lyrical feet. Here is how Imani Perry transcribes one striking metaphor from LL Cool J's "I'm Bad":

> I'm like Tyson, Icin', I'm a sole jaguar
> Makin' sure you don't try to battle me no more.[21]

Stumped by the "sole jaguar"? Listen to the track carefully and it is clear that she misinterprets—mondegreens, in the linguistic parlance—verses that run as follows:

> I'm like Tyson, icin', I'm a soldier at war, makin' sure
> You don't try to battle me no more.

Most song lyrics are so banal, shrugged Paul Simon back in the days of Simon and Garfunkel, that even a spark of intelligence can earn you the title of a poet from audiences who do not know any better. "But the people who call you a poet are people who never read poetry," he argued. "They never read, say, Wallace Stevens."[22] True to his word, the majority of rap *is*, of course, banal beyond belief. But detractors who extrapolate from the bad and the ugly to the rest of the genre inevitably end up throwing out the poetry with the bathwater.

Rapped rubato over a gravelly futuristic soundscape, ranging from divinity to aeronautics to technology to a veiled allusion to *Space Odyssey: 2001*, Killah Priest's starchild soliloquy from "Heavy Mental" is only one example of "rapsody" at its finest. At one point, rushing through space, past quasars, radar beams, and spacecraft-borne astronauts, the lyrical I morphs into a disembodied beam of gas,

> Out of reach of all manners of sky examiners, heaven scanners,
> Giant antennas and high tech space cameras,
> No evidence in any cemetery or obituary,
> Not found in any library or dictionary
> Or encyclopedia or media, I'm in star mode!

With lyrical bravura and the awareness of the power of the image and rhyme comes intense pride of ownership. Rappers strut their lines, stake reps on poetic prowess, bait and debate one another, boast and toast their dexterity—in short, embrace the glaring polarity between macho swagger and lyrical deftness without a hint of irony. Familiar from the dozens, verbal braggadocio underwrites the survival of the streetest, where if you're not the baddest dog on the block, it helps to be quick with your feet, poetic or not.

Pride in one's art can at times become indistinguishable from what in highbrow circles goes by the name of self-reflexive deconstruction of one's artistry. In "Station Identification," Channel Live rap, "intellectually you're shallow, mentally you're just starving/I'm rollin' on them like Calvin Butts up in Harlem/with metaphors." In "Come Clean," Jeru the Damaja picks up the thread: "I don't gang bang or shoot out, Bang, Bang/ the relentless lyrics the only dope I slang."

The genre supplies poets with preset patterns within which to develop their individuality. Reaching for emotional harmonics—trading phrases, in the lingo—rappers take on the role of lay preachers who, as often as they boast of getting rich or laid, call on their constituencies to respond to the troubles they see. As if on cue, one of the most original rap poets of his generation acknowledges in the intro to *The Moment of Truth*, "We have certain formulas but we update them with the times" before adding, in a ringing endorsement of the original classic, "and there's always a message involved."

The Message

> FIGHT THE POWER! Those are some strong words. Can you imagine being in the American power structure and hearing those words coming from a group known as "The Black Panthers of Rap"?
>
> *Julian L. D. Shabazz, The United States v. Hip-Hop*

Calling rap lyrics smart and insightful, Candidate Obama enthused in 2008: "The way they can communicate a complex message in a very short space is remarkable."[23] These props from the soon-to-be first president to come of age in the hip-hop era were a fitting *quid pro quo* for the poetic and political endorsements he had received from the community. In 2008 the roster of celebrities plumping for Obama read like *Who's Who in Rap*, from Ice Cube and Snoop Dogg in the West to Kanye West and Jay-Z in the East. Less known but politically more engaged artists like Talib Kweli and Common had been signifying references to Obama even earlier on. In "Politics as Usual," Ludacris toasted him as "my man" and appealed to listeners to make history by painting the White House black (in a bow toward *George* Clinton), while putting down the heavyweights in the Demublican Party:

> Hillary hated on you so that bitch is irrelevant [. . .]
> McCain don't belong in any chair unless he's paralyzed,
> Yeah I said it cuz Bush is mentally handicapped.

KRS-One, Paris, Talib Kweli, A Tribe Called Quest, Digable Planets, Common, Mos Def, De La Soul, Guru, Jurassic-5, J-Live, Killah Priest, Roots, Immortal Technique, Blackalicious, Arsonists, High and Mighty, Disposable Heroes of Hiphoprisy, X-Clan, Poor Righteous Teachers. This short list of the intellectuals and teachers of rap doesn't even begin to do justice to the genre's poetical and political potential. Admittedly, as musical malcontents point out, some of their verses read on occasion like op-eds in *The Nation*. But readers of this flagship of the Left might actually prefer to get their civics rapped, for example, by Brother Ali in "Uncle Sam Goddamn."

The rapper rhetorically employs the *hypophora*, often posing questions only to immediately answer them himself. One such call that drives the track, "What you think happens to the money from taxes," gets a scornful response: "Shit the governments an addict," setting the tone for the removal of the political figleaf covering the government's "billion dollar a week kill brown people habit." The rapper even smuggles in economic statistics, jeering about all Americans working three months out of twelve to pay for their country's "savage" thirst for blood. With the media, symbolized by the white anchor Dan Rather, quiescent and complicit, the nation is trained to jump to its feet and salute while the government wraps itself in the flag and strikes up the national anthem.

In spite of and because of its passionate underground following, political rap gets virtually no spins on the commercial airwaves. The reasons are not difficult to deduce. Whereas so-called conscious rap gives a voice to generalized social commentary that has been its bread and butter at least since "The Message," hardcore political rap like Aceyalone's "Ms Amerikkka" is promulgated by artists with active and activist political agendas. This is why American audiences don't get to see incendiary tracks such as Immortal Technique's "Bin Laden" on MTV, or for that matter anywhere else. Pointing his finger at the "fake Christians, fake politicians," who run the nationwide con called War on Terrorism, the artist pulls no punches:

> They funded Al-Qaeda, and now they blame the Muslim religion
> Even though Bin Laden was a CIA tactician
> They gave him billions of dollars, and they funded his purpose
> Fahrenheit 9/11, that's just scratchin' the surface.

Emboldened by their mid-1990 multi-front war on gangsta, by the end of the decade, a coalition of conservative parental and political organizations regrouped against revolutionary rap. Ironically, even as they marginalized the radical artists even further, eight years of Bush II and Cheney led to a minor revival of engagé attitudes in commercial rappers like Jay-Z, Eminem, Kanye West, Lil' Wayne, Jadakiss, and the Game. Be that as it may, none of them came even close to the lyrical Molotov cocktails that Paris was tirelessly lobbing at the neocon administration in tracks such as "What Would You Do?"

From oil blood money to politically motivated assassinations, to "Bin Ashcroft" and his campaign to curtail constitutional freedoms, the rapper asks his audiences to "bear witness to the sickness of these dictators," before going full throttle after what he sees around him:

And with the 4th Amendment gone eyes are on the 1st
That's why I'm spittin' cyanide each and every verse
I see the Carlyle group and Harris Bank Accounts
I see 'em plead the 5th each and every session now
And while Reichstag burns see the public buy it.

After Michael Franti of the Disposable Heroes of Hiphoprisy visited Baghdad and the Occupied Territories in 2004, including the infamous Rafa Refugee camp in Gaza, his statements about the terror experienced by the Iraqi and Palestinian communities were censored in the United States, while he was placed under surveillance for advocating state *non*violence. The US authorities' antagonism may also have had something to do with the group's irrepressibly political raps such as "The Winter of the Long Hot Summer," which graphically tells the story of the invasion of Iraq:

The pilots in night vision goggles Kuwaited, and generals
masturbated 'til the fifteenth, two days later they invaded
Not a single tv station expressed dissension or hardly made mention
to the censorship of information from our kinder and gentler nation.

Incredibly enough, notwithstanding its antiestablishment ferocity, political rap has been accused of not being particularly revolutionary. Rap is about black group empowerment and self-empowerment, not a broader transformation of society, insisted one critic. The few references to socialism dead prez drops, he insisted, "are more about show than content. Radically liberal rap endorses the idea of society as a fair system of social cooperation but hardly questions whether this is ultimately compatible with capitalism. Accepting a kinder, gentler market-driven economy isn't the stuff of political revolution."[24]

So, one is compelled to ask, what is the stuff of political revolution? Stuttering AK-47s? Proletarian coups d'état? If precipitating a regime overthrow or a system change is hardly rap's job description, glossing over the awakening effected by hip-hop among the often non-voting and apolitical black Americans, such critiques claim, in effect, that Frederick Douglass and Martin Luther King were more about show than content. As for dead prez, they were too busy rapping the body politic to worry about whether their tracks such as "Police State" were revolutionary.

Presciently warning about "FBI spyin on us through the radio antennas" in the next stage of the closing of the open society, they put their political credential on the line by pledging, if necessary, to "take a slug for the cause like huey p.," in a dig at what they diss as commercial fake niggaz who merely try to copy Master P. The track gathers force, rising to a political crescendo:

> Bring the power back to the street, where the people live
> We sick of workin for crumbs and fillin up the prisons
> Dyin over money and relyin on religion
> for help, we do for self like ants in a colony
> Organize the wealth into a socialist economy.

In March 2012 all Republican would-be presidents—with the notable exception of Ron Paul—rose as one in uproar against the president. What did Obama do to unite the fractious Right? He apologized for the American troops who had once again desecrated the most sacred text of the countries they had been illegitimately pacifying for years. Who was the libertarian statesman who, regardless of political fallout, broke ranks to do the right (as opposed to Right) thing? In "Ron Paul for the Long Haul," King Solomon and Roy Shivers rhymed out his portable bio in time for the 2008 election season.

The duo's signature track begins by firing political salvos at Mitt Romney, "a whore of the business class," Rudy Giuliani "a puppet of the banks and the real ruling party—Bilderberg," plus "cokehead retard" George Bush, "big money pimpin" Hillary Clinton, and the pro-Patriot Act Barack Obama—not to mention dishonorable mentions of John McCain, Fred Thompson, Jon Edwards, Joe Biden, Tom Tancredo, Sam Brownback, Al Gore, Bill Richardson, Dennis Kucinich, and Mike Bloomberg. Having cleared the air, they pledge allegiance to the only politician to have earned their respect during the bruising campaign. Ron Paul, former doctor and Vietnam operative with ten terms in Congress behind his belt,

> Voted down Iraq war, said it was illegal, wanna bring the troops home
> and end American imperial wars, for the Constitution [. . .]

Ron Paul stood tall against the Patriot Act
All the Abu Graihb torture and never raised taxes
Voted down NAFTA, voted down CAFTA,
Says that the free trade bill's a disaster.

Call them preachy or only teachy, but odds are that most Americans have never heard a word of these poems before. With three out of four buyers being white, the consumer base is not exactly enthusiastic about paying for political art that militates against white oppression, unequal distribution of income and opportunity, and color-coded disenfranchisement at the ballot box.

Uptown to Harlem

Rap artists like Public Enemy, The 2 Live Crew, NWA, Ice Cube, Ice T are not public office holders, but they carry more political clout than a lot of politicians occupying a seat on Capitol Hill.

David Shabazz, Preface to The United States v. Hip-Hop

The 2004 election was the first serious testing ground for the effectiveness of the hip-hop vote. New political groups from the Hip-Hop Summit Action Network to the National Hip Hop Political Convention to P. Diddy's Citizen Change all went after the hip-hop nation to register and vote. Engagé as ever, dead prez summed up the spirit of the moment: "We're here for all the people, not just the political militants, but the people who need to be awakened to become political militants."[25]

This is not to say that the hip-hop generation has been abstaining from political action. The 2001 UCLA freshman survey revealed, for example, that almost half of the new entrants took part in an organized demonstration during the previous year. Astonishingly, this was three times higher than at the height of the civil rights movement. By 2004 poll after poll reported record levels of interest in presidential elections among the youngest tier eligible to vote.[26]

Amid admittedly higher than usual voter turnout and amid Ohio ballot irregularities, they lost. Bush II won. The next day, critics and self-critics fell to questioning hip-hop's political viability. And yet, how much the movement has achieved, even in its relatively short history, is clear from Amiri Baraka's program for the Black Arts Movement back in the day. Going uptown to Harlem, he recollected,

We wanted to do three things. We wanted to create an art or a poetry that was African American, let's say, as African American as Bessie Smith or

Duke Ellington. We wanted to create an art that was mass-oriented, that would come out of the universities, that would get into the street, that would reach our people . . . And the third thing we wanted to do was to create an art that was revolutionary.[27]

Fifty years down the road, the program of Black Arts Movement poets has undeniably been achieved by hip-hop poets. And yet, questions linger. What does rap in the political scheme of things stand for—and stand up for? From day one there has been no coherent platform and no political unity in the movement. Chuck D himself has evolved from a Black Power nationalist to an increasingly color-blind but class-conscious populist whose efforts to promote civic engagement and political education, much as his *bêtes noires*—political apathy, democratic malaise, corporate media—are virtually indistinguishable from Michael Moore's. "Rap is the Black CNN," he argued, only to correct himself, "the CNN for young people all over the world" (256).

Political mobilization along racial lines is an increasingly problematic, not to say quixotic, project, given hip-hop's inherent eclecticism. It may be a lyrical and musical blessing, but it is a partisan curse that has historically produced as many recipes for American apple pie as there are cooks. "They didn't want to come together for Malcolm X," shrugged Scarface, "so I know they won't look out for mine."[28]

This heterogeneity is only exacerbated by the fact that political rap is by now a global art form. A case in point is a Putin army lieutenant who earned himself exile by rapping on Russian YouTube about conditions at his St. Petersburg base. Set to Eminem's "Stan"—which itself samples the hook from Dido's "Thank You"—his homemade video "A Letter to the Minister of Defense" records images as bad as anything in US inner-city tenements. The soldier raps to the minister about the filth, the promised mortgages to buy a decent place to live, asking, like Stan, why he never got a reply to his previous email messages. His reply came in the form of his being posted to the other side of Russia, to a town known only for a military school, a statue of Lenin, and lots of trees.[29]

In 2012 a Bulgarian rapper, Big Sha, was prosecuted for offending the white, green, and red national flag. The criminal proceedings were initiated because, according to the government's broadcast council, one of his tracks associated the white with cocaine and the red with the menstrual cycle. With bloggers jeering that the state had gone nuts, the imbroglio reached even the EU, forcing the prime minister and his ruling party to deny having instigated the transparently political lawsuit.

American rap is itself no stranger to political friction. "Fuck tha Police," which lashed out at cop brutality in a mock court session with Judge Dre, goaded the FBI and the Secret Service to accuse NWA of verbal assault on law enforcement—only to goad Congressman Don Edwards (ironically, a former FBI agent) to defend the group in the name of the First Amendment. Bill Clinton ripped into Sister Souljah for her quip about replacing black-on-black violence with black-on-white. Paris had his knuckles rapped for "Bush Killa," which, in the opinion of the NSA, plotted a fictional assassination of the president. Maybe this is why Beaton never got into hot water with the US security apparatus: he killed everyone on the planet *except* the president.

Sensing political or commercial payoff, politicians and rappers resort to the same tactics and the same inflated rhetoric. The resulting arms race in reciprocal recriminations works like a dream, boosting sales on the one hand and law-and-order credentials on the other. Unfortunately, the longer it goes on, the more the public image of hip-hop as a breeding ground for all manner of asocial behaviors takes on a life of its own, drowning its poetics and politics with the help of the scandal-hungry and increasingly tabloid-minded media.

A (highly contested) share of the blame for this one-sided portrayal is attributable to rap itself, a victim not so much of censorship as of its own success. The genre that once dared to offend and innovate chose instead to chase the dollar, in the process inevitably marginalizing its artistic and political wing. In 1995 D. A. Smart could still rap in "Where Ya At?" about going to Washington to get justice, pledging to "get it or die tryin." By 2003 the message, incorporated into 50 Cent's breakout album (and his 2005 eponymous movie), became *Get Rich or Die Tryin*. His fellow hip-hop mogul Jay-Z chorused on the semi-biographical "Moment of Clarity," "I dumbed down for my audience to double my dollars." Both are as good as their word: together they are worth well in excess of half a billion dollars.

Politricks as Usual

Economics and a loyal, growing constituency is what constitutes political power.

David Shabazz, Preface to The United States v. Hip-Hop

Racial discrimination would seem to be a ghost of the past. The United States has its first mulatto president, elected in 2008 with more white votes than John Kerry secured in 2004. Nearly one in ten politicians in the House is black. The US attorney general is black. Black CEOs are running blue-chip corporations from American Express to Xerox to Merck. Even at the ground level, where historically miscegenation was a lynchable offence, a quarter of black men now tie the knot across racial lines. So why are "message" rappers so angry?

Maybe because they have been reading Derrick Bell's exhortations for racial realism that eschews symbolic victories that serve to obscure ugly economic realities. Or maybe because in spite of Obama's skin color or his liking for Jay-Z and Kanye, his administration has been all politricks as usual. There's no need to look past the 2012 Democratic National Convention, under whose auspices Joe Biden bragged that the Democrats "created 4.5 million private-sector jobs in the last 29 months."[30] Earlier that summer Obama cited the same number for the same period beginning in February 2010. Although not quite fiction, their statistics were not unlike a Malibu g-string: flashing the eye candy while concealing the vital parts.

The logical, not to say fair, date for comparing job numbers would be January 2009, when Obama took office. Instead, the Democrats reset the scale to the absolute bottom of the job slump, which happened to be February 2010. The truth behind their cherry-picked numbers is that the economy has not yet recouped the losses since the president took office. Concentrating on private-sector gains, moreover, Obama sidestepped the fact that government positions, starting with teachers and policemen, continued to go down the drain.

The title of WC and the Maad Circle's 1991 protest album *Ain't a Damn Thang Changed* said it all then and since then. Then, even as Toni Morrison publicly toasted Clinton as America's first black president, his patented "It's the economy, stupid" boom increased extreme poverty rates (less than half of the minimum needed to survive) for black Americans. Since then, wealth disparity between the two races has only widened, with gaps in household income wider today than when King led the march on Washington.

Granted, differences in life expectancy and high school graduation have all but been eliminated. But black men are more likely to rot in local, state, or federal prisons than they were half a century ago. Well into Obama's second term, blacks continue to live in poverty, drop out of school, and run afoul of the law with a frequency that would horrify white America. This is not to overlook the often-overlooked fact that in absolute numbers, there are more poor whites than blacks in the country, while most blacks are working-class and middle-class. But the long and short of it is that, as an ethnic group, they live harder and die younger.

Political conservatives often contrast blacks with "model minorities," such as Asians, as a prelude to accusing them of leeching off social programs. While conceding that the ultimate responsibility for one's life rests with the individual, defenders retort that Asians have never had to suffer centuries of "the bloody whip, the chain, the gag, the thumb-screw, cat-hauling, the cat-o'-nine-tails, the dungeon, the blood-hound" (410), as Frederick Douglass put it in *My Bondage and My Freedom*. Black Americans deserve all the help they can get, they contend, if only because you cannot put a dollar value on moral expiation.

Preoccupied with the representative minorities, neither side dwells on the fact that the United States itself was founded on ghettos, better known as Indian reservations (the Oklahoma Indian Territory was a ghetto on the scale of a state). Ghetto mentality continued to dictate federal policy in 1924, when US citizenship was extended to Indians only with the express proviso that the Bill of Rights did not apply to them. That had to wait until 1968, almost five hundred years after Columbus first proposed to resell Native American slaves in the Atlantic islands and Iberia.

The history of racial segregation cast a shadow even over nineteenth-century abolitionism, which in most ways, and most minds, was equivalent to separatism. Erstwhile slaves or assimilationist tribes like the Cherokees were not expected to be integrated, largely because they were not expected to bring much of value to white society, save for emotional scars, race riots, and relentless competition for service jobs. Not much change since the late sixteenth century, when Elizabeth I decreed that all "Negars" be expelled from the Sceptered Isle for fear of stealing jobs away from the English.

Ironically, it is the longevity and ferocity of these racial fault lines that makes the embracing of hip-hop by white audiences look like the best argument that they have finally been bridged. Young people, always more ready to rebel against the parental and social status quo, have indeed identified themselves with black culture with intensity that seems to defy old-time racial divisions. Black urban fashion and speech, not to mention avidly consumed music and videos, are irresistible magnets for today's white suburban teenagers. A non-fringe integration of hip-hop culture and lifestyle that would seem miraculous even a generation or two ago is now a fait accompli.

It is tempting to interpret this children's crusade as a sign of America evolving into a kinder and gentler nation. The truth, however, is likely to be considerably less romantic. Jazz Age Harlemania also saw a violent interest in all things black by visitors titillated by the exotic and the risqué. Van Vechten, who used to take Somerset Maugham and others on tours of ghetto nightlife, may have been a patron of black art and a lifelong friend and correspondent of Langston Hughes. But, like other whites who used to fill Harlem clubs and speakeasies, he had no desire to live with or like the blacks.

Much like the white folks who were said to be Van Vechtening in the Jazz Age ghettos, today's suburbanites may be doing no more than seeking vicarious thrills. Young people are always drawn to taboos, even as they do not always propose to smash them, and there is an undeniable frisson in crossing over to the other side of the racial tracks in the hope that some of the street toughness and coolness might rub off. Hip-hop is a potent

Figure 4.2   Human Evolution ". . . It is tempting to interpret this children's crusade as a sign of America evolving into a kinder and gentler nation . . ."
Credit: Wilmar Marques

"afrodisiac" for well-to-do white youth whose idea of being down with it is often limited to showing off brand-name banger apparel and Beats headphones.

How much of the apparent integration is knee-jerk nonconformism and how much genuine devotion to black community values is an open question at best. After all, a picture of racial relations suggested by that faithful mirror of American culture and mores, primetime television, is rather different. Almost as soon as interracial relationships appear on the small screen, they are written out of scripts, quite often pursued by a firestorm of hate mail. A kiss between the president's white daughter and his black valet at the end of "Six Meetings Before Lunch" on *The West Wing*'s opening season sparked letters so ugly that they astonished the scene's writer, Sorkin.[31]

A Postcard from the Ghetto

Too many of our brothers and sisters talk big but do nothing.

Julian L. D. Shabazz, *The United States v. Hip-Hop*

Commercialized to the bone, mainstream rap is now a popular entertainment designer brand. In this it reflects the realities of the music industry, which in the course of the last generation has been redesigned top to bottom by a wave of consolidations, corporate-controlled playlists, new monitoring technologies such as SoundScan, and not least MTV. In a sign of the times, one hip-hop scholar wrote, "A genre as novel as rap was in 1979 would never gain the spins necessary in today's radio industry to establish a viable presence."[32]

Be that as it may, the gangsta-playa tropes seem in no danger of losing their appeal to the paying white consumers. Never mind that these bestselling fictions of America's mean inner-city streets are about as authentic as the hardboiled hype of Mickey Spillane. For the fans, every rap lyric is a postcard from the ghetto, and its hoods in the 'hood are social archetypes rather than racial stereotypes.

Naturally, there is no such thing as unmediated naturalism or realism. All art is artifice. This is why it is surprising that even scholars who relish gangsta's puckish humor and ironic distancing, situating it within a long cultural tradition of tricksters and picaros, typically ignore the puckishness and distancing that runs through all of rap.[33] After all, flipping from "Dear Mama" to booty juice, from hailing community consciousness to hailing conspicuous consumption, from making art to making a profit, the genre has turned self-reflexivity into art.

Not even in the months following the publication of *Nigger Heaven* had authenticity discourse been mobilized to the degree it has been by rap apologists. They contend, not without merit, that the genre pursues the same aesthetic that Dreiser, Norris, Teague, and other naturalists had at the turn of the twentieth century. Blame the lyricists for making the social underclasses the subject of art, or for dwelling on violence, carnality, and survivalism, and you might as well blame the novelists. Not that both literary and social critics did not try to do just that as the nineteenth century drew to a close.

At the heart of these contretemps lies the cult of authenticity that has, paradoxically, driven rap's commercial success from its inception. Street cred is a priceless commodity on the super-crowded and super-competitive hip-hop market. What makes it even more so is that the paying fan base, the majority of whom know the ghetto only second-hand, finds it as difficult to separate artful storytelling from street reality as to separate the storyteller from the lyrical "I."

Never mind that the ghetto life conjured up by lyricists armed with the poetic license to thrill, chill, and kill is oftentimes little more than hyperbolic hyperreality. Never mind that street cred is little more than a buzzword used by hyphenated rappers (as in investor-mogul-entrepreneur) to generate sales. Even as competition over rap's creative resources has by now mutated into a dogfight over the capital and economic resources of the entire music-and-video industry, buyers want their rap to be real, ignoring the fact that it has always followed in *their* tracks, not the other way around.

Amid all this wrangling over what is real in rap fiction, Michael Eric Dyson stands the authenticity discourse on its head by blasting the obsession with street cred as a sufficient, or even necessary, condition for truthfulness of art. So what if Tupac did not personally live every verse of the life he rhymed so vividly on his tracks? So what if he borrowed from other people's lives or even invented them altogether? If he did, Dyson asks, "would he be any different from any other artist whose primary obligation is to make art out of imagination, fiction, and fantasy?"[34]

Stories do not have to be real to be true, and few are. Although some rap stars, like Afrika Bambaataa in NYC or Eazy-E in LA, did live the street-gang life, most came onto the scene from respectable working-class families or even straight outta college. As spoofed already in a 1994 mockumentary, *Fear of a Black Hat*, street cred is cashed out not in terms of what *is* but what *sells* in the business where top performers are diversified-portfolio brand names whose wealth is calibrated in tens and hundreds of millions of dollars.

Rappers are often accused of betraying the principles of which they sing, not least by making obscene amounts of money (by these standards, Sam Cooke should fail history and Madonna should be a virgin). Purists scorn Ice Cube, who went from "Fuck tha Police" to playing good cops in Hollywood flicks. They diss Eazy-E for paying 25 grand to lunch with Bush I at a Republican fundraiser and Snoop Dogg for selling commercials rather than delivering a message. In "No Rest for the Wicked," B-Real ripped Cube for going to school in white San Fernando Valley, and in "Checkmate" Jadakiss trashed 50 Cent for living in Connecticut suburbia—the same "the only good cop is a dead cop" 50 Cent who now hires cops for his personal security.

Michael Moore—who, like many a rapper who made it big, has also been reviled for failing to practice what he preaches—replied to *his* critics in words that cut to the heart of popular, not to say populist, art. "I'm filthy rich. You know why I'm a multi-millionaire? 'Cause multi-millions like what I do."[35] His caution against confusing a person with a persona is, however, only half the truth. The other half is personified by cheap stunts like the 2013 firestorm in a teapot over Kendrick Lamar's diss of a few fellow performers. With the social media astir over what was hyped as another blood feud, the snicker from one of those name-checked rappers, Meek Mill, said it all: "We gonna have fun with it; get money. Hip hop needed that."[36]

In her pioneering study *Black Noise: Rap Music and Black Culture in Contemporary America* (1994), Tricia Rose could still credibly maintain that most rap artists were working in the form and in the tradition with direct roots in 1970s New York City. Only three years later, Chuck D would contradict her squarely in *Fight the Power*: "rap is in total chaos right about now" (104). Wonder what he would say today.

The Left Wing

Aaron Sorkin, Lawrence O'Donnell, Jr.,
Eli Attie, et al., *The West Wing*

Pornography for Liberals

Liberals got women the right to vote, liberals got African Americans the right to vote, liberals created Social Security and lifted millions of elderly people out of poverty, liberals ended segregation, liberals passed the Civil Rights Act, the Voting Rights Act, liberals created Medicare, liberals passed the Clean Air Act, the Clean Water Act. What did conservatives do? They opposed every one of those programs, every one.

"The Debate," The West Wing

The end of an era is traditionally a time of reckoning, and on the last day of the year, the century, and the millennium, the *New York Times* critic Laura Lippman issued her report card to the TV series making waves around the country. Whatever she gave with the left hand, praising the writers and the actors, she took away with the right, excoriating *The West Wing* for being more devastating to the Democrats than any rightwing conspiracy. In her pique she resembled John Podhoretz, who earlier that same year slammed the show from the opposite end of the political spectrum as "pornography for liberals" (23).

Week after week, panned Lippman, twenty million Democrats were spoon-fed a Pollyanna presidency that lulled them into complacency when they ought to be rallying against Bush II, anointed just days before by the Supreme Court. The fact that *The West Wing* was smart enough to teach real-life politicians something about partisan tactics was beside the point. Take back the White House from the Republicans, rang her thinly veiled battle cry, and everything would be back to normal.

Normal as in "snafu," perhaps. The 2000 recount kicked up such a perfect partisan storm that Democrats began to mouth "dog eat dog" only left to right, and Republicans the other way round. Be that as it may, there was something on which even Lippman and Podhoretz did agree: namely that *The West Wing* peddled opium to the masses. "Masses," in this context, was a numerical rather than a class denominator. After all, the show has consistently rated highest with upscale, educated, politically hip yuppies *à la* Vince Lennox from *A Planet for the President* (and, consequently, with premium-rate advertisers, with thirty-second spots priced at $300,000 per).

Either way, there was no doubt that at the turn of the millennium, America was as hooked on Sorkin as Sorkin was on freebase cocaine. This was as true of Lippman's twenty million loyal viewers—half of whom, according to Nielsen, were actually Republicans—as of Podhoretz himself, who would end up as the show's paid consultant. That, however, would not stop others from raking the show over the coals again. "*The West Wing* has always been a didactic series," grumbled *Time* in a prelude to an all-out pan of "Isaac and Ishmael," an episode scripted, produced, and aired in a record three weeks following 9/11.[1] No sooner had the final credits rolled across the screens than it became crucified in the conservative media for presuming to be important—while being only earnest—in airing a message of peace to a record twenty-five million Americans who had tuned in.

If it is easy to knock such mass-audience didacticism, it is because there is no easy way to measure its effects. Feelings of panic or anger, or incidents of hatred or unrest that would never have occurred in the first place are ontologically indistinguishable from those that had not because someone drew solace or understanding from a televised homily contrived to do just that. But if something cannot be counted, it does not follow that it can be discounted. In fact, if *The West Wing* was anywhere near as persuasive as its leftwing and rightwing critics complained, it must have been very effective indeed in seeding a message of cohabitation and peace.

What is remarkable about these and other broadsides fired over the years at *The West Wing* is their shared conviction of its impact on the real world. Why else would a real Virginia senator urge a boycott of NBC after a fictional hate group that ambushed the presidential cavalcade in the finale of the first season was identified as West Virginia White Pride at the start of the second? Why else would viewers ask the Warner Brothers front desk for Josh's email address to send him real get-well cards after he was injured in the same West Virginia White Pride assassination attempt?[2]

The assumption of the back-and-forth between reel and real life was only bolstered by the fact that most featured members of the cast not only played committed Democrats but *were* committed Democrats off-screen. Rob Lowe, for instance, cut his political teeth on Michael Dukakis's 1988 presidential campaign, while Martin Sheen and Bradley Whitford worked on Gore's ill-fated 2000 run. Reinforcing this partisan double-take were the 2000 and 2004 Democratic National Conventions at which *The West Wing* stars, in attendance both as actors and as card-carrying Democrats, were mobbed for interviews and photo ops as often as the candidates and party bigwigs.

Who could say what was real anyway, with so many of the lead cast based more or less openly on members of Clinton's inner circle: Sam (Rob Lowe) as George Stephanopoulos, Josh (Bradley Whitford) as Paul Begala, Toby (Richard Schiff) as Gene Sperling, C. J. (Allison Janney) as Dee Dee Myers—to say nothing of second-tier roles, from Mandy (Moira Kelly) as Mandy Grunwald to Bruno (Ron Silver) as maverick election strategist Dick Morris. In 2000 *TV Guide* even ran a story linking the dots between *Who's Who* in reel and real life. There was also the *Documentary Special* aired in 2002 in the program's regular time slot. Ostensibly a tribute to the people who had served in the White House, it reeled off clips from the first three seasons interspersed with interviews with Clinton, Carter, Ford, Dee Dee Myers, Paul Begala, Peggy Noonan, Karl Rove, and many others.[3]

With Clinton's staffers openly commenting on new episodes, with "Bartlet for President" badges sold during the 2000 and 2004 campaigns, with cars sporting "Don't blame me, I voted for Bartlet" bumper stickers during Bush II's two terms, who could blame the viewers for projecting the reel White House onto the real thing? Especially when a few weeks after touring swing states on John Kerry's 2004 "Vote for Change" campaign, James Taylor appeared as himself to sing "A Change Is Gonna Come" for the reel White House and millions of real voters across America?

In October 2002 the National Education Association, the largest teachers' union in the country, issued a press communiqué that stated in part, "The president can be sure that the members of the NEA will do our share to make public schools great for every child."[4] Their rebuke of Bush II would have been par for the course, except that it referred to a fictional speech given by President Bartlet against the backdrop of a banner (used by permission) with the real union's slogan "Making Public Schools Great for Every Child."

In 2008 Sorkin knit the threads of reel and real life even tighter by putting words in both Bartlet's and Obama's mouth in a mini-screenplay that ran as a *New York Times* op-ed by Maureen Dowd (herself the prototype for Karen Cahill in "The Leadership Breakfast"). After conceding that he did not have to be the leader of all Americans, just those who watched *The West Wing*, the television president flayed the adversaries of the soon-to-be real one:

> McCain decried agents of intolerance, then chose a running mate who had
> to ask if she was allowed to ban books from a public library. It's not bad

enough she thinks the planet Earth was created in six days 6,000 years ago complete with a man, a woman and a talking snake, she wants schools to teach the rest of our kids to deny geology, anthropology, archaeology and common sense too?[5]

There is no doubt that reel fiction can sometimes feel as compelling as fact. This is what, among numerous other journalists, the former White House correspondent for *The New Republic* had in mind when he decreed *The West Wing* "more truthful than reporting."[6] Literally, of course, this is an oxymoron. How can fiction be more truthful than nonfiction? How can drama tinted with melodrama and comedrama trump real-life reportage? Easy, shrugged Roger Ebert. Summing up Michael Moore's breakthrough documentary, he wrote, "Parts of 'Roger & Me' are factual. Parts are not. All of the movie is true."

God Bless America

I didn't make the political choice here, I made the right choice.

"The Debate," The West Wing

"I would disagree that this is a liberal show," argued Sorkin against pretty much everyone else.[7] As evidence, he pointed to the fact that it has shown the president praying on his knees in the Oval Office, presumably what the conservative Republicans would want to see in real life. Be that as it may, partisan sniping by Sorkin and other members of the cast so rankled Team Bush that in 2002 it canceled the show's annual visit to the White House. It may have also had to do with "The Midterms," an episode about failing to get a clear electoral mandate, which aired during the Bush-Gore recount (the *West Wing* political cycle runs two years out of phase with the real one).

A little over a year earlier, Martin Sheen caused a brouhaha by first calling candidate Bush "full of shit" and then scorning an invitation to the latter's White House.[8] This was the same Sheen whose hard-nosed liberal commitments raised questions during the casting stage whether he would tailor the Bartlet presidency to his political activism, for which he had been arrested scores of times at various demonstrations and sit-ins. In the end, Sorkin's lobbying on his behalf carried the day, although the actor did get a contract clause exempting him for being on the set when pending bail.

Wading into the murky waters of the real and reel Potomac, Sheen and other cast members only reinforced many viewers' conviction that, as he put it on *The Today Show*, *The West Wing* was "a civics lesson with a heart."[9]

Agree with him or not, it was without doubt more than standard-issue entertainment. It may have spun a moth-eaten melodrama of virtue triumphant, but it suborned it to the task of dramatizing the most complex political rhetoric ever heard on primetime television.

One reason why, in contrast to *Left Behind*, *The West Wing* could so well interpose popular entertainment with political enlightenment was its deep pool of talent. On most soaps plots are pitched and sketched collectively before being assigned to staff writers, who then submit teleplays to the show's creator for the final focus and polish. Not on *The West Wing*, where for the first four years, Sorkin himself wrote most of the episodes, albeit—as pointedly stressed by co-writer Eli Attie—"from a lot of smart, heavily researched material from a very hardworking staff."[10]

Sorkin, who had honed his chops under the New York playwright Peter Parnell, luxuriated in Heller-like rapid-fire dialogue that could take as many twists and turns as the corridors of the White House set that Steadicams had to negotiate during their vaunted walks-and-talks. Unlike Heller, however, he could also drown in schmaltz, like in the final scene of "The Midterms," which all too artlessly reflected his vision of the show as "a valentine to public service":[11]

JOSH
What do you say about a government that goes out of its way to protect even citizens that try to destroy it?
TOBY
God bless America.
SAM
(beat) God bless America.
C.J.
God bless America.
DONNA
God bless America.
JOSH
God bless America.

The other reason is the deliberation with which the show's writers put valid, or at least forceful, arguments in the mouths of the opposition. Many plotlines began, in fact, as pro/con memos that bulleted each side's argumentative thrusts and parries, which were later fleshed out into full-blown episodes. Indeed, as often as it adopted a principled stance against a Republican position, the show tackled issues—from education to campaign finance reform to the census—regardless of the center-right and right-of-center ideologies of the two wings of the Demublican party.

Although it would be a stretch to call *The West Wing* bipartisan or non-partisan, by kindling a dialogue with the liberal caucuses on both sides of the aisle, it deliberately complexified political discourse *tout court*. This is why even its Capraesque presidency wallowed in spin redolent of *Tanner '88*, a Robert Altman and Garry Trudeau mockumentary that also split the difference between political fiction and reality TV. Aesthetically harking to *Citizen Kane*, down to handheld cameras and multi-character dialogue, *The West Wing* turned television series into serious television.

Of course, even as it attempted to complexify the binomial rhetoric of Washington politics, it remained first and last a vehicle for commercial entertainment. For all their Beltway savvy, the scriptwriters lifted lids off hot-button issues without tackling, let alone resolving, anything. Therein, of course, lies the difference between verisimilitude and veracity. The behind-the-scenes politicking endemic to the White House, so expertly satirized by Beaton—cutthroat rivalry for access to the president, palace intrigue, groupthink, sycophancy—is conspicuously absent. On *The West Wing*, the highest political office in the land is wiped clean of office politics.

Some commentators took exception to such narrative license. Jeff Riley, a former White House aide, even posted a series of online critiques in which he drew a straight line from his years in the Bush I and Clinton administrations to *The West Wing*. His running theme was that, from the things the president would never say to the physical layout of the set, *The West Wing* could not be trusted in its depiction of Washington. He was, of course, right. Giving the lie to "Mr. Willis of Ohio," for example, the House no longer votes by show of hands but electronically.

Be that as it may, this type of criticism misses the point highlighted by Sorkin's remark that in moviemaking (and, one might add, in politics), the appearance of reality is more important than reality itself.[12] Side by side with unvarnished reality, any television series will be found deficient if realism is gauged by one-to-one correspondence to the world. Naturally, if audiences were interested in unvarnished reality, network producers would be airing 24/7 footage from convenience store or parking lot surveillance cameras. But realism or even naturalism consists in more than streaming raw life into the living room. The legendary police procedural *Dragnet* did not need to employ real corpses in sundry stages of decomposition to break new ground in television realism.

A more valid framework for viewing *The West Wing* is side by side with previous primetime political TV series. Those include the 1992 *The Powers That Be*, which followed the political life of a senator (canceled after 21 episodes), and the eponymous 1995 *Women of the House* (canceled after 13), to say nothing of earlier flops such as Fox's *Mr. President*, ABC's *Hail to the Chief*, or NBC's own *The Senator*. It is at this point that the show's political complexity—not to call it realism—comes into its own, paving the way for mature and literate political series such as the darkly Machiavellian *House of Cards* or Europe's equally dark and Machiavellian *Borgen*.

The Debate

I've watched every televised presidential debate this country has ever had, and every time I heard them recite the rules I always thought "That means they are not going to have a real debate."

"The Debate," The West Wing

"We got lucky on a lot of the stuff—we're not that smart," protested one of *The West Wing*'s key writers and producers when asked about their knack for scripting plotlines that would subsequently surface as headline news.[13] It had been generating a buzz right from the beginning of Season One, when the foreign policy angle on the border tensions between India and Pakistan ("Lord John Marbury" and "He Shall, From Time to Time . . .") drew praise even from Clinton's hawkish secretary of state Madeleine Albright.

The extent to which the universe of *The West Wing* paralleled ours was often nothing short of unreal. It went beyond celebrities appearing as themselves, or characters mirroring the actors who portrayed them—from working for the Democrats to, in the case of Ron Silver's Bruno, leaving the party to cozy up to the Republicans. The original plotline, for example, envisioned for the Republican Senator Vinick to win the election in Season Seven and continue as president in Season Eight. After the death of John Spencer (Leo McGarry), the writers and producers decided to end the show at the natural caesura of the presidential race, even as—to heighten the drama—they gave the victory to the Democratic Congressman Santos and his dead running mate McGarry.

But nothing came close to crystal-balling the 2008 election. By mid-November, when a charismatic, non-Caucasian newcomer had come from behind to beat the Democratic front-runner with links to the Oval Office and then gone on to win an underdog campaign against a seasoned centrist Republican maverick, it seemed as if Obama had been lifted left, right, and center from the show's color-coded script books. Compounding the déjà vu, not only did Obama and Santos share the same year of birth, but both campaigned on the idea of hope. Was it the reel or the real politician who barnstormed America with:

Hope is real. In a life of trials, in the world of challenges, hope is real. In a country where families go without health care, where some go without food, some don't even have a home to speak of, hope is real. In a time of global chaos and instability, where our faiths collide as often as our weapons, hope is real. Hope is what gives us the courage to take on our greatest challenges, to move forward together. We live in cynical times, I know that. But hope is not up for debate. There is such a thing as false science, there is such a thing as false promises, and I am sure I will have my share of false starts. But there is no such thing as false hope. There is only hope.[14]

The doppelganger effect was rooted in the fact that in Washington, there are few degrees of separation. When a former speechwriter for Gore, Eli Attie, was given the task of developing the character of Santos (played by Jimmy Smits), he reached out to Obama's campaign strategist, David Axelrod, for background. Like the writer, so the actor. Smits closely studied Obama's breakout keynote at the 2004 Convention as well as the politician himself, even meeting him once at a rally where they were both speaking.

Running against Santos was Arnold Vinick (played by Alan Alda), whose candidacy bore an equally uncanny resemblance to John McCain's. Both were centrists with substantial cross-over appeal, which actually put them in a bind insofar as the religious and conservative caucuses in their party did not reckon them Republican enough. Even Vinick's selection of a young, born-again hardliner as a running mate to shore up his conservative base was reenacted two years later in McCain's uneasy alliance with Sarah Palin. But the line between real and reel political theater blurred even further when *The West Wing* hosted a televised presidential debate.

For the first and last time on the show, the broadcast went out live, just like in a real debate, albeit in two takes—the first for the East Coast and the other for the West (the later telecast features in the box set—the other has gone the way of Jimmy Hoffa). By all accounts, the stars were invigorated by the thespian challenge, including for the first and only time the permission to go off-script to simulate heat-of-the-moment extemporizing. Under the pressure to get arguments and soundbites right, admitted Smits, "Alan Alda and myself prepared as if we were candidates."[15] Adding to the air of democracy caught in the act was the moderator, former *ABC News* and *NBC News* anchor Forrest Sawyer, cast in the role he was born to play: himself. With ten million viewers, "The Debate" tied for the second-most watched episode from the last season.

Interestingly, even as it exemplified the idea of *The West Wing* as a mass-audience forum for civic advocacy, "The Debate" broke almost every rule of engagement from the preceding six years. Not only did it not unveil multiple plotlines, it even lacked a story. Although scripted, it leaned, rap-like, on structured improvisation. In lieu of ensemble performance, it starred a two-mic cipher. Longer than a regular episode, it dispensed with the music track, intercutting, and the signature verbal rat-a-tat, with words flying faster than assassins' bullets. It even stood out on the visual level, being shot for the first and only time in 35mm, making for a crisper and more color-saturated video.

But in its didactic quotient, "The Debate" was a perfect correlative for the series. In its reel version of a "real" debate, rules were ditched to create an "authentic" public forum where issues and policies could be hammered out "live" in front of voters, on the assumption that they would reward not the juiciest soundbite, but the soundest argument. Staging an alternative to staged electoral debates, "The Debate" embodied *The West Wing* and its almost unreasonable faith in reforming American political culture.

Paradoxically, however, even as it strove to elaborate an alternative to present-day American politics, the episode—much as the entire series— was premised on the status quo. With every speech and every argument, it reinforced the sanctity of the presidency, the representational system of government, and the constitutional premises on which they rest. As such, far from challenging the political establishment, *The West Wing* endorsed it for the millions who watched it every week. The American system might need fine-tuning—which country's does not? But even if the body politic was bent out of shape, its engine of democracy was humming along just fine.

Like the Beatles, *The West Wing* caught the zeitgeist of its times. The proof is in the critical harvest: a bibliography that by a conservative estimate exceeds a thousand entries in popular and scholarly outlets. But even as there is little new to be said about the show itself, a lot remains to be said about what this most political of shows had to say about American politics. And what it had to say was enunciated by the president in "The Lame Duck Congress":

> In all the talk about democracy, we forget it's not a democracy, it's a republic. People don't make the decisions, they choose the people who make the decisions. Could they do a better job of choosing? Yeah. But when we consider the alternatives . . .

Much as campaign advisers on and off *The West Wing* advise not to buy into the tacit premises of a debate, I want to contest this pat dismissal of the alternatives by the fictional president and the real people behind him: the writing cadre of Washington insiders, the politicians they had served, the tens of millions of American viewers, and the United States at large. In the spirit of "The Debate," I want to open a critical debate with the republican premises of the American system of government in order to defend the political grail of all post-Periclean states: people's and not politicians' democracy.

A Government We Can Believe In

All of us, Democrats, Republicans, liberals, conservatives, we all want a government we can believe in.

"The Debate," The West Wing

Like all foundational myths, the myth of American democracy is nationally syndicated via textbooks, radio, television, the press, the Internet, movies, and other mass-media and mass-culture platforms, including prominently *The West Wing*. But with the line between spin and fact drawn in invisible ink, myths can sometimes overshadow the truth. This is not an accident. To preserve the status quo, political elites worldwide sanction a variety of compensatory mechanisms designed to maintain an illusion of people's power.

In the United States, the foremost among them is the quadrennial pageant of presidential elections. Even as voters cast ballots under the illusion that they elect the CEO of the USA, behind the scenes party bosses, cloaked as caucuses and the electoral college, steal the show. Sometimes, however, their theft is caught on candid camera, as it was in the episode broadcast nationwide on November 7, 2000. The Election Day putsch robbed many black Floridians of their ballots, whipped up a TV network stampede to prematurely declare Bush II the winner, and flung itself into the arms of Reagan's Supreme Court, which halted the recount that duly would have sent Al Gore to four years in a federal institution.

The orchestrated nature of the putsch becomes apparent in the light of one universally overlooked fact. During the recount, a reexamination of ballots produced a net gain for Gore at more than three times the rate of Bush. This massive asymmetry flies in the face of the null hypothesis of the contested ballots falling equally on either side, as they should if the causal factor was random. Instead, some nonrandom factor had caused the votes for Gore to be suppressed three times more than for Bush—"nonrandom" being a euphemism for "manmade."

But this real-life episode of *Big Brother* concealed an even more inconvenient truth. Nationwide, in the popular vote, Gore scored a solid victory over his rival. If the American people really elected the president and the ruling party, he should have become POTUS no. 43. Instead, the electorate got a politician they did not elect, one who polled more than a million votes less than his rival. *Quod erat demonstrandum.* Just like the recommendation to close the Patent and Trademark Office, the American presidential elections are at bottom a great political fiction.

Neither was the election of 2000 the only such wake-up call. Back in 1876 the Republican Party fielded Rutherford B. Hayes, a decorated Civil War brigade commander. His opponent was Samuel J. Tilden, a reformer famous for taking on Tammany Hall. Hayes ran such a shadowy campaign

Speak softly and carry a big shovel.

Figure 5.1 Speak Softly and Carry a Big Shovel ". . . But this real-life episode of Big Brother concealed an even more inconvenient truth . . ."
Credit: Brian Narelle

that it earned him the nickname of Ruther*fraud* B. Hayes. Perhaps for that reason, the winner in the popular vote was Tilden, who, in accordance with the myth of the American people electing the president, should have received the keys to the West Wing. Yet because Hayes eked out a razor-sharp majority in the electoral college—185 to Tilden's 184—he became the nineteenth president of the United States.

Naturally, myths can be as potent as historical facts, not least when the history in question is as ancient as the myth of people's power. Famous as the birthplace of direct democracy, ancient Greece conjures up chiton-clad tableaux of the Athenian Assembly enjoying a remarkably high level of day-to-day civic participation and face-to-face interaction. In reality, in a page taken from *Picture This*, Hellenic *demokratia* was a power grab by another name. Pericles instututed democracy in Athens in mid-fourth century BC to found his own political base independent of the hereditary aristocracy who opposed his imperial designs.

His people's power reversed the legislative balance between the land-owners' Areopagus and the people's Assembly and enfranchised all adult males to participate in public affairs, even as it excluded women, slaves, and foreign-born Athenians. However, even though most public officials and jurymen were indeed selected by lot, the poor could ill afford to hold office, as they needed to scratch out a living. Power to the people meant, in practice, power to Pericles and a clique of kingmakers at the top.

Ironically, the principle of people's power also became incorporated by the ruling bodies of Athens' perennial military and political foe, Sparta. Its method of electing Council members by the Shout was, in turn, similar to the practice in colonial-era New England's township assemblies. As *The West Wing* vividly depicts, however, the American government of today looks askance at people's democracy. In lieu of the Athenian *isegoria* (the universal right to address the Assembly), America keeps politics away from the public forum, where the founding father of democracy, not to mention some of the Founding Fathers of the American state, thought it belonged.[16]

The result? Political apathy.[17] Denied their birthright, American citizens who vote conscientiously, engage in civic affairs, and consult with their elected representatives on matters of state are found mostly in State Department pamphlets, alongside popular myths such as "One Person, One Vote." Even as it is frequently cited as the cornerstone of the American political system, the system blatantly violates OPOV by endorsing unequal equality. How so? By following the majority of political federations—which comprise a third of the world—in granting federated entities equal political status regardless of demographics.

In Australia some half a million Tasmanians elect the same number of representatives to the upper chamber as New South Wales, which covers Sydney and Melbourne—seven million people in total. In Canada the pint-sized Prince Edward Island boasts the same number of senators as the goliath of Ontario. In the European Parliament, which cannot even defend itself with arguments of historical nature, some half a million Greek Cypriots have twice as many representatives as the 1.2 million voters of Northern Ireland. In the US Senate, half a million people of Wyoming are served by the same number of senators as 38 million Californians. This means that a California senator represents seventy-five times more people than his counterpart in Wyoming, making each voter seventy-five times less important than in the Cowboy State.

Vox Populi

> They [the people] will remain silent until the end of the debate, when we can all give democracy a big round of applause.
>
> "The Debate," *The West Wing*

It is not that the US Constitution forbids referenda or other tools of direct democracy. In 2010 animal rights activists in Missouri collected two hundred thousand signatures in support of the Puppy Mill Cruelty Prevention Act. Later that year their grassroots initiative became law.[18] Once in a blue moon, citizens may even be asked to vote in referendums put forth by state legislatures. But fewer than half of the states have the basic tools of direct democracy—initiative or referendum—in place. Fewer still have provisions to recall bad politicians from office. And fewer still use these tools on anything like a regular basis. When in 2012 Wisconsin Republican governor Scott Walker survived an attempt to oust him from office, he was just the third ever to face a recall vote.

The result is a staggering disparity. Of the more than two thousand statewide initiatives in American history, the lion's share was confined to California, with Oregon and Colorado trailing a distant second and third. But California matters, not only because its version of people's power has been branded a failure on the scale of Three Mile Island. With one out of eight Americans living there, it is the most populous state in the nation. Despite being labeled ungovernable and dysfunctional, its economy would be listed in the world's top ten countries. And its experiment in direct democracy is unique in the United States, both in the scale and the avidity with which it has been put to work.

The key terms of people's democracy form a triangle. A referendum allows citizens to vote on laws that have been passed by the legislature. A recall allows elected politicians to be removed before their term runs out. And an initiative—once it is on the ballot, it's called a proposition and given a consecutive number in a ten-year cycle—is a measure drawn up by the people of California to be considered as a statewide law. Even on the first glance, this is a very different triangle from that formed by the executive, legislative, and judiciary branches of the federal system, and for a reason. Most Founding Fathers were appalled at the idea of people's democracy, arguing that minority factions and special interests might hijack the entire system, much like their aristocratic republican faction did.

As young James Madison recorded, delegates at the Constitutional Convention repeatedly blamed their difficulties on too much democracy, deriding it as mobocracy. For that matter, what democracy there is in the United States owes as much to the Constitution as to its fiercest opponent, Patrick Henry. Asking how it was possible that this paean to liberty did not vouchsafe freedom of speech, freedom of the press, or freedom of religion, this prominent slaveholder oversaw the passage of the Bill of Rights. In the end, over Jefferson's and Franklin's objections, America would become a republic with power in the hands of professional politicians. There would be no people's democracy. No fourth branch of the government.

In defiance, in 1911 California governor Hiram Johnson arranged a special election to empower *vox populi* with three new ways of balloting: referenda, initiatives, and recalls. His state was not the first to do so—South Dakota adopted initiatives in 1898—but it would practice them on a scale that would outstrip all others put together. From the start, however, there was a significant asymmetry. Although it was difficult to repeal a law already passed by the legislature, it was relatively straightforward to drum up an initiative to bypass that law. Instead of fostering compromise, as the Swiss direct democracy does, California made it easy for petitioners and lawmakers to go tit-for-tat.

Critics who claim that direct democracy in California is a textbook case of the tyranny of the majority stop short of answering how that is worse than Washington. But in one respect, at least, the difference is very real. In California all it takes to repeal a burdensome law is to start a petition and convince enough voters to sign on. This is the essence of democracy. It's not that everyone gets what they want. It's that everyone gets a chance to get what they want, if they get involved. The rest is up to the voters and not the politicians—at least in theory. The practice is determined by details such as the relatively short period (150 days) to collect signatures. This, combined with sprawling geography and scant public access to mass media, means that in California, like everywhere else, money often trumps grassroots activism.

Initiatives have spawned a political machine at the beck and call of whoever can foot the bills submitted by petition-management companies and professional signature collectors. When several states (not California) tried to outlaw paid circulation in a bid to return to volunteer sign-ups, the 1988 Supreme Court outlawed their efforts as a suppression of free speech. It is true that deep pockets can afford to pay for signature collection and media campaigns launched to convince (or just con) people into voting for an initiative. Voters can certainly be led astray—as if they could not by elected politicians. But well-educated and well-informed voters are more difficult to hoodwink than you might think. Ultimately, this is the whole point of people's democracy: you get to sleep in the bed *you* make.

For much of the twentieth century, initiatives in California were like a novelty item: proudly displayed, rarely used. But after the Second World War, correlating with increased funding for education, growing numbers of state universities, and growing cohorts of graduates, each ten-year cycle brought more activism and participation. In the 1960s less than ten propositions were voted on. In the 1970s that number more than doubled, then in the 1980s more than doubled again, peaking at more than seventy during the 2000s.

But something went spectacularly awry in 1978. The people passed Proposition 13, an anti-tax measure that blew a hole the size of California in every subsequent budget. Suddenly the state's hands were tied when it came to collecting money—Prop 13 required two-thirds supermajorities for any tax hike—but the appetite for state services only grew. While the Swiss consistently voted down longer unpaid holidays, Californians voted to eat the cake they did not have. Yet the proof that direct democracy does work as it should is the recent political reversal engineered by the same people and the same system that got it into hot water in the first place.

During the last few years, voters voted into law several initiatives to remake the bed in which they were sleeping. In 2010 they put a stop to gerrymandering, a notorious electoral practice of drawing up voting districts to keep expected supporters in and opponents out. Instead of mixing them randomly and thus equally, with the net effect of nurturing compromise, gerrymandering polarizes and antagonizes. California used to be a place where runaway deficits, gridlocked budgets, and apocalyptic partisanship were as familiar as Santa Ana brushfires, just because lawmakers had no incentive to put them out. To no one's surprise, nonpartisan redistricting had the salutary effect of making electoral districts more competitive and, as such, more centrist.

In the same vein, Californians approved "top-two" state primaries, in which everyone votes in the same primary and the top two winners, regardless of party affiliation, go to the runoff. Now politicians have to seek approval of the entire political spectrum, which brings them to the center and makes them try to represent larger and more diverse interests than those of their own party. Ironically, one of the first casualties of this revamped system was Republican David Dreier, the same who had praised *The West Wing* for attracting larger and more diverse audiences than what a politician has access to (it did not help that he was embezzling campaign contributions).

Every Man a King

What you've heard, over and above the many important policy differences, were different philosophies of government.

"The Debate," The West Wing

You might think that the complexity of modern states exceeds the capacity of citizens to oversee their business. If so, you agree with *The West Wing*'s President Bartlet, who, stymied by a test ban treaty, did not mince words with his communications director:

I couldn't give a damn what the people think. The complexities of a global arms treaty, the technological, military—the diplomatic nuance of it is staggering, Toby. Eighty-two percent of the people can't possibly be expected to reach an informed opinion. ("Lame Duck Congress")

What he forgot to say is that few politicians understand the ins and outs of any but their own pet issues either (appropriation bills alone can run into thousands of pages), habitually relying on précis or just recommendations from staffers.

But direct democracy in the twenty-first century is not only feasible but practiced with ringing success, foremost in Switzerland. Swiss local, cantonal, and federal-level referendums take power away from politicians and put it in the hands of regular folks in a type of *demokratia* unpracticed in America since the popular assemblies of the colonial era. In one such still-surviving type of assembly (*Landsgemeinde*), some Swiss villages gather to receive face-to-face reports from local representatives, as well as to elect them and to vote on new initiatives by a public show of hands.[19]

Europe and North America may seem worlds apart, but there are a number of historical and political affinities between Switzerland and the United States.[20] To take only one example, in 1848 when Switzerland was modernizing its constitution, it adopted the American bicameral system. Thus the Swiss Federal Assembly is modeled on the US Congress, with the National Council and the States Council corresponding, respectively, to the House and the Senate. On the other hand, the biggest difference between the two countries lies in the role of citizens in political decision-making—the very difference that made Mark Twain praise the Swiss history in "The Cradle of Liberty" as "worthy to be taught in all schools and studied by all races and peoples" (50).

The cornerstone of Swiss democracy is the referendum. Inasmuch as the parliament proposes rather than disposes, laws already ratified can be nullified by the people's vote. The 1848 Right of Referendum obligates the government to put *any* act of parliament to national vote, provided fifty thousand citizens so demand within three months of its passage. Direct democracy is further enshrined in the 1891 Right of Initiative. It grants any citizen the right to propose a constitutional amendment, provided he gets the support of 99,999 others within eighteen months. In short, the government rules by the consent of the nation. It is people's power all the way. If a requisite number of signatures is secured within a given time, there *must* be a vote (constitutional amendments require a simple majority in the popular and cantonal vote).[21]

Before a constitutional vote, citizens receive a novelette-size election guide (covers are also used) that prints all the information needed to make an informed decision. Among others, it includes the full legal text; competing summaries of the initiative; the parliamentary counterproposal; reports on benefits and hazards; tabulations of costs; editorials by pro and con committees; counterarguments by the executive branch; and, not least, the breakdown of the parliamentary vote. This being Switzerland, the vote by the legislature is only a nonbinding recommendation.

California also prints official voter-information guides before every ballot. On the plus side, they are thorough and impartial in presenting the rival theses and antitheses. On the other hand, they are government publications: fat and full of legalese. As a consequence, the majority of the public go for information to the media, which is to say to attack ads, which form the bulk of paid advertising. Anything that simplifies choice will be seized on by voters to cut through the thickets of political information, misinformation, and disinformation, and attack ads do just that. Belying "The Debate," political discourse degenerates into a *dialogue de sourds,* with rival lobbies embroiled in a shouting match like football kibitzers.

Whichever way you look at it, the key element of Swiss democracy is the delegation of political power to the people. Elected officeholders are not power brokers but executors of the nation's will—revocable delegates who wield authority by virtue of the mandate of the people. As such, they are largely left to themselves. Unlike the United States, top-tier politicians walk by themselves or use public transport without getting mobbed or shot

Figure 5.2   Money Talks, Bullshit Walks ". . . Without resorting to Huey Long's pork-barrel politics, Switzerland, it seems, found a way to implement his populist slogan: Every Man a King . . ."

Credit: John Jonik

at. Assassinations are unknown, because to disrupt the system, you would have to eliminate all those who wield the power: the electorate. Without resorting to Huey Long's pork-barrel politics, Switzerland, it seems, found a way to implement his populist slogan: Every Man a King.

This isn't to say that there is no voter fatigue about mundane issues. Some referendums feel like neverendums, political footballs kicked about in front of empty bleachers. Interest is typically highest in political action initiated by regular folks or by local organizations, as opposed to organized parties or lobbies. No less typically, the system usually yields a compromise. Initiatives can go too far, but the fact that they are set in motion in the first place spurs politicians to enact changes that may even cause the original initiative to be withdrawn.

Aided by proportional representation, the Swiss system favors compromise over competition. The parliamentary multiplicity of parties, factions, and interests fosters a culture of *quid pro quo* whereby political platforms are cut, ideological planks splintered, and policy edges filed off in pursuit of conciliatory or, if you like, satisficing solutions: somewhere between fully satisfying and merely sufficing. On the other hand, that same inclusiveness, which solicits input from all parties, unions, chambers, commissions, and citizens' groups, makes Swiss laws a mosaic of progressive conservatism and pragmatic idealism (women did not get the full vote until 1971).

In contrast, the American winner-take-all system churns out horse races that produce political winners rather than political leaders. The idea of a collective and constructive debate on merits of policies seems quaint, if not quixotic, in a culture dominated by inflammatory rhetoric. With few exceptions, American candidates run all-or-nothing campaigns that, in the words of one prominent politician, make for "24-hour, slash-and-burn, negative-ad, bickering, small-minded politics."[22] Longtime aide in the Senate and writer of "The Debate" Lawrence O'Donnell agreed: "The newer generation of politicians are a win-at-all-costs group. Winning isn't the only thing that matters."[23]

Granted, Switzerland is small, and America is big. One has less than eight million, the other more than three hundred million people. In area, Switzerland is 10 percent of California. What works for a small country, no matter how heterogeneous, may not be feasible in a colossus like the United States—or so maintain the skeptics. Saturated as it is with smartphones and Internet outlets, however, not to mention the post office and the voting booth, the United States could institute national referendums with relative ease. Far from being too big for direct democracy, it lacks not the technology but the political will to embrace national referendums and other instruments of people's power that, as research shows, enhance political stability and personal well-being.[24]

After all, California itself is about halfway between Switzerland and the United States in size. Whatever else its century-old experiment with people's power proves, it proves that direct democracy is not limited by population size, area, or homogeneity. Betting its future on this, Intellitics, a digital engagement startup in—where else—California, helps the public, private, and nonprofit sector apply technology to public initiatives and other types of democratic processes. After all, since the birth of modern Switzerland under the 1848 constitution, that country held more than 150 referendums on constitutional amendments, not to mention tens of thousands of cantonal and local ones. Outside the Bill of Rights, the US Constitution has been amended just seventeen times.

Eurocracy

> When you go to work tomorrow and you're talking about this debate, talk about the qualities that you want in the President, the leadership qualities.
>
> "The Debate," The West Wing

"Voters seem increasingly indifferent to politics. Party membership and election turnout are both declining. Increasingly, citizens protest or call referendums instead."[25] The attitudes reported by The Economist in 2011 are so commonplace that they could apply to almost any developed nation. And although the reference to referendums points to Europe—in this case, Germany—it is highly ironic, given the EU's history of evasion when it comes to consulting its citizens.

Remember the "done deal" European Constitution that screeched to a halt in 2005 when the French and the Dutch gave it thumbs down? Next time around it was the Irish who voted no to the EU Constitution-by-another-name that is the Treaty of Lisbon, only to be made to vote again. Among attitudes like that, with the Treaty coming into effect in December 2009, in June 2009 the famously low turnouts in the European Parliament elections set the record for the lowest ever.

So, to placate the angry and woo the indifferent, the Lisbon treaty came with a provision for direct democracy, something that few member countries would embrace at the national level. Finland, for example, held only two referendums in its history: in 1931 on prohibition and in 1994 on joining the EU. Britain's last national referendum was in 2011, on replacing its voting system (first-past-the-post) with ranked voting. Before then, the last national referendum was in 1975, when Margaret Thatcher blasted all referendums as "a splendid weapon for demagogues and dictators."[26]

Coincidentally, the British rejected ranked (aka preferential) voting, even though, as the Irish or Australian experience shows, it improves voter turnout. Instead of picking politicians from a menu supplied by parties or caucuses, people can express how they personally feel about candidates by ranking them against others. Also, even before anyone heads to the booth, ranked-voting systems tend to improve the political climate by steering candidates toward civility and compromise ("If I rein in my attacks, I could be ranked second by those who would never put me tops").

In Europe, the keystone of the revamped structure is the European Citizens' Initiative (ECI), modeled on the Swiss Right to Initiative. Because the EU is a supranational entity, there is an extra stipulation that proposals must have support across member states. The European Commission's original minimum was a third of the states—more than required to found a political party. The European Parliament preferred five. The Commission wanted a 12-month limit on signature collection. The MEPs suggested 18 to 24. The Commission asked for hard ID checks on the authenticity of signatures. The MEPs did not.

The final version is a million signatories—proportionately less than in Switzerland—collected from a quarter of the member countries within a year of registration, with the EC looking to act within four months thereafter. The Commission, which drafts all EU laws, retains the power to vet (not veto, although they may be indistinguishable in practice) all initiatives. This is to guard, in their words, against manifestly abusive, frivolous, or vexatious proposals, perhaps like the already rejected one for singing the European Anthem in Esperanto. The lowest national thresholds are in the smallest countries like Cyprus, Estonia, Malta, and Luxemburg, which need only 4,500 signatures. The highest is in Germany with 74,250.

In a crucial difference from Switzerland, citizens' initiatives do not automatically result in politically binding referendums. Eurocrats are only obliged to *respond* to petitions that have cleared all the legal hurdles. The experience from more than a dozen initiatives approved since the launch of the ECI in 2002—from "Central Public Online Collection Platform for the ECI" to "High Quality European Education for All"—suggests that proposals vetted by Brussels are forwarded for a hearing and a vote to the European Parliament.[27]

Some MEPs have been pushing for mandatory public hearings even if—perhaps especially if—an initiative is turned down by the Commission. Others waved away the scent of a democratic revolution: "It's not a Swiss-style system of initiatives and referendums. It's dipping the toe in the water of participatory democracy."[28] One factor that caught everyone off guard was the effect of the Internet and social networks, whose ubiquity makes organizing supranational petitions a cinch. Just whip up a website, generate momentum in the blogosphere, and watch the initiative ricochet from a myriad posts at the speed of light. It saves not only time but also money, obviating the need for California-style on-commission signature hunters.

Globally, the direct-democracy tortoise may be slowly gaining on the politicians' democracy Achilles. Countries as dissimilar as Uruguay, Brazil, New Zealand, and South Korea have partially adopted direct democracy on the national scale. Together with Democracy International (the European lobby group that had campaigned for the ECI), Initiative and Referendum Institute Europe (IRI-E) documents that during the last generation, half of the world introduced some sort of direct voting, albeit mostly infrequent and nonbinding. Japan runs local polls almost every month. Italy, Latvia, Lithuania, and Liechtenstein hold national votes on citizen initiatives. Not impressed? You shouldn't be. In 2009 Venezuela's populist dictator Hugo Chávez annulled term limits on his presidency by means of a popular vote.

The ECI apart, getting people, especially young people, to engage in politics is always a challenge. So, in the spring of 2014, MEPs have seized on another revolutionary means of propagating democracy: a rap cipher at the Parliament in Brussels. As in any political debate, beginning with *The West Wing*'s, politicians were quizzed on hot-button topics, from the euro to immigration. But, bringing Warren Beatty's political comedy *Bulworth* to life, they expressed their platforms in the idiom of hip-hop.[29] With help from freestyle professionals, the legislators dueled cipher-style until the winner was picked by the appreciative (if not exactly moshing) crowd—all in the hope of translating the vibe from the beatbox to the ballot box.

Education Is Everything

Head Start doesn't work. I wish Head Start did work. But it doesn't. By Grade Four and Five Head Start graduates do no better academically than their equally poor classmates who didn't attend Head Start. Our whole school system has been slipping now for years.

"The Debate," The West Wing

Not long after the popular television series *The Wire* had run its course, its creator David Simon complained that despite all the critical applause and publicity, its political message remained utterly ignored. Even as the city's police commissioner slammed Simon for ruining Baltimore's image—only to be slammed back for ruining Baltimore itself—the city stayed as it was: drug-ravaged, politically corrupt, racially divided.[30]

Just like with *The West Wing*, the remarkable thing about this spat was the assumed correlation between reel and real life. Both the people on the show and the Baltimore civil servants did not need to be convinced of the effects of the series on the circumstances of the city. They took it for granted. As such, Simon's complaint should be measured not just against the durability of the political status quo but against the norm of television programming, where low expectations are all too often duly met.

In *Viewing America* (2013), Christopher Bigsby suggested that, in concert with other network series like *The Sopranos, Generation Kill*, and *Treme, The Wire* and *The West Wing* marked a turning point in American culture whereby television surpassed not just Hollywood but even theater in producing quality drama. In the end, *The Wire* and *The West Wing* may not have become the political catalysts for reform that some of their creators had hoped for, but they did become lightning rods for debates about political education and mass "entartainment."

Echoing Sorkin, director and producer Thomas Schlamme has demurred, saying that *The West Wing* was "not a history lesson or civics lesson."[31] This might seem like gainsaying, given that long before it went off the air, *The West Wing* became a fixture in American civics and history classrooms. What Sorkin and Schlamme meant, of course, was that the series was not intended as an audiovisual teaching aid—it never would have got the funding, the cast, or the airtime, a cynic might point out—but as commercially viable television. Be that as it may, even Frank Luntz, a Republican pollster and (for a spell) a consultant on the show, echoed the prevailing opinion that "for better or worse, Americans by the millions get their information about politics from *The West Wing*."[32]

Even as one hopes that this brilliant soap will not be the end of Americans' education about their government, as a starting point it could hardly be better, turning politics into an experience as personal and gripping as a peddler's clasp at a Marrakesh bazaar. *The West Wing* set the golden standard when it came to political education, so much so that among its string of accolades were back-to-back Peabody Awards in recognition of distinguished and meritorious public service. Education, it contended time and again, is the silver bullet in the battle to transform America. In "Six Meetings Before Lunch," Sam Seaborn orated, in an impromptu manifesto,

> Education is everything. We don't need little changes, we need gigantic changes. Schools should be palaces. The competition for the best teachers should be fierce, they should be making six-figure salaries. Schools should be incredibly expensive for government and absolutely free of charge to its citizens, just like national defense.

In 2002 Talib Kweli rapped out his variant of this message in "The Proud": "Niggaz with knowledge is more dangerous than niggaz with guns/They make the guns easy to get and try to keep niggaz dumb." Symptomatically, of course, even as Bartlet is called the Education President, his education secretary is nowhere near his inner circle or even his "kitchen cabinet." In this, once again *The West Wing* accurately reflects the political reality of Washington.

But education is more than a shield against political spin. In many ways it is a branch of politics, not least seeing how frequently reason and common sense fall victim to partisan rhetoric. The paradigmatic example may be how our innate risk-aversion biases are exploited by spin doctors. Take two plans for national recovery from an economic affliction of great proportion. Plan A will appropriate funds to immediately and directly help one million Americans. Plan B, iffy from the start, has only one chance in ten of aiding ten million. If you stack the choices this way, more people will line behind Plan A, even though the expected returns are equivalent.

You can tap the same biases to redirect public support to the other side. All you need to do is reframe the picture. Suppose you are cautioned that the president's overseas military intervention will result in the deaths of a thousand American soldiers. The Pentagon's own plan is much safer: the invasion will cost zero American lives with a likelihood of one in ten, and ten thousand with a likelihood of nine in ten. Although the numbers are again equivalent, more people will opt for door number two with its spin of "zero American lives."

Here is a historical rather than hypothetical example of politricks in need of a silver bullet. In 1999 the Clinton administration altered the way in which the Consumer Price Index (CPI) is calculated: from arithmetic mean to geometric mean. Sounds esoteric and irrelevant, doesn't it? A little math exposes the dirty trick. Calculated over the same quantities, the geometric mean is *never* greater than the arithmetic mean, and usually lower. This is vital because the higher the CPI, the higher the calculated inflation, which requires higher levels of intervention by the government. Now, with one computer keystroke, the government lowered the CPI, pocketing billions in Social Security payouts that otherwise would have gone to those in need.

Given that any matter of state may be submitted to the vote of the people, in Switzerland no effort is spared to educate the decision-makers. Unlike the United States, where one hundred million remain functionally illiterate or a step above, the Swiss political system is founded on literacy and numeracy. This is not to say, however, that its schools aim at producing intellectual elites. Rather, the system—which includes a surprisingly high number of high-quality trade and vocational schools—aims to deliver solid, comprehensive, practical education to everyone. Right or wrong, the Swiss take pride both in their education and in their education system, which enjoys a comparatively higher social standing than in the United States.

The greatest difference, however, which I have observed over years of visits and street interviews, lies in political attitudes exemplified in the wake of a divisive national initiative whose aftershocks still reverberate throughout the country. In 2014 the Swiss narrowly voted to cancel the bilateral treaty with the EU on free movement of people. The breakdown was 50.3 to 49.7, almost unheard of in being so close, especially with the winning side edging ahead only at the finish line (typically initiatives lose momentum as the voting day nears). In these and other aspects, the initiative and the vote reflected the jitters of a small and prosperous state landlocked inside teeming, multiethnic Europe.

During the past decade, Switzerland has experienced very high per-capita rates of immigration (Basel alone is nearly 50 percent non-Swiss). Although foreign nationals have always formed a sizable segment of the population, unlike the United States, Switzerland has never identified itself as a nation of immigrants. Now city infrastructures had to expand rapidly, problems arose in schools where children not only could not understand the teachers but did not even have a common language among themselves, public outlays began to swell, etc. With many benefits of the treaty being indirect and diffuse, the majority of non-urban and non-French-speaking inhabitants protested their short-term pain over the long-term gain.

The initiative gives the government three years to implement the results of the vote, which opens enough of a window to seek a compromise between the yes and no camps. And a compromise will likely be sought and found, even as minority voices from the losing side call for initiating another vote. It is at this point that the typically Swiss attitudes are most salient. As one losing-side voter told me, "I am against it. I don't think one should repeat votes so quickly. It is an insult to the winners whom one accuses of not knowing what they wanted . . . In a few years we'll know what the new Switzerland looks like and then we can have a repeat vote on our relationship with our neighbours, but not now."

The Marquess of Queensberry

Level the playing field.

"The Debate," The West Wing

Democracy, especially direct democracy, is predicated on good schools and open channels of information. It cannot function properly without them, if people are to make educated and informed decisions. In short, giving the lie to what the *West Wing* president said about the American people, democracy presumes citizens capable of weighing (and weighing in on) sometimes-nuanced social, economic, and political matters. On this point, one of the Founding Fathers and one of the most revered presidents in American history took a position that could hardly be more at odds with Bartlet's:

> A popular Government without popular information, or the means of acquiring it, is but a Prologue to a Farce or a Tragedy; or perhaps, both. Knowledge will forever govern ignorance: And a people who mean to be their own Governors, must arm themselves with the power which knowledge gives . . . Learned Institutions ought to be favorite objects with every free people. They throw that light over the public mind which is the best security against crafty and dangerous encroachments on the public liberty.[33]

The cardinal element of democracy, as de Tocqueville remarked, is that the political process must be transparent. Democracy presumes access to information, especially in today's information society. In this respect voters are like computers: informational garbage in, decisional garbage out. As if to underscore this point, in 2007 Obama tore into his soon-to-be predecessor, saying that it was "no coincidence that one of the most secretive administrations in our nation's history has favored special interests and pursued policies that could not stand up to the sunlight."[34] Once he got in the saddle, however, his Justice Department evoked the Espionage Act to press criminal charges against leakers more than all previous presidents combined, including the paranoid Nixon, while his administration spied on everyone around, from regular citizens to US senators.

Obama's secrecy and ruthlessness in punishing all those who would bring sensitive (even if unclassified) data into the public domain matches his predecessor's resolve to keep records and information from the public eye. The defining moment of this undeclared war on democracy was when Bush II's chief of staff sneered to the *New Yorker*, "In our democracy . . . I don't believe [the press has] a check-and-balance function."[35] In one mouthful the leader of the free world moved from the democratic "right to know" to the autocratic "need to know." Sir Humphrey Appleby, of *Yes Minister* and *Yes, Prime Minister* fame, would be proud.

Understandably in our scandal-hungry culture, no one wants to find himself at the wrong side of the torrent of leaks that have crippled more than one administration. The new political role model is Dick Cheney, who not only stayed away from his letterhead like the devil stays away from holy water, but did not even use email, lest his secrecy be compromised. Unlike the utopia of *The West Wing*, today's politically connected Washingtonians do not answer email for fear of incriminating themselves, to say nothing of refusing to talk unless your degree of separation from the Oval is less than theirs.

As for the fourth estate, in the face of commercial pressures, these days exacerbated by the Internet and social networks, the press and the broadcast media have long since stopped reporting on the political process as too complex and too difficult to track anyway. Instead, the focus is on the political event. The short, sharp shock of a news flash has replaced open-ended, context-sensitive reportage. The biggest loser in this new state of affairs is the American citizen, and the biggest winner is the network commentary, as reflected in the diminution of the already humble soundbite.

In his critique of the news media's distortion of America's political process, Thomas E. Patterson documented the shrinkage of the soundbite over just two decades of presidential campaigns. In the year that Robert Kennedy was assassinated, the average soundbite was 42 seconds in duration. Significantly, most of the time the candidates were shown on the screen when speaking their lines. By the time Bush I ran against Dukakis, the average political statement had shriveled to less than ten seconds, while candidates became wallpaper for reporters' commentary.[36]

Not even campaign debates let candidates spread their oratorical wings. As accurately depicted on *The West Wing*, the scarcity and rigid format of these public forums reduces them to little more than round-robin soundbite recitals. Needless to say, this is where *The West Wing* has an edge over real life. It can script a "reality TV" episode in which candidates seemingly forswear the scripted Marquess of Queensberry rules in order to duke it out verbally—albeit still politely and with panache—in front of the electorate.

All the same, today we are witnessing a tectonic shift in political reporting. In the developed world, news increasingly travels not by air but by the click of the mouse. Crowdsourcing also significantly usurps the informational structure that used to be the domain of paid professionals. Online programs streamed live on broadband are perhaps the clearest reminder of how much the role of the broadcast and print media has changed since the coming of age of the Internet and its image-and-text-sharing platforms.

Even as television, radio, and papers lose ground in the struggle for the attention of younger audiences, live streaming emerges as an inexpensive and democratic alternative to media conglomerates that routinely edit content for length, format, and political slant. Uploaded in real time, raw footage has a proven record of drawing viewers skeptical, not to say suspicious, of the news reported (or not) by mainstream broadcasters and newspapers. Interested sectors of the public can verify what appears in the national or local media or, even better, get hold of information that does not make it there at all. Nor has this new delivery platform escaped the attention of marginalized political parties, public figures, and regular citizens discontented with the six o'clock news.

All take advantage of the opportunities offered by the Internet by uploading footage by the truckload (YouTube is said to upload almost thirty hours of video every minute), bypassing not just the censors but also the prohibitively expensive network airtime. Also, unlike private broadcasters, who are crucially dependent on advertising revenue, online services are often supported by paying users. This allows streaming services to run programs that mainstream and even local TV stations would not for fear of backlash from sponsors.

The mainstream media defend themselves with the cub reporter's truism that you cannot report everything. The question is, however, who does the selecting, and who selects the selectors? Time and again, evidence shows that mainstream news providers—broadcast and broadband—snap to their corporate owners' heels. Their selectivity could easily be mistaken for media bias consistent over programs, news crews, and networks. The bias favors the myth of laissez-faire over social planning, affluent WASPs over low-income ethnics, management over labor, and corporations over communities. Given who owns the media, such distortions are less errors of omission than errors of commission perpetrated in the name of vested, suited, and cravatted interests.[37]

Social Capital

> The market has the power to change what we think, to change what we want. The government can't do that.
>
> *"The Debate," The West Wing*

The West Wing was scheduled to go on the air in 1998, but history got in the way. With the furore over Clinton getting oral relief from an intern in the hallowed halls of the White House (as if JFK's late-night dinners never happened), the producers doubted that anyone would take the reel president seriously. Ironically, it was the level of public interest in *l'affaire* Lewinsky that eventually convinced NBC that it might be profitable to put *The West Wing* on. When, with a year's delay, it received the go-ahead, the network asked only for a balanced treatment of political issues, otherwise giving the writers and producers *carte blanche*.

Whether *The West Wing* was balanced is open to argument. What is not is that it created political theater at its finest. Once again "The Debate" exemplifies the series' edutainment quotient, demonstrating how real-life political debates are in practice indistinguishable from scripted television. With screenplays, cue cards, read-throughs, and dress rehearsals, today's politicians are all character actors, coached in their body language, acting out their speechwriters' lines, and directed by professional filmmakers against the backdrop of apposite mise-en-scène, with sound effects (including on-cue or canned applause) and music completing the picture.

The overall effect is to dramatize the verbal delivery and manipulate emotions by turning listeners into viewers. Everyone knows that hardly anyone can recall the contents of political speeches, although no one has difficulty ranking each candidate's performance on a scale of 1 to 10. The corresponding shift from issues to candidates is both the cause and an effect of this Hollywoodization of the political process. Issues change from day to day, but the candidate's character does not, becoming the focus and the barometer of most campaigns.

If all politicians are actors, this is especially so for American politicians, who—as both de Tocqueville and *The West Wing* underscored—are forever running for office. Before they even declare for a race, they need to publicly act out the persona befitting the office they want to occupy, not to mention acting out the collective hopes and fears of the voters whose endorsement they hope to corral. In a nonstop election season, the public persona can never come down, lest it reveal a tired, often clueless, yet always ambitious person underneath.

The patent way to take off the public mask is, of course, to transfer power from politicians to the people. In Season Six of *The West Wing*, in an episode entitled, appropriately enough, "The Wake Up Call," the maverick White House communications director confronts a constitutional expert in the only scene that hints at problems with the political status quo, even as it carefully locates them outside the country's borders:

> Maybe we should push beyond American-style government . . . Half the faculty at Yale Law describes the American presidential system as one of this country's most dangerous exports responsible for wreaking havoc in over thirty countries around the globe.

Trying to convince Americans of it, however, is like trying to convince an on-a-roll gambler that his winning streak won't last forever. In the meantime, evidence for a direct link between direct democracy and social happiness mounts. Strikingly, it suggests that higher levels of happiness are linked not just to desired political outcomes but to the political process itself. Direct democracy, it seems, is good for you in more ways than one.[38]

Contemporary debates about individual and social happiness trace back to Daniel Bell's *The Coming of Post-Industrial Society* (1973). Four decades hence, we know that what motivates people most powerfully is not a fat paycheck or brute power but rather what they offer in social terms: autonomy, release from worry about necessities, social status and esteem, health, and self-development. We also know that the income gap between the rich and the poor correlates with a healthy society. As income disparity shrinks, so do social dysfunctions such as acute anxiety, drug use, teenage pregnancies, high school dropout rates, and not least crime. And although the United States has the biggest economy, the prestigious Legatum Institute's 2011 rankings put it after Norway, Denmark, Australia, New Zealand, Sweden, Canada, Finland, Switzerland, and Holland in terms of prosperity.

In a parallel view of social happiness in America, in *Bowling Alone* (2000), Robert Putnam documented a massive decline in civic engagement between the middle and the end of the twentieth century. Institutionally and individually, professionally and privately, Americans as a nation and as a people have become atomized and disconnected from families, friends, neighbors, and social groups. Voting rates in presidential elections are near the bottom of all developed countries, trade unions and PTAs are ghosts of their former selves, and healthy family structures and social behaviors can be found mostly in the bastions of family values in American life—the sitcoms.

In trends particularly salient since the Nixon era, family dinners are in steep decline, whereas family vacations with school-age kids are wholly a thing of the past. Quality family time—discussions, playtime, budgeting—is practically unheard of. Fewer people have friends over to dinner and less often, and more people in general live more closed and isolated lives. They have fewer intimate friends, and fewer intimate conversations with them. At least a quarter of Americans live alone, more than ever in the history of the country (and more than three times that of 1940). Other social data corroborate this bleak picture, with the mean size of social networks dropping from almost three in 1985 to barely above two in 2004.[39]

In May 1989, Vice President Dan Quayle grandstanded, "I believe we are on an irreversible trend toward more freedom and democracy, but that could change."[40] This solecism, so typical of the man and of his profession, does nevertheless contain a grain of truth. If bad governments are elected by good people who don't vote, the United States and the rest of the world need a system that will reward good people for voting. And we have one: people's democracy, which, remarkably, appears to promote not only civic participation but also social happiness. And even though the road to real democracy in America is likely to be long and winding, experience around the world shows that once the direct democracy genie is released from the bottle, it is hard to put it back.

Put another way, people like to exercise political power, showing every citizen to be a natural-born politician.

Notes

Introduction

1. For *The Economist* perpetuating the Patent Office myth, see April 13, 1991, page 83.
2. See Sass.
3. Book publication in 1906.
4. Swirski (2006).
5. For more on eliterary critiques and nobrow artertainment, see Swirski (2005).
6. Carlin, et al., online.
7. Reagan's first inaugural, January 20, 1981.
8. For background and analysis, see Hess; also excellent study by Lamb.
9. This and following quote in Conason, 78.
10. BBC News, "Obama: Mitt Romney wrong."
11. NYC cabbies in Bryson and McKay, 24; on regulated economy, Goldin and Libecap; on welfare for Big Business, Schlosser, 72, 102.
12. For an informed critique from the perspective of a Wall Street trader, see Taleb; for a frontal assault on the neoliberal programs of economic austerity and political repression, see Klein; Collins and Yeskel; documentary *Walmart*.
13. In Kohut, 28.
14. Orwell, 318.
15. Storey, 5; McCabe, 6; Altschull, 424.
16. Kelly, 19.
17. "From falsehood, anything follows."
18. Calder; also Swirski (2010), Introduction.
19. In *The Economist*, February 19, 2011: 79.
20. Prominently Gianos; Giglio.
21. *The Economist* (2011).
22. For more examples, see Swirski (2010); Tavakoli-Far. My thanks to Alice Tse for her help with the images.

Chapter 1

1. In Powers, 137; parts of this research are based on Swirski (2009).
2. Haynes, 19.

3. In Moyers, 279.
4. Ruderman, 10.
5. In Krassner, 276–77.
6. Green, 57; bottom of paragraph, Ruderman, 179.
7. In Zagorin, 28; next quote 30; Shakespeare did not spare the Trojan War in *Troilus and Cressida*.
8. Swirski (2011).
9. Sagan, 2; for examples of contemporary democratic malpractice, Trend.
10. Eliot, 13–14; also Jerome, 158 and 172.
11. Shapiro, 68.
12. Zinn, 354.
13. George W. Bush, online.
14. Thucydides, 178; see also Zagorin, 72.
15. In Stromseth, 872.
16. In Klein, 46.
17. Schlesinger, 141; below, unidentified Bush aide quoted in Suskind, 51. On American empire, see Robin; Mann; Kegley, Lefever; Mirra; Ferguson; David and Grondin; www.americanempireproject.com.
18. Kristol and Kegan, 12; on the limits of benevolent hegemony, Fukuyama, 111–113; below, US DoD, "Full Spectrum Dominance," 6.
19. US DoD (2003).
20. Office of the Coordinator for Counterterrorism.
21. White House, 1970, online; on American involvement in Latin America, see Wiarda; Chomsky.
22. In Stokes, 60; before, fumigation war in Chomsky, 59–60; Senate hearings in Huggins, 4.
23. Much of the dossier was extracted from a single article in the *Middle East Review of International Affairs* dating back to 1993; for parallel accounts, see Lashmar; Halper and Clarke; film *Uncovered: The Whole Truth About Iraqi War*.
24. Caldicott, xxi–xxv; Armstrong; other prominent neoconservatives involved at various stages in the plan were Richard Perle, Lewis Libby, Stephen Hadley, William Kristol, and Robert Kagan.
25. Powell, 24.
26. In Hegghammer, 30.
27. Akbarzadeh; Duskin; Racizade.
28. Tonnesson, 333.
29. Stockholm International Peace Research Institute; American figures reflect the Pentagon budget plus annual appropriations for the wars in Afghanistan and Iraq.
30. Wilson, 42; for background, Cook.
31. Plato, 135.
32. US DoD, "FY 2003."
33. Data from Brandes, 264, 265, 275; see also documentary, *Why We Fight?*
34. Grimmet, online.
35. Briody, 234.

36. Chevron online; Abate; Caldicott, 190–202; Rampton and Stauber.
37. Lintott.
38. In their original *Lancet* study, Burnham et al. estimated the number to be six hundred thousand; for a legal formulation of a murder case against Bush II, see Bugliosi.

Chapter 2

1. For the dimensions of LaHaye's educational and political empire, see Standaert; the opening parts of this research are based on Swirski (2014).
2. On Kemp campaign, see Dreyfuss; Boston; Huckabee quote in Chafets.
3. Morrison, 2–3.
4. See Sizer; Wilkinson; Weremchuk.
5. On Darby's textual exegeses, see Frey; Shuck.
6. Co-written with John Castle; Buck Williams may be based on Tom Hammond, bachelor journalist hero of the early twentieth-century premillennialist novels of Sydney Watson.
7. Page 200; all subsequent references are to *Left Behind* unless indicated otherwise.
8. Page 267.
9. See, for example, *Apollyon*, 157, 303, 330.
10. This point is elaborated upon by just about every ecclesiastical commentator on the series, including Price; Bergen; Mathewson; Chapman.
11. On biblical transmissions, corruptions, and restorations, see Metzger; the Gospel of Judas in Kasser, Meyer, and Wurst.
12. "About the Author," in *The Bible's Influence*, 83.
13. O'Leary, 182; Boyer, 141.
14. For plot précis, see Price; Shuck; Gribben (chapter 7) tracks other prophecy fictions after the LBS.
15. *Time* magazine, July, 1, 2002; see also *The Guardian* (2003).
16. Page 394; see also 237; *The Mark*, 196; *The Remnant*, 275.
17. "Trends in Large U.S. Church Membership from 1960."
18. Sizer, 23.
19. *Bible's Influence*, 33; for background, see Guyatt, esp. 245–277.
20. Page 247; for background, see Bernstein.
21. Kristof, A23.
22. Page xiv; see also *The Mark*, 142.
23. See also Gold, 40; below, Price, 294.
24. Frey, especially Introduction; in *Marks of the Beast*, Shucks deliberately separates the two terms (and favors the first); for behavioral engineering and charismatic leadership, see Swirski (2011).
25. Wacker, chapter 13.
26. Gribben; Dykstra.
27. Page 27.
28. Gribben 21; for a broader analysis, see Swirski (2010).
29. Sabato and Simpson, 149.

30. In Twitchell, 8.
31. See documentary film *The Revisionists* (2012).
32. Swirski (2010), chapter 5.
33. Data from T.C. Davis, et al., 96–97; and Cole, 16.
34. Data in this paragraph from the American Federation of Teachers, online; Yovanovich, 57; Sanchez online; Kaufman, A19.
35. Yovanovich; Kozol; for the lobbying role of NEA and AFT in these school/business partnerships, see Boyles, 99–105.
36. 2009 Program for International Student Assessment.
37. Kessler.
38. In Allen, 74; see also Pelikan, 157.
39. See Robinson.
40. With buyers also circulating the books through personal networks; see Frykholm.
41. Paul; Luhrmann re-articulates the coping mechanism thesis on page 320.
42. Kramnick and Moore, 22; Harris in Dershowitz, 117. For the US senators James Inhofe (R-Oklahoma) and Don Nickles (R-Oklahoma), see Freddoso.

Chapter 3

1. *The Mail*, 64; *Church Times* online; *The Scotsman* online.
2. Page 20; see also Felsenthal.
3. Email, February 2013.
4. Both co-written with Andy Hamilton.
5. In Byrne.
6. Johnson (2008).
7. See documentaries: *Meltdown*; *Overdose: The Next Financial Crisis*; *Inside Job*.
8. In Hall; below, Rumsfeld in Van Susteren.
9. Chaddock; Welna; Herman.
10. Savage; Byrne; Cassata.
11. Page 170; below, same paragraph, see Holtzman; Froomkin.
12. Turley; see also Kain.
13. Farmer; below, Feller; Savage and Landler. On the pattern of the executive branch ignoring the War Powers Resulution, see Fisher.
14. Burkeman; next paragraph, in DeYoung and Jaffe.
15. Brechin and Freeman, 10–12.
16. Goldenberg (2009); see also (2011).
17. In Hirsch; see also Associated Press (2004); same paragraph below, Amos; Associated Press (2006).
18. Hoggan with Littlemore, 186.
19. For PR disasters, see Wagner; Howard; Harnden; Eilperin and Wallsten; Jansen; Bull.
20. Goldenberg (2011).
21. In Kennard; see also Broder and Frosh.

22. *The Guardian*, 2002; "poodle factor" in Woodward, 107.
23. Bush in *The New York Times*; below, Harnden.
24. Shipman; below, on Wikileaks, see Moore.
25. Meining, 247; Sale, 386; for background, see Crosby.
26. Sunshine Project; Sample.
27. Swirski (2009).
28. On sociobiological roots of xenophobia, see David Livingstone Smith; Swirski (2011).
29. BBC 2003 "US Congress."
30. In Schorer, 352.
31. On Roth, see Swirski (2011), chapter 5.
32. Swirski (2010), chapter 3.
33. Byrne; Booth, 46.
34. Email, April 2013.

Chapter 4

1. In Gates and Jarrett, 114.
2. In Watkins, 21.
3. Previously the only number-one albums were by party rappers Tone Loc and MC Hammer and white rappers Beastie Boys and Vanilla Ice.
4. Joyce Marie Jackson; Gerald L. Davis; standard accounts of hip-hop's history are Rose; Keyes; George; Forman; Chang.
5. In Fuentes, 20.
6. Rap's first double CD; George Clinton, who sang on one track from *All Eyes on Me*, released a series of albums with presampled riffs from his two bands, inviting rappers to remix them.
7. In Perkins, 18.
8. Weingarten.
9. In a rare reversal, Mace, one of the more successful Harlem rappers in the 1990s, semiretired to pursue his calling as a Christian minister.
10. Marsalis, 22.
11. Jones, 189.
12. Philips.
13. Morris, 146.
14. Thomas.
15. Swirski (2005), chapter 2.
16. Nelson, 42.
17. In Gates and Jarrett, 232.
18. In Smith, Zadie.
19. Abu-Jamal.
20. See Pattillo-McCoy.
21. Page 81; on mondegreening and other elements of our cognitive apparatus, see Swirski (2007).

22. In Greenfeld.
23. In Kot; also YouTube, "USA President Barack Obama Opinion on Hip-Hop & Rap 2008."
24. McPherson, 182.
25. dead prez (2004).
26. Chang, 454.
27. In Keyes, 32–33.
28. In Mitchell.
29. BBC News, "Rap"; below, Vladov.
30. Biden, "Transcripts."
31. In Deggans, "Too subtle."
32. Watkins, 17–18.
33. Rosen and Marks.
34. Dyson, 157.
35. Blair.
36. SkyNews, "Kendrick Lamar."

Chapter 5

1. Poniewozik.
2. *Pace* Sorkin in Zap2it.com.
3. See also Patterson (2000).
4. Wear, 23.
5. Dowd (2008).
6. In Miller, 90; below Ebert, 5.
7. In Tucker.
8. In Waxman, 55.
9. 18 October, 2002.
10. In McCabe, 35.
11. Sorkin, *PBS NewsHour*.
12. Sorkin, *PBS NewsHour*; for a view dissenting from Riley's, see Anderson.
13. In Ballard.
14. Season 6, Episode 10, "Faith-Based Initiative."
15. In Ballard; in the last season, NBC rescheduled the show from Wednesday night to ultracompetitive Sunday, with a significant drop in ratings.
16. A related term, *parrhesia,* refers more closely to the practice—as opposed to the ideal—of free speech at the Assembly; for background, see Bond, et al.; for democracy prior to Pericles, see Isakhan and Stockwell.
17. See Eliasoph.
18. Subsequent revision of the Act reduced its impact; on direct democracy in USA, see Zimmerman; Waters; Schmidt; Cronin, Bilakovics.
19. Fishkin, 28; strictly speaking, Switzerland (like California) is a semi-direct democracy.
20. For more on "sister republics," see Huston; Swirski (2011), chapter 2.

21. The so-called half-cantons (Basel city and Basel county) have only a half-vote; for background, see Church; Hughes.
22. Obama (2006), 25.
23. In Hinds, 1.
24. See the empirical work of Bruno S. Frey at Switzerland's Center for Research in Economics Management and the Arts.
25. *The Economist*, "Guttby."
26. Page 307, quoting former PM Attlee.
27. The European Ombudsman is currently seeking feedback on the experience with initiatives at: http://www.ombudsman.europa.eu/en/press/release.faces/en/53306/html.bookmark.
28. In Laurence.
29. See Swirski (2010), chapter 4.
30. *The Baltimore Sun* (2011).
31. In Elber.
32. Page A19; see also Whitford, in Topping, 66.
33. Madison, "Letter to W. T. Barry."
34. *USA Today*, "Obama Unveils"; below, same paragraph, *BBC News* "Senate intelligence" and "Barack Obama: 'Full confidence.'"
35. In Fritz, et al., 32; see also Schmitt and Pound.
36. Patterson, 73–75.
37. Swirski (2010), chapter 4.
38. Frey and Stutzer; Weiner.
39. McPherson, et al.
40. To *Wall Street Journal*, May 26, 1989; see Shapiro, 624.

Bibliography

Abate, Tom. (2003). "Military Waste Under Fire: $1 Trillion Missing, Bush Plan Targets Pentagon Accounting." *San Francisco Chronicle,* May 18. http://www.sfgate.com/cgi-bin/article.cgi?f=/c/a/2003/05/18/MN251738.DTL&hw=Military+Waste+under+Fire&sn=001&sc=1000.

Abu-Jamal, Mumia. (1996). "2Pacalypse Now." *Louisiana Weekly,* September 30: A5.

Agee, Marilyn J. (1994). *The End of an Age.* New York: Avon.

Agee, Marilyn J. (1998). *Revelations 2000: Your Guide to Biblical Prophecy for the New Millennium.* New York: Avon.

Akbarzadeh, Shahram. (2004). "Keeping Central Asia Stable." *Third World Quarterly* 25: 689–705.

Allen, Brooke. (2006). *Moral Minority: Our Skeptical Founding Fathers.* Chicago: Ivan R. Dee.

Altschull, J. Herbert. (1995). *Agents of Power: The Media and Public Policy.* White Plains, New York: Pearson.

Amos, Jonathan. (2006). "US scientists reject interference." *BBC News,* December 14. http://news.bbc.co.uk/2/hi/science/nature/6178213.stm.

Anderson, Roger. (2000). "The West Wing is a hit—even if it's not always true to life." *Detroit News,* April 19: O5.

Aristotle. (1961). *Poetics.* Trans. S. H. Butcher. Introduction by Francis Fergusson. New York: Hill and Wang.

Armstrong, David. (2005). "Dick Cheney's Song of America: Drafting a Plan for Global Dominance." In Carl Mirra, ed., *Enduring Freedom or Enduring War? Prospects and Costs of the New American 21st Century.* Washington, DC: Maisonneuve Press.

Associated Press. (2004). "NASA scientist rips Bush on global warming." NBC News, October 27. http://www.msnbc.msn.com/id/6341451/ns/us_news-environment/t/nasa-scientist-rips-bush-global-warming/.

Associated Press. (2006). "New Budget Plan Squeezes Education, Medicare: Bush's $2.77 trillion proposal boosts defense spending, cuts other programs." NBC News, February 6. http://www.today.com/id/11100952/ns/politics/43986774 -.UWUCtBzpFY4.

Associated Press. (2006). "Terror Attacks Worldwide Rose 25 Percent in '06, State Department Says Most Attacks in Iraq, Afghanistan." NBC News, April 30. http://www.msnbc.msn.com/id/18399660/-storyContinued.

Auster, Albert. (2001). "The West Wing: to an outsider, it celebrated the importance of public service." *Television Quarterly* 32(1): 39–42.

Baker, Houston A., Jr. (1993). *Black Studies: Rap and the Academy.* Chicago: U. of Chicago Press.

Ballard, Janette. (2008). "Haven't we seen this election before?" BBC News Magazine, September 15. http://news.bbc.co.uk/2/hi/uk_news/magazine/7616333.stm.

Balmer, Randall. (1989). *Mine Eyes Have Seen the Glory: A Journey into the Evangelical Subculture in America.* Oxford: Oxford UP.

Barber, Kathleen L. (2000). *A Right to Representation: Proportional Election Systems for the Twenty-first Century.* Columbus, OH: Ohio State UP.

Barr, James. (1977). *Fundamentalism.* Philadelphia: Westminster.

BBC2 Newsnight Review. (2007). "Alistair Beaton. Alistair Beaton is Britain's leading writer of political satire." March 16. http://news.bbc.co.uk/2/hi/programmes/newsnight/review/6457707.stm.

BBC News. (2003). "US Congress opts for 'freedom fries.'" March 12. http://news.bbc.co.uk/2/hi/americas/2842493.stm.

BBC News. (2008). "New Study Says 151,000 Iraqi Dead." 10 January 10. http://news.bbc.co.uk/2/hi/middle_east/7180055.stm.

BBC News. (2008). "Rap earns Russian soldier 'exile.'" September 30. http://news.bbc.co.uk/go/pr/fr/-/2/hi/europe/7645252.stm.

BBC News. (2010). "Tea Party Activists Fund Sign Linking Obama to Hitler." July 14. http://www.bbc.co.uk/news/world-us+canada-10636746.

BBC News. (2012). "Obama: Mitt Romney wrong to call Americans victims." September 19. http://www.bbc.co.uk/news/world-us-canada-19644448.

BBC News. (2014). "Barack Obama: 'Full confidence' in CIA director." August 1. http://www.bbc.com/news/world-us-canada-28616553.

BBC News. (2014). "Senate intelligence head says CIA 'searched computers.'" March 11. http://www.bbc.com/news/world-us-canada-26533323.

Beard, Charles Austin. (2004). *An Economic Interpretation of the Constitution of the United States.* Mineola, NY: Dover. (Orig. 1913).

Beaton, Alistair. (2005). "An affair to dismember." *The Guardian,* October 10. http://www.guardian.co.uk/media/2005/oct/10/mondaymediasection11.

Beaton, Alistair. (2001). "I positively refuse to tell you where I buy my shoelaces." *The Observer,* May 6. http://www.guardian.co.uk/theobserver/2001/may/06/featuresreview.review2.

Beaton, Alistair. (2003). "Stop the world, I'm writing a play." *The Guardian,* June 25. http://www.guardian.co.uk/stage/2003/jun/25/theatre.artsfeatures.

Beaton, Alistair. (2004). *A Planet for the President.* London, UK: Orion.

Begala, Paul. (2002). *It's Still the Economy, Stupid: George W. Bush, The GOP's CEO.* New York: Simon and Schuster.

Bell, Derrick. (1987). *And We Are Not Saved: The Elusive Quest for Racial Justice.* New York: Basic.

Bell, Derrick. (1993). *Faces at the Bottom of the Well: The Permanence of Racism.* New York: Basic.

Berens, Jessica. (2001). "Groomed for High Office: Wild, Funny and No Stranger to the Barricades, Martin Sheen is Nobody's Idea of a President." *Calgary Herald,* February 5: final edition B6.

Bergen, Wesley J. (2008). "The New Apocalyptic: Modern American Apocalyptic Fiction and its Ancient and Modern Cousins." *Journal of Religion and Popular Culture* 20(3). http://scifilit.pbworks.com/w/file/fetch/62662590/The%20New%20Apocalyptic%20Modern%20American%20Apocalyptic%20Fiction%20and%20its%20Ancient%20and%20Modern%20Cousins.pdf.

Bernstein, Michael A. (1994). *Foregone Conclusions: Against Apocalyptic History.* Berkeley: U of California Press.

Bianco, Robert. (2001). "'West Wing' Lectured More Than Entertained." *USA Today*, October 4.

Biden, Joe. (2012). "Transcripts: Democratic National Convention." *CNN*, September 6. http://transcripts.cnn.com/TRANSCRIPTS/1209/06/se.03.html.

Bigsby, Christopher. (2013). *Viewing America: Twenty-First-Century Television Drama.* Cambridge: Cambridge UP.

Bilakovics, Steven. (2012). *Democracy Without Politics.* Cambridge, MA: Harvard UP.

Blackstock, Nelson. (1975). *COINTELPRO: The FBI's Secret War on Political Freedom.* New York: Vintage.

Blinder, Alan S. (2004). *The Quiet Revolution.* Yale: Yale UP.

Bloom, Harold, ed. (1995). *Black American Poets and Dramatists of the Harlem Renaissance.* New York: Chelsea House.

Bok, Chip. (2005). *The Recent History of the United States in Political Cartoons.* Ohio: University of Akron Press.

Bond, Jon R., et al. (2006). *The Promise and Performance of American Democracy.* Belmont, CA: Thomson/Wadsworth.

Bond, Jon R. (2009). "Bush 2004 Campaign Pledges to Restore Honor and Dignity to White House." *The Onion*, April 15, http://www.theonion.com/content/news/bush_2004_campaign_pledges_to.

Booth, Lauren. (2001). "The Feelgood Factor." *New Statesman*, February 19: 45–46.

Bork, Robert H. (1996). *Slouching Towards Gomorrah: Modern Liberalism and American Decline.* New York: Harper Collins.

Boyd, Todd. (1997). *Am I Black Enough for You: Popular Culture from the 'Hood and Beyond.* Bloomington, IN: Indiana UP.

Boyer, Paul S. (1992). *When Time Shall Be No More: Prophecy Belief in Modern American Culture.* Cambridge, MA: Belknap.

Boyles, Deron. (1998). *American Education and Corporations: The Free Market Goes to School.* New York: Garland.

Brandes, Stuart D. (1997). *Warhogs: A History of War Profits in America.* Lexington, KY: University Press of Kentucky.

Branegan, Jay. (2000). "You could call it a wonk thing." *Time*, May 15: 82–85.

Brechin, Steven R., and Freeman, Daniel A. (2004). "Public Support for Both the Environment and an Anti-Environmental President: Possible Explanations for the George W. Bush Anomaly." *The Forum: A Journal of Applied Research in Contemporary Politics* 2:1 (Article 6). http://www.bepress.com/forum/vol2/iss1/art6.

Brill, Steven. (2000). "Truth of fiction: pick one: fictional *West Wing* bests many reporters in depicting a nuanced Washington." *Brill's Content* 3: 2.

Briody, Dan. (2004). *The Halliburton Agenda: The Politics of Oil and Money.* New Jersey: Wiley & Sons.

Broder, John. M, and Dan Frosch. (2011). "U. S. Delays Decision on Pipeline Until After Election." *The New York Times,* November 10. http://www.nytimes.com/2011/11/11/us/politics/administration-to-delay-pipeline-decision-past-12-election.html?pagewanted=all&_r=0.

Bryson, Alex, and Stephen McKay, eds. (1994). *Is It Worth Working?* London: PSI Publishing.

Buckley, Christopher Taylor. (2012). *They Eat Puppies, Don't They?* New York: Twelve.

Bugliosi, Vincent. (2008). *The Prosecution of George W. Bush for Murder.* New York: Vanguard.

Bull, Alister. (2009). "Obama: Copenhagen paves way for action on climate." Reuters, December 19. http://www.reuters.com/article/2009/12/19/us-climate-copenhagen-obama-idUSTRE5BH1QZ20091219.

Bull, Martin, and James Newell. (2003). *Corruption in Contemporary Politics.* New York: Palgrave Macmillan.

Burbach, Roger, and Jim Tarbell. (2004). *Imperial Overstretch: George W. Bush and the Hubris of Empire.* London, New York: Zed Books.

Burkeman, Oliver. (2009). "Obama administration says goodbye to 'war on terror.'" *The Guardian,* March 25. http://www.guardian.co.uk/world/2009/mar/25/obama-war-terror-overseas-contingency-operations.

Burnham, Gilbert, et al. (2006). "The Human Cost of the War in Iraq: A Mortality Study, 2002–2006." *The Lancet,* October 11. Indexed 2007. http://web.mit.edu/CIS/pdf/Human_Cost_of_War.pdf

Bush, George W. (2001). "Remarks on Transmitting the Tax Relief Plan to the Congress." In Woolley, John T., and Gerhard Peters. *The American Presidency Project.* Santa Barbara, CA. http://www.presidency.ucsb.edu/ws/index.php?pid=45937.

Bush, George W. (2001). "Transcript of President Bush's Address to a Joint Session of Congress." CNN.com. http://archives.cnn.com/2001/US/09/20/gen.bush.transcript/.

Bush, George W. (2003). "Bush's Words to Britons: 'Both Our Nations Serve the Cause of Freedom.'" *The New York Times,* November 20. http://www.nytimes.com/2003/11/20/international/europe/20PTEX.html?pagewanted=5.

Bush, George W. (2010). *Decision Points.* New York: Crown.

Business Week Online. (2003). "Is Wal-Mart Too Powerful?" October 6. http://www.kuratrading.com/PDF/Walmart2.pdf.

Byrne, Ciar. (2006). "Politics and humour: Is Alistair Beaton Britain's greatest living satirist?" *The Independent,* April 5. http://www.independent.co.uk/news/uk/politics/politics-and-humour-is-alistair-beaton-britains-greatest-living-satirist-472856.html.

Byrne, John. (2009). "Obama Administration quietly expands Bush's legal defense of wiretapping program." The Raw Story, April 7. http://rawstory.com/news/2008/Obama_Administration_quietly_expands_Bushs_legal_0407.html.

Cacioppo, John, and William Patrick. (2000). *Loneliness.* New York, Norton.

Calder, Peter. (2009). "A Less Than Revolutionary Che." *Time Out*, November 26: 13.

Caldicott, Helen. (2004). *The New Nuclear Danger: George W. Bush's Military-Industrial Complex*. New York: New Press.

Carlin, Brendan, George Jones, and Toby Helm. (2006). "Blair's whips fooled by West Wing plot." *The Telegraph,* February 2. http://www.telegraph.co.uk/news/uknews/1509435/Blairs-whips-fooled-by-West-Wing-plot.html.

Cassata, Donna. (2011). "National Defense Authorization Act: House And Senate Negotiators Agree On Bill Hoping To Avoid Obama Veto." The Huffington Post. http://www.huffingtonpost.com/2011/12/13/national-defense-authorization-act-ndaa-obama-detainee-policy_n_1145407.html.

CBCNews: Politics. (2008). "Transcript: Final Presidential Debate." October 16. http://www.cbsnews.com/stories/2008/10/16/politics/2008debates/main4525254.shtml.

Chaddock, Gail Russell. (2011). "Patriot Act: three controversial provisions that Congress voted to keep." *The Christian Science Monitor,* May 27. http://www.csmonitor.com/USA/Politics/2011/0527/Patriot-Act-three-controversial-provisions-that-Congress-voted-to-keep.

Chafets, Zev. (2007). "The Huckabee Factor." *New York Times Magazine,* December 12. http://www.nytimes.com/2007/12/12/magazine/16huckabee.html?pagewanted=all&_r=0.

Chang, Jeff. (2005). *Can't Stop Won't Stop: A History of the Hip-Hop Generation*. New York: St. Martin's.

Chapman, Jennie. (2009). "Tender Warriors: Muscular Christians, Promise Keepers, and the Crisis of Masculinity in *Left Behind*." *Journal of Religion and Popular Culture* 21(3). https://www.academia.edu/329198/Tender_Warriors_Muscular_Christians_Promise_Keepers_and_the_Crisis_of_Masculinity_In_Left_Behind.

Chomsky, Noam. (2003). *Hegemony or Survival: America's Quest for Global Dominance*. New York: Henry Holt and Company.

Church, J. Forrester. (1989). "Introduction." In Jefferson, Thomas. *The Jefferson Bible: The Life and Morals of Jesus of Nazareth*. Boston: Beacon.

Church Times. (2006). "A Planet for the President." November 2. http://www.churchtimes.co.uk/articles/2004/26-november/reviews/book-reviews/a-planet-for-the-president.

Cole, M. R. (2000). "The High Risk of Low Health Literacy." *Nursing Spectrum* 13 (May 15): 16.

Collins, Chuck, and Felice Yeskel. (2005). *Economic Apartheid in America: A Primer on Economic Inequality and Insecurity*. New York: New Press.

Conason, Joe. (2003). *Big Lies: The Right-Wing Propaganda Machine and How it Distorts the Truth*. New York: Thomas Dunne.

Cook, Harold J. (2007). *Matters of Exchange: Commerce, Medicine, and Science in the Dutch Golden Age*. Yale: Yale UP.

Corn, David. (2003). *The Lies of George W. Bush: Mastering the Politics of Deception*. New York: Crown Publishers.

Crawley, Melissa. (2006). *Mr. Sorkin Goes to Washington: Shaping the President on Television's The West Wing*. Jefferson, NC: McFarland and Co.

Crosby, Alfred W. (1986). *Ecological Imperialism: The Biological Expansion of Europe, 900–1900*. Second edition. Cambridge: Cambridge UP.

Currinder, Marian. (2005). "Campaign Finance: Funding the Presidential and Congressional Elections." In Michael Nelson, ed., *The Elections of 2004*. Washington, DC: Congressional Quarterly Press.

D., Chuck, and Yusuf Jah. (1997). *Fight the Power: Rap, Race, and Reality*. New York: Delacorte.

David, Charles-Philippe, and David Grondin. (2006). *Hegemony or Empire? The Redefinition of US Power under George W. Bush*. Aldershot, England: Ashgate.

Davies, Katie. (2013). "Five years after The Wire left screens." MailOnline, April 11. http://www.dailymail.co.uk/news/article-2307221/Baltimore-poverty-plagued-city-5-years-TV-The-Wire-left-screens.html.

Davis Gerald L. (1985). *I Got the Wind in Me and I Can Sing It, You Know: A Study of the Performed African-American Sermon*. Philadelphia: U. of Pennsylvania Press.

Day, Amber. (2011). *Satire and Dissent: Interventions in Contemporary Political Debate*. Bloomington, IN: Indiana UP.

dead prez. (2004). "M1 Interview at Designer Magazine." Designer Magazine. http://designermagazine.tripod.com/DeadPrezINT2.html.

Deggans, Eric. (2001). "New opponents to besiege *West Wing*." *St. Petersburg Times*, February 6. http://www.sptimes.com/News/020601/Floridian/New_opponents_to_besi.shtml.

Deggans, Eric. (2001). "Too subtle for the small screen." *St. Petersburg Times*, February 26. http://www.sptimes.com/News/022601/Columns/Too_subtle_for_the_sm.shtml.

DeMar, Gary. (2009). *Left Behind: Separating Fact from Fiction*. Powder Springs, Georgia.

Demographia. (2005). "Trends in Large U. S. Church Membership from 1960." http://demographia.com/db-religlarge.htm.

Denselow, Robin. (1990). *When the Music's Over: The Story of Political Pop*. London: Faber and Faber.

Dershowitz, Alan. (2007). *Blasphemy: How the Religious Right Is Hijacking Our Declaration of Independence*. Hoboken, NJ: John Wiley and Sons.

Dewey, Donald. (2007). *The Art of Ill Will: The Story of American Political Cartoons*. New York: New York UP.

DeYoung, Karen, and Greg Jaffe. (2010). "U. S. 'secret war' expands globally as Special Operations forces take larger role." *Washington Post*, June 4. http://www.washingtonpost.com/wp-dyn/content/article/2010/06/03/AR2010060304965.html.

Douglass, Frederick. (1983). *My Bondage and My Freedom*. New York: Auburn, Miller, Orton, & Co. Expanded as *Life and Times of Frederic Douglass; Written by Himself*. Hartford, CN: Park Pub. Co., 1881. Reprinted: Secaucus, NJ: Citadel Press. (Orig. 1857.)

Dowd, Maureen. (2004). "The Thief of Baghdad." *The New York Times*, February 15. http://www.nytimes.com/2004/02/15/opinion/the-thief-of-baghdad.html.

Dowd, Maureen. (2008). "Aaron Sorkin conjures a meeting of Obama and Bartlet." *New York Times*, September 20. http://www.nytimes.com/2008/09/21/opinion/21dowd-sorkin.html.

Dreyfuss, Robert. (2004). "Reverend Doomsday: According to Tim LaHaye, the Apocalypse is now." *Rolling Stone,* January 28: 35–38.

Drinkard, Jim. (2006). "House softens lobbying measure." *USA Today,* April 23. http://www.usatoday.com/news/washington/2006-04-23-lobbying_x.htm.

Duskin, J. Eric. (2002). "Permanent Installation." *In These Times,* March 29. http://www.inthesetimes.com/issue/26/11/feature2.shtml.

Dykstra, Ursa. (2012). "*Left Behind* as a Stage for Resolution of the Internal Tensions and Insecurities of Evangelical American Fundamentalism." Unpublished MA thesis, University of Helsinki.

Dyson, Michael, Eric. (2001). *Holler If You Hear Me: Searching for Tupac Shakur.* New York: Basic Civitas Books.

Ebert, Roger. (1990). "The Cheapest Shots Attacks on 'Roger & Me' Completely Miss Point of Film." *Chicago Sun-Times,* February 11: 5.

Eilperin, Juliet, and Peter Wallsten. (2011). "Obama's decision on smog rule offers hints on regulation strategy." *The Washington Post,* September 4. http://www.washingtonpost.com/politics/obamas-decision-on-smog-rule-offers-hints-on-environmental-strategy/2011/09/03/gIQAX4EzzJ_story.html.

Elber, Lynn. (2002). "*West Wing* walks fine line of fiction, political reality." *Napa Valley Register,* April 23. http://napavalleyregister.com/lifestyles/west-wing-walks-fine-line-of-fiction-political-reality/article_7138ad97-4864-5c88-8f32-686396cdc7fa.html.

Eliasoph, Nina. (1998). *Avoiding Politics: How Americans Produce Apathy in Everyday Life.* Cambridge, UK: Cambridge UP.

Eliot, George Fielding. (1950). *The H Bomb.* New York: Didier.

Engelhardt, Tom. (2010). *The American Way of War: How Bush's Wars Became Obama's.* Chicago: Haymarket Books.

Ewen, Stewart. (1996). *PR! A Social History of Spin.* New York: Basic Books.

Falwell, Jerry. (1987). *Strength for the Journey: An Autobiography.* New York: Simon & Schuster.

Farmer, Ben. (2011). "US troops may stay in Afghanistan until 2024." *The Telegraph,* August 19. http://www.telegraph.co.uk/news/worldnews/asia/afghanistan/8712701/US-troops-may-stay-in-Afghanistan-until-2024.html.

Feller, Ben. (2011). "Obama Libya Speech Strongly Defends Intervention." *The Huffington Post,* March 28. http://www.huffingtonpost.com/2011/03/28/obama-libya-speech-_n_841311.html.

Felsenthal, Carol. (2001). "The Don: A Look at Former Defense Secretary Donald Rumsfeld." *Chicago Magazine,* June. http://www.chicagomag.com/Chicago-Magazine/June-2001/The-Don-A-Look-at-Former-Defense-Secretary-Donald-Rumsfeld/.

Ferguson, Niall. (2004). *Colossus: The Price of America's Empire.* New York: Penguin.

Fisher, Louis (1987). *Presidential War Power.* Lawrence, KS: University Press of Kansas.

Fisher, Roger A. (1995). *Them Damned Pictures: Explorations in American Political Cartoon Art.* Hamden, CT: Archon Books.

Fishkin, James S. (1995). *The Voice of the People: Public Opinion and Democracy.* New Haven: Yale UP.

Forbes, Bruce David, and Jeanne Halgren Kilde, eds. (2004). *Rapture, Revelation, and the End Times: Exploring the Left Behind Series*. New York: Palgrave Macmillan.

Forman, Murray. (2002). *The 'Hood Comes First: Race, Space and Place in Rap and Hip-Hop*. Middletown, CN: Wesleyan UP.

Forman, Murray, and Mark Anthony Neal, eds. (2004). *That's the Joint! The Hip-Hop Studies Reader*. New York: Routledge.

Franklin, John Hope, and Alfred J. Moss, Jr. (1994). *From Slavery to Freedom: A History of African Americans*. New York: Knopf.

Freddoso, David. (2002). "Who Would Confirm an Atheist to the Supreme Court?" *Human Events* 58(26) (July 15): 3.

Freddoso, David. (2008). *The Case Against Barack Obama: The Unlikely Rise and Unexamined Agenda of the Media's Favorite Candidate Since 1947*. Washington, DC: Regnery.

French, Blaire Atherton (1982). *The Presidential Press Conference: Its History and Role in the American Political System*. Washington, DC: University Press of America.

Frey, Bruno S. (2008). *Happiness: A Revolution in Economics*. Cambridge, MA: MIT Press.

Frey, Bruno S., and Alois Stutzer. (2000). "Happiness prospers in democracy." *Journal of Happiness Studies* 1: 79–102.

Frey, Bruno S., and Alois Stutzer. (2002). *Happiness and Economics: How the Economy and Institutions Affect Human Beings*. Princeton: Princeton UP.

Frey, Bruno S., and Alois Stutzer. (2007). *Economics and Psychology: A Promising New Cross-Disciplinary Field*. Cambridge, MA: MIT Press.

Frey, Rebecca Joyce. (2007). *Fundamentalism (Global Issues)*. New York: Facts on File.

Fritz, Ben, et al. (2004). *All the President's Spin: George W. Bush, the Media, and the Truth*. New York: Touchstone.

Froomkin, Dan. (2010). "Bush's waterboarding admission prompts calls for criminal probe." The Huffington Post, November 11. http://www.huffingtonpost.com/2010/11/11/calls-for-criminal-invest_n_782354.html.

Frykholm, Amy. (2004). *Rapture Culture: Left Behind in Evangelical America*. Oxford: Oxford UP.

Fuentes, Annette. (1985). "The Hollis rappers: hometown boys make good." *City Limits*, December: 16–21.

Fukuyama, Francis. (2004). *America at the Crossroads: Democracy, Power and the Neoconservative Legacy*. Yale: Yale University Press.

George, Nelson. (1998). *Hip Hop America*. New York: Penguin.

Gianos, Philip L. (1998). *Politics and Politicians in American Film*. Westport, CN: Praeger.

Gibbs, Nancy. (2002). "The Bible and the Apocalypse: The Biggest Book of the Summer Is About the End of the World. It's Also a Sign of Our Troubled Times." *Time*, July 1.

Giglio, Ernest. (2000). *Here's Looking at You: Hollywood, Film, and Politics*. New York: Peter Lang.

Gladstone, Brooke. (2000). "Bartlet 2000: The Fictional President from the West Wing has Real-Life Appeal." *Detroit Free Press*, October 1.

Gladstone, Brooke. (2000). "Politics in Movies: Morning Edition." Washington, DC: National Public Radio, September 7.

Gold, Malcolm. (2006). "The *Left Behind* Series as Sacred Text?" In Elizabeth Arweck and Peter Collins, eds. *Reading Religion in Text and Context: Reflections of Faith and Practice in Religious Materials*, 34–49. Hampshire, England: Ashgate.

Goldenberg, Suzanne. (2009). "The worst of times: Bush's environmental legacy examined." *The Guardian*, January 16. http://www.guardian.co.uk/politics/2009/jan/16/greenpolitics-georgebush.

Goldenberg, Suzanne. (2011). "Report highlights Obama's broken environmental promises." *The Guardian*, November 28. http://www.guardian.co.uk/environment/blog/2011/nov/28/report-obama-broken-environmental-promises.

Goldin, Claudia, and Gary D. Libecap, eds. (1994). *The Regulated Economy: A Historical Approach to Political Economy*. Chicago: Chicago UP.

Government Accountability Office. (2006). "Media Contracts: Activities and Financial Obligations for Seven Federal Departments." January.

Gray, Jonathan, Jeffrey P. Jones, and Ethan Thompson. (2009). *Satire TV: Politics and Comedy in the Post-Network Era*. New York: New York UP.

Green, Robert. (1988). "Picturing Heller." *Baltimore Jewish Times*, October 21: 56–58.

Greenfeld, Josh. (1968). "For Simon and Garfunkel all is groovy." *New York Times Magazine*, October 13: 48–49, 168–184.

Gribben, Crawford. (2006). "After *Left Behind*: The Paradox of Evangelical Pessimism." In Kenneth G. C. Newport and Crawford Gribben, eds. *Expecting the End: Millennialism in Social and Historical Context*, 113–130. Waco, Texas: Baylor UP.

Gribben, Crawford. (2009). *Prophecy Fiction in Evangelical America*. Oxford: Oxford UP.

Guyatt, Nicholas. (2007). *Have a Nice Doomsday: Why Millions of Americans Are Looking Forward to the End of the World*. London: Ebury.

Hall, Richard. (2009). "'Little difference' between Bush and Obama in substance: Noam Chomsky interviewed by Richard Hall." *Daily Star*, June 24. http://www.chomsky.info/interviews/20090624.htm.

Halper, Stefan, and Jonathan Clarke. (2004). *America Alone: The Neo-Conservatives and the Global Order*. New York: Cambridge UP.

Halperin, Mark, and John F. Harris. (2006). *The Way to Win: Taking the White House in 2008*. New York: Random House.

Hanahoe, Tom. (2003). *America Rules: US Foreign Policy, Globalization, and Corporate USA*. Dingle: Brandon.

Harding, Susan. (1994). "Imagining the Last Days: The Politics of Apocalyptic Language." In Martin B. Marty and R. Scott Appleby, eds. *Accounting for Fundamentalisms: The Dynamic Character of Movements*. Chicago and London: U. of Chicago Press. 57–78.

Hardt, Michael, and Antonio Negri. *Empire*. (2000). Cambridge, MA: Harvard UP.

Harnden, Toby. (2006). "Britain's 'special relationship' just a myth." *The Telegraph*, November 30. http://www.telegraph.co.uk/news/worldnews/1535639/Britains-special-relationship-just-a-myth.html.

Harnden, Toby. (2011). "Collapse of solar power giant an embarrassment for Obama administration." *The Telegraph*, September 15. http://www.telegraph.

co.uk/earth/energy/solarpower/8766476/Collapse-of-solar-power-giant-an-embarrassment-for-Obama-administration.html.

Haynes, Kevin. (1993). "Contemplating Joseph Heller." In Adam J. Sorkin, ed. *Conversations with Joseph Heller.* Jackson: University Press of Mississippi, 290–292.

Hegghammer, Thomas. (2006). "Global Jihadism after the Iraq War." *The Middle East Journal* 60:11–32.

Heller, Joseph. (1979). *Good as Gold.* London: Black Swan.

Heller, Joseph. (1988). *Picture This.* New York: Ballantine Books.

Hendershot, Heather. (2004). *Shaking the World for Jesus: Media and Conservative Evangelical Culture.* Chicago: U. of Chicago Press.

Herbert, Bob. (2004). "Masters of Deception." *The New York Times,* January 16. http://www.nytimes.com/2004/01/16/opinion/16HERB.html

Herman, Susan N. (2011). *Taking Liberties: The War on Terror and the Erosion of American Democracy.* New York: Oxford UP.

Herzog, Rudolph. (2011). *Dead Funny: Humor in Hitler's Germany.* Trans. Jefferson Chase. Melville House Publishing.

Hess, Stephen. (1975). *The Ungentlemanly Art: A History of American Political Cartoons.* New York: MacMillan Publishing Company.

Hess, Stephen. (1996). *Drawn & Quartered: The History of American Political Cartoons.* Montgomery, AL: Elliott & Clark Publishing.

Hinds, Julie. (2000). "Bartlet 2000: The fictional president from 'The West Wing' has real-life appeal." *Detroit Free Press,* October 1: 1.

Hirsch, Tim. (2004). "US rejects climate policy attacks." *BBC News,* December 8. http://news.bbc.co.uk/2/hi/science/nature/4077137.stm.

Hofstadter, Richard. (1967). *The Paranoid Style in American Politics and Other Essays.* New York: Vintage.

Hoggan, James, with Richard Littlemore. (2009). *Climate Cover-Up: The Crusade to Deny Global Warming.* Vancouver: Greystone Books.

Holtzman, Elizabeth. (2010). "Damn Wrong: Bush Admission on Torture Should Draw Special Prosecutor." The Huffington Post, November 15. http://www.huffingtonpost.com/elizabeth-holtzman/damn-wrong-bush-admission_b_783001.html.

Honig, Bonnie. (1993). *Political Theory and the Displacement of Politics.* Ithaca: Cornell UP.

Hornick, Ed. (2009). "Democrats voice concerns on Obama's Iraq drawdown plan." *CNN,* February 27. http://articles.cnn.com/2009-02-27/politics/iraq.dems_1_troop-plan-troop-level-forces?_s=PM:POLITICS.

Howard, Jordan. (2011). "Obama to Expand Drilling Off Alaska, In Gulf." The Huffington Post, November 8. http://www.huffingtonpost.com/2011/11/08/obama-alaska-gulf-drilling_n_1082191.html.

Hudson, William E. (2006). *American Democracy in Peril: Eight Challenges to America's Future.* Washington, DC: CQ Press.

Huggins, Martha K. (1998). *Political Policing: The United States and Latin America.* Durham, NC: Duke UP.

Huggins, Nathan Irvin. (1971). *Harlem Renaissance.* New York: Oxford UP.

ICasualties.org. (2007). "Iraq Coalition Casualty Count." December 29. http://icasual ties.org

Illich, Ivan. (1973). *Tools for Conviviality*. London, UK: Marion Boyars Publishers.

Isakhan, Benjamin, and Stephen Stockwell, eds. (2012). *The Secret History of Democracy*. New York: Palgrave Macmillan.

Ivanovich, David. (2007). "Halliburton Defends Its Dealings: Subsidiary's Work in Iran Was Not Against Law, Executive Contends." *Knight Rider Tribune Business News,* May 1: 1.

Jackson, Joyce Marie. (1981). "The Black American folk preacher and the chanted sermon: parallels with a West African Tradition." In Card, Caroline, et al. *Discourse in Ethnomusicology II*. Bloomington, IN: Indiana UP.

Jacoby, Susan. (2008). *The Age of American Unreason*. New York: Pantheon.

Jansen, Lesa. (2011). "Obama announces steps to speed oil drilling." *CNN,* May 14. http://articles.cnn.com/2011-05-14/politics/obama.weekly.address_1_oil-drill ing-bp-oil-oil-companies?_s=PM:POLITICS.

Jefferson, Thomas. (1989). *The Jefferson Bible: The Life and Morals of Jesus of Nazareth*. Boston: Beacon.

Jerome, Fred. (2002). *The Einstein File: J. Edgar Hoover's Secret War Against the World's Most Famous Scientist*. New York: St. Martin's.

Johnson, Alex M. (2008). "Obama blasts Bush's 'failed presidency.'" NBC News, August 29. http://www.msnbc.msn.com/id/26436143/.

Jones, Darryl. (2006). "The Liberal Antichrist: *Left Behind* in America." In Kenneth G. C. Newport and Crawford Gribben, eds. *Expecting the End: Millennialism in Social and Historical Context*. 97–112. Waco, Texas: Baylor UP.

Jones, Jeffrey, P. (2009). *Entertaining Politics: Satiric Television and Political Engagement*. Second edition. New York: Rowman, Littlefield.

Jones, LeRoi. (1963). *Blues People: Negro Music in White America*. New York: William Morrow & Company.

Kain, Erik. (2011). "The National Defense Authorization Act is the Greatest Threat to Civil Liberties Americans Face." *Forbes,* December 5. http://www.forbes.com/ sites/erikkain/2011/12/05/the-national-defense-authorization-act-is-the-greatest-threat-to-civil-liberties-americans-face/.

Kasser, Rodolphe, Marvin Meyer, and Gregor Wurst, eds. (2006). *The Gospel of Judas: From Codex Tchacos*. Washington, DC: National Geographic.

Kauffman, Bill. (2004). "Heil to the Chief." *The American Conservative,* September 27. http://www.amconmag.com/article/2004/sep/27/00028/

Kegley, Charles W. Jr., and Gregory A. Raymond. (2007). *After Iraq: The Imperiled American Imperium*. New York: Oxford UP.

Kelly, Alison. (2008). "Welcome to America: Lorrie Moore's fiction as a national register." *The Times Literary Supplement,* May 2:19.

Kennard, Matt. (2011). "Gore Criticises Obama on Global Warming." *Financial Times,* June 22. http://www.ft.com/intl/cms/s/0/dd89a13e-9cf8-11e0-8678-00144feabdc0 .html#axzz1gRUAogfv.

Kennedy, Paul. (1989). *The Rise and Fall of the Great Powers: Economic Change and Military Conflict from 1500–2000*. New York: Vintage.

Kessler, Glenn. (2011). "The Fact Checker." *The Washington Post*, January 28. http://voices.washingtonpost.com/fact-checker/2011/01/bachmann_on_slavery_and_the_na.html.

Keyes, Cheryl L. (2002). *Rap Music and Street Consciousness*. Urbana, Chicago: U. of Illinois.

Klein, Joe. (2006). "Lieberman's Last Stand." *Time*, July 31: 46.

Klein, Naomi. (2007). *The Shock Doctrine*. London: Penguin.

Knightly, Philip. (1975). *The First Casualty: From the Crimea to Vietnam: The War Correspondent as Hero, Propagandist, and Myth Maker*. New York: Harcourt, Brace, Jovanovich.

Koch, Adrienne, and William Peden. (1993). *The Life and Selected Writings of Thomas Jefferson*. New York: Random.

Kohut. Andrew. (2000). "Getting voters to engage." *Columbia Journalism Review* 39: 28.

Kot, Greg. (2008). "Barack Obama, first president to come of age in hip-hop era." *Chicago Tribune*, November 9. http://articles.chicagotribune.com/2008-11-09/news/0811070250_1_artists-that-i-love-hip-hop-community-kanye-west-and-common/2.

Kozol, Jonathan. (1991). *Savage Inequalities: Children in American Schools*. New York: Crown.

Kramnick, Isaac, and R. Laurence Moore. (1991). *The Godless Constitution: The Case Against Religious Correctness*. New York: Norton.

Krassner, Paul. (1973). "An Impolite Interview with Joseph Heller." In Frederick T. Kiley and Walter McDonald, eds. *A "Catch-22" Casebook*. New York: Crowell, 273–293.

Krauthammer, Charles. "The Unipolar Moment." *Foreign Affairs* 70:1 (1990/91): 23–34.

Kristof, Nicholas D. (2004). "Apocalypse (Almost) Now." *The New York Times*, November 24: A23.

Kristol, William, and Robert Kagan. (2000). *Present Dangers: Crisis and Opportunity in American Foreign and Defense Policy*. San Francisco: Encounter.

Kumar, Krishna. (2002). "Religious Fundamentalism in India and Beyond." *Parameters* 32: 17–34.

LaHaye, Tim. (1976). *The Bible's Influence on American History*. San Diego: Christian Heritage College, MasterBooks.

LaHaye, Tim, and Jerry B. Jenkins. (1995). *Left Behind: A Novel of the Earth's Last Days*. Wheaton, IL: Tyndale House.

LaHaye, Tim, and Jerry B. Jenkins. (1996). *Tribulation Force: The Continuing Drama of Those Left Behind*. Wheaton, IL: Tyndale House.

LaHaye, Tim, and Jerry B. Jenkins. (1997). *Nicolae: The Rise of the Antichrist*. Wheaton, IL: Tyndale House.

LaHaye, Tim, and Jerry B. Jenkins. (1998). *Soul Harvest: The World Takes Sides*. Wheaton, IL: Tyndale House.

LaHaye, Tim, and Jerry B. Jenkins. (1999). *Apollyon: The Destroyer Is Unleashed*. Wheaton, IL: Tyndale House.

LaHaye, Tim, and Jerry B. Jenkins. (1999). *Are We Living in the End Times? Current Events Foretold in Scripture and What They Mean.* Nashville, TN: Tyndale House.

LaHaye, Tim, and Jerry B. Jenkins. (1999). *Assassins: Assignment: Jerusalem, Target: Antichrist.* Wheaton, IL: Tyndale House.

LaHaye, Tim, and Jerry B. Jenkins. (2000). *The Indwelling: The Beast Takes Possession.* Wheaton, IL: Tyndale House.

LaHaye, Tim, and Jerry B. Jenkins. (2000). *The Mark: The Beast Rules the World.* Wheaton, IL: Tyndale House.

LaHaye, Tim, and Jerry B. Jenkins. (2001). *Desecration: Antichrist Takes the Throne.* Wheaton, IL: Tyndale House.

LaHaye, Tim, and Jerry B. Jenkins. (2002). *The Remnant: On the Brink of Armageddon.* Wheaton, IL: Tyndale House.

LaHaye, Tim, and Jerry B. Jenkins. (2003). *Armageddon: The Cosmic Battle of the Ages.* Wheaton, IL: Tyndale House.

LaHaye, Tim, and Jerry B. Jenkins. (2004). *Glorious Appearing: The End of Days.* Wheaton, IL: Tyndale House.

LaHaye, Tim, and Jerry B. Jenkins. (2005). *The Rising: Antichrist is Born.* Wheaton, IL: Tyndale House.

LaHaye, Tim, and Jerry B. Jenkins. (2007). *Kingdom Come: The Final Victory.* Wheaton, IL: Tyndale House.

LaHaye, Tim, Jerry B. Jenkins, and Sandi L. Swanson. (2005). *The Authorized Left Behind Handbook.* Wheaton, IL: Tyndale House.

Lamb, Chris. (2004). *Drawn to Extremes: The Use and Abuse of Editorial Cartoons in the United States.* New York: Columbia UP.

Lardner, James, and David Smith. (2005). *Inequality Matters: The Growing Economic Divide in America and Its Poisonous Consequences.* New York: New Press.

Lasher, Lawrence M., ed. (1991). *Conversations with Bernard Malamud.* Jackson, MI: University Press of Mississippi.

Lashmar, Paul. (2003). "On the Brink of War: The Spies' Revolt M16 and CIA: The New Enemy Within." *The Independent,* February 9: 13.

Lee, Earl. (2003). *Kiss My Left Behind.* Aventine.

Lee, Earl. (2004). *Kiss My Left Behind 2: The Tribulation Farce.* Outskirts Press.

Lee, Spike. (2012). Twitter, December 22. https://twitter.com/SpikeLee/status/282611091777941504.

Lefever, Ernest W. (1999). *America's Imperial Burden: Is the Past Prologue?* Boulder: Westview Press.

Lelchuk, Alan. (1992). "On Satirizing Presidents." In George J. Searles, ed. *Conversations with Philip Roth.* Jackson, MI: University Press of Mississippi.

Levine, Michael L. (1996). *African Americans and Civil Rights, From 1619 to Present.* Phoenix: Oryx.

Levy, Peter B. (1998). *The Civil Rights Movement.* Westport, CN: Greenwood.

Lewis, Ann F. (2001). "The West Wing: An Insider Calls It the Insider's View of Democracy." *Television Quarterly* 32(1): 36–38.

Lewis, David Levering, ed. (1995). *W. E. B. Du Bois: A Reader.* New York: Henry Holt.

Lewis, Sinclair. (1930). "Nobel Lecture." December 12. http://www.nobelprize.org/nobel_prizes/literature/laureates/1930/lewis-lecture.html.

Lewis, Sinclair. (1936). *It Can't Happen Here: A Novel.* Garden City, NY: Doubleday, Doran, and Company.

Lindsey, Hal, with Carole C. Carlson. (1970). *The Late Planet Earth.* Grand Rapids, MI: Zondervan.

Lindsey, Hal. (1994). *Planet Earth—2000 A.D. Will Mankind Survive?* Palos Verdes, CA: Western Front.

Lintott, Andrew. (2008). *Cicero as Evidence: A Historian's Companion.* New York: Oxford UP.

Lippman, Laura. (2000). "The lovable liberal behind Bush's victory." *The New York Times,* December 31. http://www.nytimes.com/2000/12/31/arts/television-radio-the-lovable-liberal-behind-bush-s-victory.html.

Locke, Alain LeRoy. (2007). "The New Negro." In Henry Louis Gates and Gene Andrew Jarrett, eds. *The New Negro: Readings on Race, Representation, and African American Culture, 1892–1938.* Princeton, NJ: Princeton UP. (Orig. 1925.)

Long, Tom. (2000). "West Wing Fiction Wins over Reality with Idealism." *Detroit News,* October 5: C1.

Luhrmann, T. M. (2012). *When God Talks Back: Understanding the American Evangelical Relationship with God.* New York: Knopf.

Luntz, Frank. (2002). "President Bartlet, please take me back." *The New York Times,* December 28: A19.

MacRone, Michael. (1997). *Naughty Shakespeare.* New York: Cader Books.

Madison, James. "Letter to W. T. Barry." *The Founders' Constitution.* Volume 1, Chapter 18, Document 35. http://press-pubs.uchicago.edu/founders/documents/v1ch18s35.html.

Mann, Michael. (2005). *Incoherent Empire.* London and New York: Verso.

Marsalis, Wynton. (1989). "Marsalis Rips Rap and Heavy Metal Musicians." *Jet,* November 6: 22.

Marsden, George. (1991). *Understanding Fundamentalism and Evangelicalism.* Grand Rapids: William B. Eerdmans.

Marx, Gary T. (1974). "Thoughts on a Neglected Category of Social Movement Participant: The Agent Provocateur and the Informant." *American Journal of Sociology* 80: 402–42.

Mathewson, Dan. (2009). "End Times Entertainment: The *Left Behind* Series, Evangelicals, and Death Pornography." *Journal of Contemporary Religion* 24(3): 319–337.

Maxwell, Dominic. (2007). "His Islamic Majesty requests . . ." *The Times Theatre,* February 26. http://www.thetimes.co.uk/tto/arts/stage/theatre/article1867877.ece.

McAlister, Melani. (2003). "Prophecy, Politics, and the Popular: The *Left Behind* Series and Christian Fundamentalism's New World Order." *South Atlantic Quarterly* 102(4): 773–797.

McCabe, Janet. (2013). *The West Wing.* Detroit: Wayne State UP.

McConnell, Terry. (2003). "Liberty Is Dealt Another Blow." *The Edmonton Journal,* March 9: D2.

McKissack, Fred. (2000). "The West Wing Is Not a Wet Dream." *The Progressive* 64(5): 39.

McPherson, Lionel K. (2005). "Halfway Revolution: From That Gangsta Hobbes to Radical Liberals." In Derrick Darby and Tommie Shelby, eds. *Hip Hop and Philosophy*. Chicago: Open Court Publishing. 173–182.

McPherson, Miller, Lynn Smith-Lovin, and Matthew Brashears. (2006). "Social Isolation in America: Changes in Core Discussion Networks over Two Decades." *American Sociological Review* 71(3): 353–375.

Meacham, John. (2006). *American Gospel: God, the Founding Fathers, and the Making of a Nation*. New York: Random.

Meining, D. W. (1986). *The Shaping of America. A Geographical Perspective on 500 Years of History. Vol 1*. New Haven: Yale UP.

Metzger, Bruce M. (1992). *The Text of the New Testament: Its Transmission, Corruption, and Restoration*. Third ed. New York: Oxford UP.

Meyerson, Harold. (2005). "President of Fabricated Crises." *The Washington Post*, January 12. http://www.washingtonpost.com/ac2/wp-dyn/A2304-2005Jan11?language.

Miller, Matthew. (2000). "The real White House." *Brill's Content*, March 3: 88–95, 113.

Miller, Merle. (1974). *Plain Speaking: An Oral Biography of Harry S. Truman*. New York: Putnam.

Mink, Eric. (2000). "'West Wing' boldly confronts disease." *New York Daily News*, January 19. http://www.nydailynews.com/archives/entertainment/west-wing-boldly-confronts-disease-article-1.874838.

Mirra, Carl, ed. (2005). *Enduring Freedom or Enduring War? Prospects and Costs of the New American 21st Century*. Washington, DC: Maisonneuve Press.

Mitchell, Rick. (1993). "Mr. Scarface for himself." *Houston Chronicle*, October 10.

Mohamad, Husam. (2009). "Protestant Evangelicals and U. S. Policy Towards Israel." In Karolyn Kinane and Michael A. Ryan, eds. *End of Days: Essays on the Apocalypse from Antiquity to Modernity*. Jefferson, North Carolina: McFarland and Company. 199–215.

Monahan, Torin. (2008). "Marketing the beast: *Left Behind* and the apocalypse industry." *Media, Culture, and Society* 30: 814–830.

Moore, Matthew. (2011). "Wikileaks Cables: US Agrees to Tell Russia Britain's Nuclear Secrets." *The Telegraph*, February 4. http://www.telegraph.co.uk/news/worldnews/wikileaks/8304654/WikiLeaks-cables-US-agrees-to-tell-Russia-Britains-nuclear-secrets.html#.

Morris, Chris. (1998). "Future divined in a new 'trendsetters study.'" *Billboard*, September 26: 5, 146–147.

Morris, Edmund. (1999). *Dutch: A Memoir of Ronald Reagan*. New York: Modern Library.

Morrison, Richard. (2002). "Armageddon Ahead: Please Fasten Your Bible Belt." *The Times*, September 20: T2, 2–3.

Morrison, Toni. (1998). "Talk of the town: comment." *The New Yorker*, October 5. http://www.newyorker.com/archive/1998/10/05/1998_10_05_031_TNY_LIBRY_000016504.

Moyers, Bill. (1993). "Joseph Heller, Novelist." In Adam J. Sorkin, ed. *Conversations with Joseph Heller*. Jackson: University Press of Mississippi. 276–289.

Mueller, James E. (2006). *Towel Snapping the Press: Bush's Journey from Locker-Room Antics to Message Control*. Lanham, Md.: Rowman & Littlefield.

Murphy, Mary. (2000). "House Call." *TV Guide*, July 22: 15–16, 18, 20, 22, 24.

Nelson, Michael, ed. (2000). *The Presidency and the Political System*. Washington, DC: CQ Press.

Nussbaum, Martha. (2007). *The Clash Within: Democracy, Religious Violence, and India's Future*. Cambridge, MA: Belknap.

O'Leary, Stephen D. (1994). *Arguing the Apocalypse: A Theory of Millennial Rhetoric*. Oxford: Oxford UP.

Obama, Barack. (2006). *The Audacity of Hope*. New York: Three Rivers Press.

Obama, Barack. (2007). *Barack Obama in His Own Words*. Lisa Rogak, ed. New York: Carroll & Graf.

Office of the Coordinator for Counterterrorism; United States Department of State Publication 11409. (2007). "Country Reports on Terrorism." April 2007. http://www.state.gov/s/ct/rls/crt/2006/.

Ogbar, Jeffrey O. G. (2007). *Hip-Hop Revolution: The Culture and Politics of Rap*. Kansas: UP of Kansas.

Orssag, Rica Roadman. (2001). "Do You Recognize the Clinton West Wing in *The West Wing*?" *The Atlantic Monthly,* March. http://www.theatlantic.com/issues/2001/03/lehmann-rorszag.htm.

Orwell, George. (1998). "Why I Write." In Peter Davison, ed. *The Complete Works of George Orwell, vol. 18. Smothered Under Journalism 1946*. London: Secker and Warburg. 316–21.

Owe, Rob. (2000). "West Wing Elects to Keep Its Idealistic Platform." *Pittsburgh Post-Gazette*, October 4: E1.

Oxfeld, Jesse. (2000). "Census Consensus: *The West Wing* covered it better." *Brill's Content* 3(2): 94.

Parry-Giles, Trevor, and Shawn J. Parry-Giles. (2006). *The Prime-Time Presidency: The West Wing and U. S. Nationalism*. Urbana, IL: U. of Illinois Press.

Patterson, Bradley H. (2000). *The White House Staff: Inside The West Wing and Beyond*. Washington: Brookings Institution Press.

Pattillo-McCoy, Mary. (1999). *Black Picket Fences: Privilege and Peril Among the Black Middle Class*. Chicago: Chicago UP.

Paul, Gregory. (2009). "The Chronic Dependence of Popular Religiosity upon Dysfunctional Social Conditions." *Evolutionary Psychology* 7(3): 398–441.

Pautz, Johann. (2009). "The End Times Narratives of the American Far-Right." In Karolyn Kinane and Michael A. Ryan, eds. *End of Days: Essays on the Apocalypse from Antiquity to Modernity*. Jefferson, North Carolina: McFarland and Company. 265–286.

Pelikan, Jaroslav. (1989). "Afterword." In Thomas Jefferson. *The Jefferson Bible: The Life and Morals of Jesus of Nazareth*. Boston: Beacon.

Perkins, William Eric, ed. (1996). *Droppin' Science: Critical Essays on Rap Music and Hip Hop Culture*. Philadelphia: Temple UP.

Perry, Imani. (2004). *Prophets of the Hood: Politics and Poetics in Hip Hop*. Durham, London: Duke UP.

Peter, Laurence. (2010). "Power to the People EU-style." *BBC News,* November 22. http://www.bbc.co.uk/news/world-europe-11773647.

Philips, Chuck. (1993). "Rap Defense Doesn't Stop Death Penalty." *Los Angeles Times,* July 15. http://www.latimes.com/local/la-me-tupactxverdict15jul1593-story.html#page=1.

Plato. (1999). *Laws, Book VIII*. Trans. R. G. Bury. Cambridge, MA: Harvard UP.

Podhoretz, John. (2000). "The Liberal Imagination." *The Weekly Standard,* March 27: 23–27.

Poniewozik, James. (2001). "*West Wing*: Terrorism 101." *Time,* October 4. http://content.time.com/time/arts/article/0,8599,178042,00.html.

Popper, Karl R. (1945). *The Open Society and Its Enemies*. London: Routledge.

Porter, Dennis. (1981). *The Pursuit of Crime: Art and Ideology in Detective Fiction*. New Haven: Yale UP.

Potter, Russell A. (1995). *Spectacular Vernaculars: Hip-Hop and the Politics of Postmodernism*. Albany: SUNY Press.

Powell, Colin L. (2004). "A Strategy of Partnerships." *Foreign Affairs* 83:1 (Jan/Feb): 22–34.

Powers, Charles T. (1993). "Joe Heller, Author on Top of the World." In Adam J. Sorkin, ed. *Conversations with Joseph Heller*. Jackson: University Press of Mississippi. 137–143.

Price, Robert M. (2007). *The Paperback Apocalypse: How the Christian Church Was Left Behind*. Amherst, NY: Prometheus.

Putnam, Robert. (2000). *Bowling Alone*. New York: Simon and Schuster.

Quinn, Eithne. (2005). *Nothin' but a "G" Thang*. New York: Columbia UP.

Rampton, Sheldon, and John Stauber. (2006). *The Best War Ever: Lies, Damned Lies, and the Mess in Iraq*. New York: Penguin.

Rangwala, Glen. (2003). "British Intelligence Iraq Dossier Relies on Recycled Academic Articles." *Global Policy Forum,* February 5. http://www.globalpolicy.org/security/issues/iraq/attack/2003/0205plagiarism.htm.

Rasizade, Alec. (2002). "The New 'Great Game' in Central Asia after Afghanistan." *Alternatives: Turkish Journal of International Relations* 1:2. http://www.alternatives journal.net/volume1/number2/rasizade.htm.

Reagan, Ronald. (1981). "First inaugural, 20 January 1981." http://avalon.law.yale.edu/20th_century/reagan1.asp.

Reed, David A. (2008). *LEFT BEHIND Answered Verse by Verse*. Morrisville, NC: Lulu.com.

Reed, Julia. (1986). "The War Is Over, But There's Still a Catch." *U. S. News and World Report,* October 13: 67–68.

Richler, Mordecai. (1964). "A Captivating but Distorted Image." *Book Week (Sunday Herald Tribune),* September 13: 4, 19.

Riley, Jeff. (2002). "The West Wing." FindLaw Entertainment. http://e.findlaw.com/reviews/westwing/.

Boston, Rob. "If Best-Selling End-Times Author Tim LaHaye Has His Way, Church-State Separation Will Be . . . Left Behind." Americans United for Separation of Church and State, February 2002. https://www.au.org/church-state/february-2002-church-state/featured/left-behind.

Roberts, Sam. (2013). "Race Equality Is Still a Work in Progress, Survey Finds." *The New York Times,* August 22. http://www.nytimes.com/2013/08/23/us/americans-see-racial-equality-as-a-work-in-progress-pew-poll-finds.html?ref=us&_r=0&pagewanted=print.

Robin, Corey. (2004). *Remembrance of Empires Past: 9/11 and the End of the Cold War*. New York: New Press.

Robinson, Nina. (2012). "Misbehaving pupils ending up in court." *BBC News,* April 10. http://www.bbc.com/news/magazine-17664075.

Rollins, Peter C., and John O'Connor, eds. (2003). *The West Wing: The American Presidency as Television Drama.* Syracuse, NY: Syracuse UP.

Rose, Tricia. (1994). *Black Noise: Rap Music and Black Culture in Contemporary America.* Hanover, NH: Wesleyan UP.

Rosen, Ralph, and Donald Marks. (1999). "Comedies of transgression in gangsta rap and ancient classical poetry." *New Literary History* 30. 897–928.

Rossing, Barbara R. (2004). *The Rapture Exposed: The Message of Hope in the Book of Revelation.* New York: Basic.

Rowe, H. Edward. (1976). "Foreword." In Tim LaHaye. *The Bible's Influence on American History.* San Diego: Master Books/Christian Heritage College.

Rushe, Dominic. (2011). "The Bush-era tax cuts that sank the supercommittee." *The Guardian,* November 21. http://www.guardian.co.uk/business/2011/nov/21/bush-era-tax-cuts-supercommittee.

Sagan, Eli. (1991). *The Honey and the Hemlock: Democracy and Paranoia in Ancient Athens and Modern America.* Princeton: Princeton UP.

Sale, K. (1990). *The Conquest of Paradise: Christopher Columbus and the Columbian Legacy.* New York: Knopf.

Sample, Ian. (2005). "From frozen Alaska to the lab: a virus 39,000 times more virulent than flu." *The Guardian,* October 6. http://www.guardian.co.uk/society/2005/oct/06/health.medicineandhealth2.

Santayana, George, with Logan Pearsall Smith. (1920). "Ideal Immorality." *Little Essays: Drawn from the Writings of George Santayana.* London: Constable.

Sass, Samuel. (1989). "A Patently False Patent Myth." *Skeptical Inquirer* 13: 310–313.

Savage, Charlie. (2004). "Secrecy in the Bush Administration. Prepared by the US House of Representatives, Committee on Government Reform—Minority Staff Special Interest Division, September 14." http://oversight.house.gov/features/secrecy_report/pdf/pdf_secrecy_report.pd.

Savage, Charlie. (2007). *Takeover: The Return of the Imperial Presidency and the Subversion of American Democracy.* New York: Little, Brown.

Savage, Charlie. (2009). "Obama's war on terror may resemble Bush's in some areas." *The New York Times,* February 19. http://www.nytimes.com/2009/02/18/us/politics/18policy.html?_r=1&.

Savage, Charlie, and Mark Landler. (2011). "White House Defends Continuing U. S. Role in Libya Operation." *The New York Times,* June 16. http://www.nytimes.com/2011/06/16/us/politics/16powers.html?pagewanted=all.

Schama, Simon. (1987). *The Embarrassment of Riches: An Interpretation of Dutch Culture in the Golden Age.* New York: Knopf.

Schlesinger, Arthur M., Jr. (1986). *The Cycles of American History.* Boston: Houghton Mifflin.

Schlosser, Eric. (2004). *Reefer Madness: Sex, Drugs, and Cheap Labor in the American Black Market.* Boston: Mariner.

Schmitt, Christopher H. and Edward T. Pound. (2003). "Keeping Secrets." *U. S. News,* December 22. http://www.usnews.com/usnews/news/articles/secrecy/22secrecy.htm.

Schorer, Mark. (1961). *Sinclair Lewis: An American Life*. New York: McGraw-Hill.

Schumpeter, Joseph. (1950). *Capitalism, Socialism, and Democracy*. New York: Harper & Bros.

Schweizer, Peter. (2005). *Do As I Say (Not As I Do): Profiles in Liberal Hypocrisy*. New York: Doubleday.

Scotsman.com. (2005). "The spitting image of a true satirist." June 26. http://www.scotsman.com/lifestyle/books/features/the-spitting-image-of-a-true-satirist-1-1391345.

Scott-Tyson, Ann. (2003). "Rumsfeld: Moral Warrior." *The Edmonton Journal*, January 4: A12.

Searles, George J., ed. (1992). *Conversations with Philip Roth*. Jackson, MI: University Press of Mississippi.

Seed, David. (1989). *The Fiction of Joseph Heller: Against the Grain*. Basingstoke: Macmillan.

Shabazz, Julian L. D. (1992). *United States vs. Hip Hop: the Historical and Political Significance of Rap Music*. Conquering Books.

Shapiro, David. (1965). *Neurotic Styles*. New York: Basic.

Shapiro, Fred R. (2006). *The Yale Book of Quotations*. New Haven: Yale UP.

Shipman, Tim. (2009). "Barack Obama Sends Bust of Winston Churchill on Its Way Back to Britain." *The Telegraph*, February 14. http://www.telegraph.co.uk/news/worldnews/barackobama/4623148/Barack-Obama-sends-bust-of-Winston-Churchill-on-its-way-back-to-Britain.html.

Shuck, Glenn W. (2005). *Marks of the Beast: The Left Behind Novels and the Struggle for Evangelical Identity*. New York: New York UP.

Shusterman, Richard. (1992). "The Fine Art of Rap." *Pragmatist Aesthetics*. Oxford: Blackwell.

Sizer, Stephen R. (2004). *Christian Zionism: Road-Map to Armageddon?* Leicester, UK: IVP.

SkyNews. (2013). "Kendrick Lamar: 50 Cent, Diddy & Lohan Respond." August 15. http://news.sky.com/story/1128980/kendrick-lamar-50-cent-diddy-and-lohan-respond.

Smail, J. Kenneth. (1995). "Confronting the 21st Century's Hidden Crisis: Reducing Human Numbers by 80 Percent." *NPG (Negative Population Growth) Forum Series*. http://www.npg.org/forum_series/Confronting21stCenturyHIddenCrisis019.pdf.

Smith, Christian. (1998). *American Evangelism: Embattled and Thriving*. Chicago, U. of Chicago Press.

Smith, David Livingstone. (2007). *The Most Dangerous Animal: Human Nature and the Origins of War*. New York: St. Martin's Griffin.

Smith, Zadie. (2005). "The Zen of Eminem." *Vibe*, January: 91–98.

Sorkin, Aaron. (2000). *PBS NewsHour*, September 27. http://www.pbs.org/newshour/media/west_wing/sorkin.html.

Sorkin, Aaron. (2003). *The West Wing: Seasons 3 and 4: The Shooting Scripts*. New York: Newmarket Press.

Sorkin, Adam J., ed. *Conversations with Joseph Heller*. Jackson: University Press of Mississippi, 1993.

Standaert, Michael. (2006). *Skipping Towards Armageddon: The Politics and Propaganda of the Left Behind Novels and the LaHaye Empire*. Brooklyn, New York: Soft Skull.

Stockholm International Peace Research Institute. (2002). "Chapter 8: Military Expenditure." *SIPRI Yearbook 2005: Armaments, Disarmament and International Security*. Oxford: Oxford University Press. http://yearbook2005.sipri.org/ch8/app8A.

Stokes, Doug. (2005). *America's Other War: Terrorizing Colombia*. London, New York: Zed Books.

Storey, John. (1993). *An Introductory Guide to Cultural Theory and Popular Culture*. Athens, GA: U. of Georgia Press.

Strauss, Leo. (1964). *The City and Man*. Chicago: University of Chicago Press.

Strombeck, Matthew. (2006). "Invest in Jesus: Neoliberalism and the *Left Behind* Novels." *Cultural Critique* 64: 161–194.

Stromseth, Jane E. (1996), "Understanding Constitutional War Powers Today: Why Methodology Matters: Presidential War Power." *The Yale Law Journal* 106(3): 845–915.

Suskind, Ron. (2004). "Without a Doubt." *New York Times Magazine*, October 17: 44–51; 64; 102; 106.

Swirski, Peter. (2005). *From Lowbrow to Nobrow*. Montreal, London: McGill-Queen's UP.

Swirski, Peter. (2006). "Upton Sinclair: *The Jungle* (1906); *Oil* (1927)." In *Magill Survey of American Literature; Revised Edition*. Pasadena: Salem. 2335–2341.

Swirski, Peter. (2009). "The Historature of the American Empire: Joseph Heller's *Picture This*." *I Sing the Body Politic: History as Prophecy in Contemporary American Literature*. Montreal, London: McGill-Queen's UP.

Swirski, Peter. (2010). *Ars Americana, Ars Politica: Partisan Expression in Contemporary American Literature and Culture*. Montreal, London: McGill-Queen's UP.

Swirski, Peter. (2011). *American Utopia and Social Engineering in Literature, Social Thought, and Political History*. New York: Routledge.

Swirski, Peter. (2014). "To Sacrifice One's Intellect Is More Demonic Than Divine: American Literature and Politics in *Left Behind: A Novel of the Earth's Last Days*." *European Journal of American Studies* 9:2. http://ejas.revues.org/10342.

Swofford, Anthony. *Jarhead: A Marine's Chronicle of the Gulf War and Other Battles*. New York: Scribner, 2003.

Taleb, Nassim Nicholas. (2007). *Fooled by Randomness: The Hidden Role of Chance in Life and In the Markets*. London: Penguin.

Tavakoli-Far, Nastaran. (2013). "Artists Use Data to Make Political Statements." *BBC News*, February 7. http://www.bbc.co.uk/news/magazine-21018205.

Thatcher, Margaret. (1975). "House of Commons Speech, 1975, March 11." Margaret Thatcher Foundation, Hansard HC [888/304–17].

The Baltimore Sun. (2011). "'Wire' creator responds to top cop's criticism." January 18. http://weblogs.baltimoresun.com/news/crime/blog/2011/01/simon_responds_to_bealefelds_c.html.

The Economist. (2011). "Teaching Standards: Don't Know Much About History." February 19: 44.

The Economist. (2011). "Guttbye Guttenberg." March 5: 32.

The Guardian. (2002). "50% see Blair as Bush's lapdog." November 14. http://www.guardian.co.uk/politics/2002/nov/14/foreignpolicy.uk1

The Guardian. (2003). "Apocalypse Now." June 12. http://www.theguardian.com/books/2003/jun/12/londonreviewofbooks.

The Mail on Sunday. (2005). "A Planet for the President, by Alistair Beaton." June 12: 64.

The Sunshine Project. (2003). "Lethal Virus from 1918 Genetically Reconstructed: US Army scientists create 'Spanish Flu' virus in laboratory—medical benefit questionable." October 9. http://www.sunshine-project.org/publications/pr/pr091003.html.

Theatre Voice. (2007). "Ace-satirist Alistair Beaton laughs at power." March 28. http://www.theatrevoice.com/2165/interview-alistair-beaton-the-award-winning-satirist-and-pl/ - .UTf56hyKVJk.

Thomas, Don. (1986). "Putting the Rap on 'Rap Attacks.'" *Big Red,* July 26: 20–21.

Thucydides. *The History of the Peloponnesian War.* Trans. William Smith. London: John Watts, 1753. Eighteenth Century Collections Online. Gale Group. http://galenet.galegroup.com/servlet/ECCO.

Thurman, Scott, dir. (2012). *The Revisionaries.* Documentary film.

Tillich, Paul. (1948). *The Shaking of the Foundations.* New York: Scribner's.

Tonneson, Stein. (2004). "The Imperial Temptation." *Security Dialogue* 35(3): 329–343.

Topping, Keith. (2002). *The West Wing: Inside Bartlet's White House.* London: Virgin.

Trend, David. (1996). *Radical Democracy: Identity, Citizenship and the State.* New York: Routledge.

Tucker, Ken. (2000). "Meet the Prez." *Entertainment Weekly,* February 25. http://www.ew.com/ew/article/0,,275497,00.html.

Turley, Jonathan. (2011). "Obama: A disaster for civil liberties." *Los Angeles Times,* September 29. http://articles.latimes.com/2011/sep/29/opinion/la-oe-turley-civil-liberties-20110929.

Twain, Mark. (1992). "The Cradle of Liberty." *Collected Tales, Sketches, Speeches and Essays, 1891–1910.* New York: Library of America. (Orig. 1892.)

Twitchell, James B. (2007). *Shopping for God: How Christianity Went from In Your Heart to In Your Face.* New York: Simon and Schuster.

US Army Special Warfare School. (1962). *Concepts for US Army Counterinsurgency Activities.* http://www.adtdl.army.mil/rtddltextv.html.

US Department of Defense. (2003). "Base Structure Report: Fiscal Year 2003 Baseline." http://www.defenselink.mil/news/Jun2003/basestructure2003.pdf.

US Department of Defense. (2000). "Joint Vision 2020, Full Spectrum Dominance." May 2000. http://www.dtic.mil/jointvision/jv2020a.pdf.

US Department of Defense. (2003). "FY 2003 International Affairs Request—Summary." *State Department budget.* http://www.state.gov/s/d/rm/rls/iab/2003/7807.htm.

US Energy Information Administration. (2011). "Annual Energy Review 2011." http://www.eia.gov/totalenergy/data/annual/pdf/sec1.pdf.

US Government Printing Office. (2002). *Authorization for Use of Military Force Against Iraq Resolution of 2002.* http://frwebgate.access.gpo.gov/cgi-bin/getdoc.cgi?dbname=107_cong_public_laws&docid=f:publ243.107.

USA Today. (2007). "Obama Unveils Innovation Agenda at Google." *USA Today,* November 14. http://usatoday30.usatoday.com/news/pdf/obama-at-google-11-14-2007.pdf.

Van Susteren, Greta. (2011). "Rumsfeld Reflects on 9/11, 10 Years Later and U. S. Troop Reduction in Iraq." *Fox News,* September 6. http://www.foxnews.com/on-air/on-the-record/2011/09/07/rumsfeld-reflects-911-10-years-later-and-us-troop-reduction-iraq.

Vernon, Alex, with Neal Creighton Jr., Greg Downey, Rob Holmes, and Dave Trybula. (1999). *The Eyes of Orion: Five Tank Lieutenants in the Persian Gulf War.* Kent, Ohio: Kent State UP.

Vidal, Gore. (1999). "True Gore." Salon, May 11. http://www.salon.com/1999/05/10/vidal/.

Vladov, Andrei. (2012). "Bulgaria prosecutes rapper Misho Shamara over flag." *BBC News,* October 3. http://www.bbc.com/news/world-europe-19799358.

Wacker, Grant. (2001). *Heaven Below.* Cambridge, MA: Harvard UP.

Wagner, Alex. (2010). "Obama's Oil Spill Response: On Top of It, or Too Little Too Late?" *Politics Daily,* May 28. http://www.politicsdaily.com/2010/05/28/obamas-oil-spill-response-on-top-of-it-or-too-little-too-lat/.

Wal-Mart: The High Cost of Low Price. (2005). Dir. Robert Greenwald. Brave New Films DVD.

Watkins, S. Craig. (1998). *Representing Hip Hop Culture and the Production of Black Culture.* Chicago: U. of Chicago Press.

Watkins, C. Craig. (2005). *Hip Hop Matters: Politics, Pop Culture, and the Struggle for the Soul of the Movement.* Boston: Beacon Press.

Waxman, Sharon. (2000). "Inside *The West Wing*'s new world." *George,* November: 54–59.

Wear, Ben. (2002). "Federal File." *Education Weekly* 22: 7, 23.

Weiner, Eric. (2008). "Will democracy make you happy? *Foreign Policy,* February 19. http://www.foreignpolicy.com/articles/2008/02/19/will_democracy_make_you_happy.

Weingarten, Marc. (1998). "Large and in Charge." *Los Angeles Times,* July 26: 8–9, 81.

Welna, David. (2011). "Patriot Act Extension Came Down To The Wire." NPR. http://www.npr.org/2011/05/27/136704247/renewing-the-patriot-act-came-down-to-the-wire.

Whisenant, Edgar C. (1988). *88 Reasons Why the Rapture Will Be in 1988.* Nashville, TN: Whisenant/World Bible Society.

White House. (1970). "CIA, Notes on Meeting with the President on Chile, September 15, 1970." *Chile and the United States: Declassified Documents relating to the Military Coup, 1970–1976.* http://www2.gwu.edu/~nsarchiv/NSAEBB/NSAEBB8/nsaebb8.htm.

White House. (2002). "The National Security Strategy of the United States of America September 2002." White House: Washington, DC, September 17. http://www.whitehouse.gov/nsc/nss.pdf.

Whitehouse, Sheldon. (2008). "Whitehouse: Bush's Lies 'Rot the Very Fiber of Democracy.'" June 5. http://emptywheel.firedoglake.com/2008/06/05/whitehouse-bushs-lies-rot-the-very-fiber-of-democracy/.

Why We Fight. (2006). Jarecki, Eugene, dir. Sony DVD.

Wiarda, Howard J. (2007). *Latin American Politics and Development*. Boulder: Westview Press.

Wigglesworth, Michael. (2012). *The Day of Doom, or a Poetical Description of the Great and Last Judgment: With Other Poems* London: Forgotten Books. (Orig. 1662.)

Wilkinson, Paul. (2007). *For Zion's Sake: Christian Zionism and the Role of John Nelson Darby*. Milton Keynes, UK: Paternoster.

Wilson, Charles. (1968). *The Dutch Republic and the Civilization of the Seventeenth Century*. London: World University Library.

Wilson, Nathan D. (2001). *Right Behind: A Parody of Last Days Goofiness*. Canon Press.

Wilson, Nathan D. (2003). *Supergeddon: A Really Big Geddon*. Canon Press.

Wolfe, Alan. 2006. *Does American Democracy Still Work?* New Haven: Yale UP.

Woodward, Bob. (2003). *Bush at War*. New York: Simon & Schuster.

Woolley, John, and Gerhard Peters. (2001). "George W. Bush. Remarks at the Swearing-In Ceremony for Ann M. Veneman as Secretary of Agriculture. March 2, 2001." *The American Presidency Project*. http://www.presidency.ucsb.edu/ws/index.php?pid=45736.

Wren, Celia. (1999). "The Inside Dope: NBC's West Wing." *Commonweal* 126 (December 3):17–19.

Wright, Jane. (2004). "Lunatics in the White House? Surely not?" *Camden New Journal*, November 19. http://www.camdennewjournal.co.uk/archive/181104/r181104_01.htm.

Yovanovich, Gordana. (2003). *The New World Order: Corporate Agenda and Parallel Reality*. Montreal: McGill-Queen's UP.

Zagorin, Perez. (2005). *Thucydides: An Introduction for the Common Reader*. Princeton: Princeton UP.

Zap2it.com. (2000). "Indecision 2000: 'West Wing'-Style." November 9.

Zinn, Howard. (2003). *The Twentieth Century: A People's History*. New York: Perennial.

Index

1000, 60
1994, 60
2 Live Crew, 120, 127
2000 National Security Strategy, 34
2004 National Military Strategy, 34
50 Cent, 118–119, 129, 134
666, 60
8 Mile, 113
88 Reasons Why the Rapture Will Be in 1988, 59

"A Change Is Gonna Come," 139
"A Disaster for Civil Liberties," 92
A General and Connected View of the Prophecies Relative to the Conversion, Restoration, Union, and Future Glory of the Houses of Judah and Israel; the Progress and Final Overthrow, of the AntiChristian Confederacy in the Land of Palestine; and the Ultimate General Diffusion of Christianity, 59
"A Good Day," 3
"A Great Day in Harlem '98," 116
"A Great Day in Harlem," 116
"A Letter to the Minister of Defense," 128
"A Modest Proposal," 105
"A Nation at Risk," 72
A Planet for the President, 2, 5, 56, 76, 81, 84–88, 94, 97, 101, 102–103–105, 138
A Question of Fact, 84
A Tribe Called Quest, 124

Abaddon, 60
Abate, Tom, 169n36
Abbott, Abbott E., 81
ABC News, 144
"About Last Night," 106
"About the Author," 169n12
Abu-Janal, Mumia, 171n19
Aceyalone, 124
Achilles (mythical character), 86
Adams, John, 16, 28, 31
Aeschines, 23
Agee, Marilyn J., 59
Agents of Power, 13
Ahmadinejad, Mahmoud, 4, 7
Ain't a Damn Thang Changed, 130
Airport, 53
Akbarzadeh, Shahram, 168n27
al-Bashir, Omar, 26
Al-Qaeda, 69
al-Zawahiri, Ayman, 37
Albright, Madeleine, 143
Alcibiades, 33
Alda, Alan, 144
Alexander the Great, 23, 41
All Eyes on Me, 113, 171n6
All in the Family, 80
All the King's Men, 105
Allen, Brooke, 170n38
Allende, Salvador, 35–36
Allnutt, Frank, 60
Alten, Steve, 16
Altman, Robert, 142
Altschull, J. Herbert, 13, 167n15
Amalric, 51
Ambler, Eric, 78

American Political Fiction, 4, 8, 14, 17
American Utopia and Social Engineering, 14
Amos, Jonathan, 170n17
Anderson, Marian, 108
Anderson, Roger, 172n12
Animal Farm, 12
Anytus, 31
Apocalypse Dawn, 61
Apocalypse, 60
Apollyon: The Destroyer Is Unleashed, 169n9
Apology, 23
Appleby, Humphrey (character), 161
Árbenz, Jacobo, 35
Archer, Iva (character), 74
Archer, Jeffrey, 50
Are We Living in the End Times?, 78
Arendt, Hanna, 97
Aristophanes, 23, 86
Aristotle Contemplating the Bust of Homer, 22
Aristotle, 21, 23–25, 27, 34, 45
Arkin, Alan, 19
Armour, J. Ogden, 2
Armstrong, Louis, 109, 168n24
Ars Americana, Ars Politica, 14
Arsonists, 124
Ashcroft, John, 33, 70, 125
Asimov, Isaac, 54
Attie, Eli, 3, 141, 144
Attlee, Clement, 173N26
Avalon, Frankie, 118
Axelrod, David, 144

B-Real, 134
Babbitt, 101–102
Bach, Johann Sebastian, 115
Bachmann, Michele, 4, 73
Baker, James, 16
Bakker, Jim, 57
Balizet, Carol, 60
Ballard, Janette, 172n13, 172n15
Balsam, Martin, 19
Bambaataa, Afrika, 113, 134

"Barack Obama: 'Full confidence' in CIA director," 173n34
Baraka, Amiri, 127
Barnes, Pastor, 52–53
Barr, James, 65
Bartlet, Josiah (character), 3, 81, 139–140, 151, 159, 161
"Base Structure Report," 34
Batten, William, 41
BBC News, 173n34
Beard, Charles Austin, 10
Beastie Boys, 171n3
Beaton, Alistair, 2, 5–6, 56, 76, 79, 81–88, 91, 93–94, 97–100, 102–105, 129, 142
Beatty, Warren, 157
BeauSeigneur, James, 60
Begala, Paul, 97, 139
Behold a Pale Horse, 60
bell hook, 119
Bell, Daniel, 164
Bell, Derrick, 130
Bennett, William, 116
Bergen, Wesley J., 169n10
Berlitz, Charles, 59
Bernanke, Ben, 89
Bernstein, Michael A., 169n20
Betzer, Dan, 60
Bible, 5, 52–53, 56–58, 60–65, 68, 76–78
Biden, Joe, 126, 130
Bilakovics, Steven, 172n18
Big Brother, 146
Big Sha, 128
Bigsby, Christopher, 158
Billboard, 110
bin Laden, Osama, 35
"Bin Laden," 124
Black Noise: Rap Music and Black Culture in Contemporary America, 135
Black Panthers, 113, 123
Blackalicious, 124
Blair, Tony, 3, 37, 84, 97–98, 172n35
Blondie, 113
Bloomberg, Mike, 126

Blues People, 114
Body By God, 62
Bolden, Buddy, 109
Bonaparte, Napoleon, 59
Bond, Jon R., 172n16
Bono, 96
Bontemps, Arna, 109
Book of Revelation, 61
Booth, Lauren, 171n33
Borgen, 143
Bork, Robert, 116–117
Boston, Rob, 169n2
Bowie, David, 115
Bowling Alone, 165
Boyd, Al, 82, 97
Boyer, Paul S., 169n13
Brandes, Stuart D., 168n33
Brechin, Steven R., 170n15
Bremer, Paul, 44
Briody, Dan, 168n35
Broder, John M., 170n21
Brother Ali, 124
Brown, Gordon, 84
Brown, Reggie, 4, 7
Brown, Sterling, 109, 111
Brownback, Sam, 126
Bubba Sparxxx (hip hop artist), 115, 121
Buchanan, Pat, 64
Buckley, Christopher, 85–86
Buckley, William F., Jr., 77–78
Buffet, Warren, 10
Bugliosi, Vincent, 169n38
Bulgakov, Mikhail, 86
Bull, Alister, 170n19
Bulworth, 157
Burkeman, Oliver, 170n14
Burnham, Gilbert, 169n38
Burns, Ken, 115
Bush at War, 81
"Bush Killa," 129
Bush, George Herbert (Bush I), 3, 9, 134, 162
Bush, George Walker (also Bush II, Dubya), 2, 5, 10, 15, 20, 22, 27, 29–31, 33–34, 36–38, 43, 47, 50, 64, 69–72, 77, 81–82, 84–96, 98, 100–101, 124–125, 127, 137, 139–140, 142, 146, 161, 168n13, 169n38, 171n23
Bush, Jeb, 81
Butler, Samuel, 27
Butts, Calvin, 117, 123
Byrne, Ciar, 170n5, 170n10, 171n33
Byrne, Vicki (character), 68
Byron, George Gordon, 84, 167n11

Caddell, Patrick, 3
Cahill, Karen (character), 139
Cain, James M., 74
Calder Peter, 167n18
Caldicott, Helen, 168n24, 169n36
Camping, Harold, 59
Capote, Truman, 25
Capra, Frank, 4, 142
Carlin, George, 11, 121
Carln, Brendan, 167n6
Carlson, Carole C., 59
Carpathia, Nicolae (character), 52–54, 57–58
Carter, Jimmy, 3, 139
Casor, John, 107
Cassandra (mythical character), 21
Cassata, Donna, 170n10
Castle, John, 169n6
Castro, Fidel, 78
Catch-22, 19–20, 22–23, 45, 81
"Cause of Death," 38
Ceausescu, Nicolae, 57
"Central Public Online Collection platform for the FCI," 156
Chaddock, Gail Russell, 170n9
Chafets, Zev, 169n2
Chambers, Frank (character), 74–75
Chandler, Raymond, 74
Chang, Jeff, 171n4, 172n26
Channel Live, 123
Chapman, Jennie, 169n10
Chavez, Cesar, 73
Chávez, Hugo, 157
Che, 13
"Checkmate," 134

Cheney, Dick, 10, 31–33, 37–38, 43–44, 47, 85, 89, 124, 161
Chiang, Kai-shek, 26
Chomsky, Noam, 91, 168n21
Christ (*see* Jesus)
Christ Clone Trilogy, 60
Chuck D, 113, 128, 135
Church Times, 81, 170n1
Church, J. Forrester, 173n21
Churchill, Winston, 28, 98
Cicero, Marcus Tullius, 46
Cinderella (character), 71
Citizen Kane, 142
Civilization's Last Hurrah, 60
Clancy, Tom, 53
Clapton, Eric, 115
Clarke, Jonathan, 168n23
Clayburn, James, 16
Cleon, 31, 86
Clinton, Bill, 3–4, 9, 16, 54, 87, 94, 96, 124, 129–130, 139, 142–143, 159, 163
Clinton, George, 124, 171n4, 171n6
Clinton, Hillary Rodham, 124, 126
Clooney, George, 77
Codex Tchacos, 57
Coen, Jan Pieterszoon, 40
Cohen, Gary, 60
Cohen, Leonard, 119
Colbert, Stephen, 15
Cole, M. R., 170n33
Collins, Chuck, 167n12
Columbus, Christopher, 98, 131
"Come Clean," 123
Common, 123–124
Conason, Joe, 167n9
Condoleezza, Rice, 82
Condon, Richard, 2
Cook, Harold, 168n30
Cooke, Sam, 134
Cooper, James Fenimore, 2
Cregg, C. J. (character), 139, 141
Crichton, Michael, 86
Cronin, Robber Barons, 172n18
Crosby, Alfred W., 171n25
Cullen, Countee, 109

Daily Life in Rembrandt's Holland, 23
Daily News, 112
Darby, John Nelson, 50–51
David, Bruce, 168n17
Davis, Gerald L., 171n4
Davis, Miles, 116
Davis, T. C., 169n33
Day-Lewis, Daniel, 73
Day, Amber, 85
De la démocratie en Amérique, 3
De La Soul, 124
de Tocqueville, Alexis, 3, 161, 164
Dead Funny: Humor in Hitler's Germany, 104
dead prez, 11–12, 125–127, 172n25
"Dear Mama," 133
Debs, Eugene V., 88
Decision Points, 92
"Defense Planning Guidance," 37
Deggans, Eric, 172n31
DeLay, Tom, 70
Dershowitz, Alan, 170n42
Descartes, René, 40
DeYoung, Karen, 170n14
Dick Tracy, 55
Dickey, James, 114
Dido, 128
Digable Planets, 124
Dion (of Syracuse), 29
Disposable Heroes of Hiphoprisy, 124–125
DJ Premier, 116
Django Unchained, 107
Documentary Special, 139
Dolan, David, 60
Dole, Bob, 116
Dome Alone with Alistair Beaton, 84
Don Juan on the Rocks, 84
"Doo Rags," 120
Doomsday 1999 A.D., 59
Dos Passos, John, 44
Double G, 116
Double Indemnity, 74
Douglass, Frederick, 126, 130
Dowd, Maureen, 139, 172n5
Downbeat, 116

Dr. Dre, 110, 113–114, 128
"Dr. Strangelove or: How I Learned to Stop Worrying and Love the Bomb," 81
Dracula, Vlad, 57
Dragnet, 142
Dreier, David, 151
Dreiser, Theodore, 133
Dreyfuss, Robert, 169n2
Drop the Dead Donkey, 84
Du Bois, W. E. B., 121
Duberstein, Kenneth, 3
Duchamp, Marcel, 116
Duell, Charles Holland, 1
Dukakis, Michael, 138, 162
Dulles, Allen, 78
Dulles, John Foster, 31
Dumas, Alexandre (*pére*), 24
Durham, Hattie (character), 54
Duskin, J. Eric, 168n27
Dylan, Bob, 119
Dyson, Michael Eric, 119, 134, 172n34

Eazy-E, 119, 134
Ebert, Roger, 140, 172n6
Ebony (magazine), 121
Edwards, Don, 129
Edwards, Jon, 126
Edwards, Jonathan, 54
Efil4ZaggiN (*see* Niggaz4Life)
Eilperin, Juliet, 170n19
Einstein, Albert, 29, 39
Eisenhower, Dwight D., 29, 39, 42, 69, 77, 89
Elber, Lynn, 173n32
Electric Ink, 84
Eliasoph, Nina, 172n17
Eliot, George Fielding, 168n10
Eliot, T. S., 109
Elizabeth I, 131
Ellington, Duke, 109, 128
Elton, Ben, 81
Emanuel, Rahm, 72
Eminem, 113, 121, 124, 128
"Enemies," 3
Esquire, 116

Ethics, 23
Evolutionary Psychology, 76

Faber, George Stanley, 59
Fahrenheit 9/11, 124
"Faith-Based Initiative," 172n14
Falwell, Jerry, 50, 62, 70
Farmer, Ben, 170n13
Fear of a Black Hat, 134
Feelgood, 84
Feller, Ben, 170n13
Felsenthal, Carol, 170n2
Ferguson, Niall, 168n17
Fight the Power, 113, 135
Firing Line, 77
Fisher, Louis, 170n13
Fishkin, James S., 172n19
Fitzgerald, Ella, 109
Fitzgerald, Francis Scott, 2
Fitzwater, Marlin, 3
Flame, 115
Flatland, 81
Fleischer, Ari, 95
Fletcher, Fletcher J. (character), 81, 83, 85–86, 91, 93–94, 96–100
Flight into Danger, 53
Flinck, Govert, 45
"For Esmé—With Love and Squalor," 100
Ford, Gerald, 22, 81, 112, 119, 139
Ford, Henry, 102
Foreign Affairs, 34
Forman, Murray, 171n4
Fortune, 111
Fourth Column, 84
Franken, Al, 15
Franklin, Benjamin, 149
Franti, Michael, 125
Frazier, Joe, 111
Freddoso, David, 72, 170n42
"Freedonia," 3
Freeman, Daniel A., 170n15
Frey, Bruno S., 169n5, 169n24, 173n24, 173n38
Fritz, Ben, 173n25
Froomkin, Dan, 170n11

Frosch, Dan, 170n21
Frykholm, Amy, 170n40
Fuchs, Klaus, 29
"Fuck tha Police," 128, 134
Fukuyama, Francis, 168n18
"Full Spectrum Dominance," 168n18
Fundamentalism, 65
Funkadelic, 113
"FY 2003 International Affairs
    Request—Summary," 168n32

Gaddafi, Muammar, 93
Galen, Claudius (of Pergamon), 24
Gang Starr, 116
Garfunkel, Art, 122
Gates, Henry Louis, 121
Gates, Robert, 90, 171n1, 171n17
Geithner, Tim, 89
Generation Kill, 158
Get Rich or Die Tryin, 129
Geto Boys, 120
Gianelli, Bruno (character), 139, 143
Gianos, Philip L., 167n20
Giglio, Ernest, 167n20
Gil Thorp, 49
Gillespie, Dizzy, 116
Gingrich, Newt, 3–4, 9, 16
Giuliani, Rudy, 126
Glorious Appearing, 55
Goatsong, 26
Gold, Malcolm, 169n23
Goldenberg, Suzanne, 170n16, 170n20
Goldin, Claudia, 167n11
Good As Gold, 45
Goodie Mob, 122
Gore, Al, 3, 69, 90, 94, 96, 126,
    139–140, 144, 146
Göring, Hermann, 104
Gospel of Judas, 57
Gramm, Phil, 9
Grandmaster Flash and the Furious
    Five, 110, 116
Grandmaster Melle Mel, 110
Green, Robert, 168n6
Greenfeld, Josh, 172n22
Gribben, Crawford, 169n14, 169n28

Grondin, David, 168n17
Grunwald, Mandy, 139
Guevara, Che, 76
Guinness World Records, 33
Guru, 116, 124
"Guttbye Guttenberg," 173n25
Guyatt, Nicholas, 169n19

Hadley, Stephen, 168n24
Hail to the Chief, 142
Hailey, Arthur, 53
Hall, Richard, 170n8
Halper, Stefan, 168n23
Hamilton, Andy, 170n4
Hammett, Dashiell, 74
Hammond, Tom, 169n6
Hampton, Mandy (character), 139
Hancock, Herbie, 116
Harnden, Toby, 170n19, 171n23
Harris, John F., 170n42
Harris, Katherine, 77
Hatfields (characters), 103
Hayes, Isaac, 114
Hayes, Roland, 108
Hayes, Rutherford B., 146–147
Haynes, Kevin, 167n2
"He Shall, From Time to Time . . ." 143
Heart of a Dog, 86
"Heavy Mental," 122
Hegghammer, Thomas, 168n26
Hellenica, 23
Heller, Joseph, 5, 19–34, 35–36, 38–42,
    44–46, 81, 141
Helms, Jesse, 70
Helms, Richard, 35
Hemingway, Ernest, 2, 100
Henderson, Fletcher, 109
Henry, Patrick, 149
Hentz, Caroline Lee, 15
Herman, Susan N., 170n9
Herzog, Rudolph, 104
Hesiod, 23
Hess, Stephen, 167n8
High and Mighty, 124
"High Quality European Education for
    All," 156

Hinds, Julie, 173n23
Hip Hop Matters, 118
Hirsch, Tim, 170n17
History of the Peloponnesian War, 23
Hitler, Adolf, 26, 102, 104
Hoff, Jimmy, 144
Hofstadter, Richard, 29
Hoggan, James, 170n18
Holt, Tom, 26
Holtzman, Elizabeth, 92, 170n11
Home to Harlem, 109
Homer, 20, 23–24, 41
Hoover, J. Edgar, 29, 78, 103
Horowitz, David, 69
House of Cards, 143
Howard, Jordon, 170n19
Huckabee, Mike, 50, 169n2
Hudson, Henry, 22
Huff, Walter (character), 75
Huggins, Martha K., 168n22
Hughes, Langston, 131, 173n21
Hussein, Saddam, 31, 33, 35, 37, 47, 98
Huston, James H., 172n30

"I Smell Pussy," 118
"I'm Bad," 119, 122
"Icarus," 96
Ice Cube, 123, 127, 134
Ice-T, 113, 127
"Ideal Immortality," 45
"Idiot Nation," 70
Immortal Technique, 38, 124
Infants of the Spring, 109
Inhofe, James, 170n42
Inside Job, 170n7
"Iraq—Its Infrastructure of Concealment, Deception and Intimidation," 36
"Isaac and Ishmael," 138
Isakhan, Benjamin, 172n16
It Can't Happen Here, 100, 102
It's Still the Economy, Stupid, 97
Ivins, Molly, 64
Ivins, Viv (character), 64

J-Live, 124
Jackson, Joyce Marie, 171n4

Jackson, Michael, 73
Jacoby, Susan, 118
Jadakiss, 125, 134
Jaffe, Greg, 170n14
Janney, Alison, 139
Jansen, Lesa, 170n19
Jarrett, Andrew, 171n1, 171n17
Jay-Z, 123–124, 129–130
"Jazz Thing," 116
Jazz, 115
Jeff, DJ Jazzy, 110
Jefferson, Thomas, 16, 28, 31–32, 74, 77, 149
Jenkins, Jerry B., 5, 50, 53–56, 59, 61, 65, 77–78
Jerome, Fred, 168n10
Jeru the Damaja, 123
Jesus, 5, 24, 41, 49, 50, 52, 55–58
Johnson, Alex M., 170n6
Johnson, Anthony, 107
Johnson, Georgia Douglas, 109
Johnson, Hiram, 149
Johnson, J. Rosamond, 109
Johnson, James Weldon, 109
Johnson, Lyndon B., 20, 22, 44
Jolie, Angelina, 76
Jones, LeRoi, 114, 171n11
Jones, Quincy, 116
Jones, Stephanie Tubbs, 16
Jurassic-5, 124

Kagan, Robert, 34, 168n18, 168n24
Kain, Erik, 170n12
Kanye West, 123–124, 130
Kasser, Rodolphe, 169n11
Kauffman, Bill, 170n34
Kazantzakis, Nikos, 56
Kegley, Charles W. Jr., 168n17
Kelly, Alison, 167n16
Kelly, Moira, 139
Kemp, Jack, 50, 169n2
"Kendrick Lamar: 50 Cent, Diddy & Lohan Respond," 172n36
Kennard, Matt, 170n21
Kennedy, John F. (also JFK), 20, 22, 73, 163

Kennedy, Paul, 39
Kennedy, Robert, 162
Kerry, John, 69, 129, 139
Kessler, Glenn, 170n37
Keyes, Cheryl L., 171n4, 172n27
Killah Priest, 120, 122, 124
Kim, Jong-Un, 7, 27
Kind of Blue, 115
King, Martin Luther, 126
King, Rodney, 97, 130
Kingdom Come, 55
Kirban, Salem, 60
Kissinger, Henry, 45, 60, 87
Klein, Naomi, 167n12, 168n16
Knibbs, Harriet (character), 105
Kohut, Andrew, 167n13
Koresh, David, 61
Kot, Greg, 172n23
Kozol, Jonathan, 170n35
Kramnick, Isaac, 170n42
Krassner, Paul, 168n5
Krauthammer, Charles, 34
Kristof, Nicholas D., 169n21
Kristol, William, 34, 168n18, 168n24
KRS-One, 124
Kucinich, Dennis, 126
Kumar, Krishna, 66
Kurtz, Walter E. (character), 44, 46
Kweli, Talib, 123–124, 158

LaHaye, Tim, 5, 44, 49–50, 52, 54–59,
    61–65, 67–71, 73, 75–78
Lalonde, Paul, 60
Lalonde, Peter, 60
Lamar, Kendrick, 134
Lamb, Chris, 167n8
"Lame Duck Congress," 151
Lancet, 169n38
Landler, Mark, 170n13
Langshite, Hickie, 105
Larson, Bob, 60
Lashmar, Paul, 168n23
Laws, 23, 42
LBS (*see* Left Behind Series)
le Carré, John, 78
Leartius, Diogenes, 23

Lee, Spike, 107, 116
Lefever Ernest W., 168n17
Left Behind (The Kids), 68
Left Behind Series, 49, 53–55, 57, 65,
    68, 169n14
Left Behind, 5, 15, 50, 52–55, 57, 63–66,
    68, 73, 75–76, 141, 169n7
Left Behind: Eternal Forces, 57
Lehmann-Haupt, Christopher, 20
Lehrer, Tom, 84, 101
Lenin, Vladimir, 128
Lennox, Vince, (character), 82–83,
    101, 138
Leone, Sergio, 107
"Letter to W. T. Barry," 173n33
Lewinsky, Monica, 163
Lewis, Sinclair, 101, 105
Libby, Lewis, 168n24
Libecap, Gary D., 167n11
Lil' Wayne, 125
Lincoln, Abraham, 15, 94
Lindsey, Hal, 59–60
Lingaard, Cheech (character), 82
Lintott, Andrew, 169n37
Lippman, Laura, 137–138
Little Book of Complete Bollocks, 84
Little England Big World, 84
Littlemore, Richard, 170n18
Lives of Eminent Philosophers, 23
LL Cool J, 113, 119, 122
Locke, Alain Leroy, 108–109
"Long Track Blues," 111
Long, Huey, 105, 154
"Lord John Marbury," 143
Los Angeles Times, 92
Louis XIV, 86
Lowe, Rob, 138–139
Ludacris, 123
Luhrmann, T. M., 170n41
Luntz, Frank, 3, 158
Lyman, Josh (character), 97,
    138–139, 141

M-1, 12
Maad Circle, 130
Mace, 171n9

MacGyver, Angus (character), 53
MacRone, Michael, 118
Madame (Emma) Bovary, 64
Madame Tussauds, 52
Madison, James, 149, 173n33
Madonna (Madonna Louise Ciccone), 134
Major, Major (character), 81
Maloney, Carolyn, 3–4
Mani (Manichean), 66
Mann, Michael, 168n17
Mao, Zedong, 26
Marco Polo, If You Can, 78
Marie Claire, 62
Marks of the Beast: The Left Behind Novels and the Struggle for Evangelical Identity, 169n24
Marks, Donald, 172n33
Marlowe, Philip (character), 75
Marquess of Queensberry, 160, 162
Marsalis, Branford, 116
Marsalis, Wynton, 115–116, 171n10
Marsh, Randy (character), 106
Marshall, Thurgood, 73
Master P, 11, 126
Mathewson, Dan, 169n10
Maugham, Somerset, 131
Mayfield, Betty, 75
MC Hammer, 171n3
McAlister, Melani, 68
McBain, Ed, 53
McCabe, Janet, 167n15, 172n10
McCain, John, 16, 106, 124, 126, 139, 144
McCarthy, Joseph, 45, 78
McCoys (characters), 103
McGarry, Leo (character), 143
McGovern, George, 42
McKay, Claude, 109, 167n11
McKinley, William, 1
McPherson, Lionel K., 172n24, 173n39
Meet John Doe, 4
Meining, D. W., 171n25
Meltdown, 170n7
"Memory Lane," 115
Metaphysics, 23
Metzger, Bruce M., 169n11

Meyer, Marvin, 169n11
Michael, George, 120
Middle East Review of International Affairs, 168n23
Mill, Meek, 134
Miller, Matthew, 172n6
Mirra, Carl, 168n17
Mirriam (Webster's Dictionary), 19
Miss Vermilyea (character), 75
Mitchell, Rick, 172n28
Mo' Better Blues, 116
Molotov, Vyacheslav, 87, 125
"Moment of Clarity," 129
Mongoose R.I.P., 78
Monk, Thelonious, 116
Moore, Laurence R., 170n42, 173n28
Moore, Lorrie, 13
Moore, Matthew, 171n24
Moore, Michael, 15, 70, 84–85, 87, 103, 128, 134, 140
Morgan, J. P., 102
Morris, Chris, 171n13
Morris, Dick, 139
Morris, Edward, 2
Morrison, Richard, 169n3
Morrison, Toni, 130
Morton, Jelly Roll, 109
Mos Def, 124
Moss, Donna (character), 141
Motley, John, 23
Moviegoer, 19
Moyer, Bill, 21, 168n3
Mozart, Wolfgang Amadeus, 115
Mr. President, 142
"Mr. Willis of Ohio," 142
"Ms Amerikkka," 124
Muhammad, Ali, 111
Musser, Joe, 60
Mussolini, Benito, 102
My Bondage and My Freedom, 130
"My Cause," 2
"My Mind Is Payin Tricks on Me," 120
Myers, Dee Dee, 3, 139

Nabokov, Vladimir, 24
Nas, 115, 120

Nast, Thomas, 6
National Review, 77
Naughty Shakespeare, 118
NBC News, 144
Necro, 121
Nelson, Kirk, 59
Nelson, Michael, 171n16
New Testament, 50, 52, 65, 74
New York Times, 49, 109, 137, 139
New Yorker, 161
Newhart, Bob, 19
Newsweek, 50
Newton, Huey, P., 126
Nickles, Don, 170n42
Niggas-4Life, 110, 119
"Niggaz 4 Life," 113
Niggaz Wit Attitudes (NWA), 110, 127, 129
Nigger Heaven, 109, 121, 133
"Niggers Are Scared of Revolution," 111
Nixon, Richard Milhous, 1, 20, 22, 35, 42, 54, 78, 93, 111, 161
"No Rest for the Wicked," 134
Noonan, Peggy, 3, 139
Norris, Frank, 133
North, Oliver, 60, 70
Nostradamus, 50, 57
Not the Nine O'Clock News, 84
Nussbaum, Martha, 26
NWA (*see* Niggaz Wit Attitudes)

O'Brien, Tim, 100
O'Donnell, Lawrence, Jr., 3, 137, 154
O'Leary, Stephen D., 169n13
O'Rourke, P. J., 103
O'Shaughnessy, Brigid, 75
Oakes, Blackford (character), 77–78
"Obama Unveils Innovation Agenda at Google," 173n34
Obama, Barack, 4–7, 29, 34, 43, 69, 72, 77, 83, 85, 87–93, 95–96, 98, 100, 103, 106, 123, 126, 130, 144, 161, 167n10, 173n22
Odom, Mel, 61

OED (see Oxford English Dictionary)
Oedipus Rex, 118
Old Testament, 50, 52, 65, 74
Oliver, King, 109
"One Step," 120
Orwell, George, 12–13, 26, 46, 102, 167n14
Osby, Greg, 116
"Our Government: What the Fuck Do They Do All Day, and Why Does It Cost So Goddamned Much Money?," 103
Overdose: The Next Financial Crisis, 170n7
Oxford English Dictionary, 19, 121

P. Diddy, 111, 127
Palm, Sarah, 143
Paradise Lost, 57
Parallel Lives, 23, 29
Paris, 125
Parliament, 113
Parker, Chalie (Bird), 116
Parnell, Peter, 141
Patillo-McCoy, Mary, 171n20
Patterson, Bradley H., 172n3, 173n36
Patterson, Thomas E., 162
Paul, Gregory, 170n41
Paul, Ron, 126–127
Pautz, Johann, 68
Pawlenty, Tim, 4
PBS NewsHour, 172n11, 172n12
Peace, Michael, 115
Perry, Imani, 118, 122
Pelikan, Jaroslav, 170n38
Pepys, Samuel, 41
Percy, Walker, 19
Peretti, Frank, 60
Pericles, 20, 26, 28–29, 32, 39, 145, 147, 172n16
Perkins, William Eric, 171n7
Perle, Richard, 168n24
Petrarch, 46
Petronius, Gaius, 105
Philip II, 23

Philips, Chuck, 171n12
Phyllis (character), 75
Picture This, 5, 19–25, 27, 29–31, 35–36, 39, 41–42, 44–46, 103, 147
Piercing the Darkness, 60
Pinochet, Augusto, 36
Planet Earth—2000 A.D., 59
Plantern's Northern Bride, 15
Plato, 23–25, 27–29, 34, 42, 45, 86, 168n31
Playback, 74
Playboy, 33, 42
Plessy v. Ferguson, 107
Plessy, Homer, 108
Plutarch, 23, 29
Podhoretz, John, 137–138
Poetics, 23, 27
Pol Pot, 26
"Police State," 126
Politics," 123
Pollyanna, 137
Pompilius, Numa, 59
Poniewozik, James, 172n1
Poor Righteous Teachers, 124
Portrait of an Artist, as an Old Man, 20, 34
Pound, Edward T., 173n35
Pound, Ezra, 109
Powell, Colin L., 33, 37, 168n25
Powers, Charles, 167n1
Pratt, Larry, 70
Price, Robert M., 169n10, 169n14
Primary Colors, 72
Public Enemy, 113–114, 127
Putin, Vladimir, 34, 128
Putnam, Robert, 165

Quayle, Dan, 165

Raising Hell, 110
Rampton, Sheldon, 169n36
Rangwala, Glen, 37, 168n27
Rap City, 110
"Rap," 172n29
"Rapper's Delight," 113

"Rapture," 113
Rather, Dan, 124
Reagan, Ronald, 1, 3, 5, 9, 20, 22, 34, 36, 50, 58, 68, 72–73, 77, 85, 119, 146, 167n7
"Rebuilding America's Defenses," 37
Red Harvest, 74
Rembrandt: His Life, His Paintings, 23
Remington Steele (character), 53
Republic, 23, 25
Revelations 2000, 59
Rhyme Pays, 113
Ricardo, David, 10
Rice, Condoleezza, 33
Richardson, Bill, 126
Richler, Mordecai, 23
Richter, Charles F., 45
Riley, Jeff, 142, 172n12
Rising Sun, 86
Ritchie, Ritchie J. (character), 79, 81
Ritchie, Robert (character), 81
Robertson, Pat, 57, 60, 62, 68–69, 70–71
Robeson, Paul, 108–109
Robin, Corey, 168n17
Robinson, Nina, 170n39
Rockefeller, John D., 102
Roger & Me, 140
Romney, Mitt, 4, 8, 10, 77, 126, 167n10
"Ron Paul for the Long Haul," 126
Roosevelt, Franklin D. (also FDR), 56, 72
Roosevelt, Theodore (also Teddy), 88–89, 94
Roots, 124
Rose, Tricia, 135, 171n4
Rosen, Ralph, 172n33
Roth, Philip, 87, 102, 171n31
Rove, Karl, 82, 139
Ruderman, Judith, 168n4
Rumsfeld, Donald, 33, 38, 81, 91, 170n8
Run-DMC, 110

Sabato, Larry J., 169n29
Sagan, Eli, 168n9

Sale, K., 171n25
Salinger, Jerome David, 100
Sample, Ian, 171n26
Sanford, Mark, 16
Santayana, George, 45
Santos, Matthew (character), 144
Sass, Samuel, 167n2
Satire and Dissent, 85
Saturday Night Live, 15
Satyricon, 105
Savage, Charlie, 170n10, 170n13
Sawyer, Forrest, 144
Scarface, 128
Schama, Simon, 23
Schiff, Richard, 139
Schlamme, Thomas, 158
Schlesinger, Arthur M., Jr., 34, 168n17
Schlosser, Eric, 167n11
Schmitt, Christopher H., 173n35
Schorer, Mark, 171n30
Schusterman, Richard, 118
Schwartz, Gary, 23
Scofield Reference Bible, 51
Scofield, Cyrus I., 51–52
Seaborn, Sam (character), 72, 139, 141, 158
"Senate intelligence head says CIA 'searched computer,'" 173n34
Seuss, Theodor, 13
Seventh Epistle, 23
Shabazz, David, 107, 127, 129
Shabazz, Julian L. D., 111, 114, 117, 120, 123, 132
Shakespeare, William, 168n7
Shakur, Tupac, 113, 134
Shapiro, David, 168n11
Shapiro, Fred R., 173n40
Sharpe, Tom, 81
Sheehan, Cindy, 31
Sheen, Martin, 19, 139–140
Sherman, William Tecumseh, 93
Shipman, Tim, 171n24
Shivers, Roy, 126
Shuck, Glenn W., 169n5, 169n14, 169n24

Sidney, Philip, 64
Silver, Ron, 139, 143
Simon, David, 157
Simon, Paul, 122
Simpson, Glenn R., 169n29
Sinclair, Upton, 2, 15
Sister Souljah, 119, 129
"Six Meetings Before Lunch," 72, 132, 158
Sizer, Stephen R, 169n4, 169n18
Skidelski, Joe (character), 81, 86
Smart, D. A., 129
Smith, Adam, 10–11
Smith, Bessie, 109, 127
Smith, David Livingstone, 171n28
Smith, Will, 110
Smith, Zadie, 171n18
Smits, Jimmy, 144
SNL (see Saturday Night Live)
Snoop Dogg, 123, 134
Snowden, Edward, 93
Socrates, 22, 24–25, 28, 45, 86
Soderbergh, Steven, 13
"Soldier's Home," 100
Solomon, King, 126
Something Happened, 20
Sorkin, Aaron, 3, 132, 137–142, 158, 172n2, 172n11
Soul Harvest, 63, 65
South Park, 103, 106
Space Odyssey: 2001, 122
Spade, Sam (character), 75
"Speaking of Courage," 100
Spectator, 16
Spencer, John, 143
Sperling, Gene, 3, 139
Spillane, Mickey, 133
Spinoza, Baruch, 23
Spitting Image, 85, 103
Stalin, Joseph, 26, 102
"Stan," 128
Standaert, Michael, 67
"Station Identification," 123
Stauber, John, 169n36
Steele, Chloe (character), 52

Steele, Rayford (character), 52–54
Stein, Gertrude, 109
Stephanopoulos, George, 139
Stevens, Wallace, 122
Stevenson, Adlai, 69
Stewart, Jon, 66
stic.man, 12
Still Standing, 122
Stockwell, Stephen, 172n16
Stokes, Doug, 168n22
Storey, John, 167n15
Strauss, Leo, 26
Stromseth, Jane E, 168n15
Stupid White Men . . . and Other Sorry Excuses for the State of the Nation!, 70, 85
Stutzer, Alois, 173n38
Suskind, Ron, 168n17
Swaggart, Timmy, 57
Swift, Gustavus, 2, 41
Swift, Jonathan, 105
Swirski, Peter, 79, 82, 85, 88, 91, 93, 97, 100, 103, 167n4, 168n8, 169n1, 170n32, 171n27, 171n28, 171n31, 172n20, 173n29, 173n37
Symposium, 23

Taft, William Howard, 88–89
Taking Liberties, 92
Taleb, Nassim Nicholas, 167n12
Tancredo, Tom, 126
Tanner 88, 142
Tarantino, Quentin, 107
Tavakoli-Far, Nastaran, 167n22
Taylor, Edward, 54
Taylor, James, 139
Teague, Mc, 133
Tenet, George, 33
"Thank You," 128
Thatcher, Margaret, 85, 119, 155
The 700 Club, 68–69
The Age of American Unreason, 118
The Anatomy Lesson of Dr. Nicolaes Tulp, 23
The Appeal to Reason, 2

The Audacity of Hope, 72
The Authorized Left Behind Handbook, 60
The Babylonians, 86
The Baltimore Sun, 173n30
The Beast: A Novel of the Coming World Dictator, 60
The Beatles, 145
The Beaton Generation, 84
The Bible's Influence on American History, 44, 49, 52, 55, 58, 62, 65, 68, 71, 73, 75, 169n12
The Bill Cosby Show, 109–110
The Chronic, 114
The City and Man, 26
The Clash Within, 26
The Closing of the American Mind, 5
The Clouds, 86
The Coming of Post-Industrial Society, 164
"The Cradle of Liberty," 152
The Day of Doom, 75
"The Debate," 137, 140, 143–146, 148, 151, 153–155, 157, 160, 160
The Economist, 1, 155, 167n1, 173n25
The Embarrassment of Riches, 23
The End of Days, 60
The End of the Age, 59–60
The Game, 125
The Gilded Age, 105
"The Gospel of Judas," 169n11
The Great Game: Afghanistan, 14
The Great Gatsby, 2
The Green Bible, 76
The Guardian, 96, 169m15, 171n22
The Ides of March, 77
The Independent, 5, 87
The Jungle, 2, 15, 64
The Knights, 86
"The Lame Duck Congress," 145
The Last Poets, 111
The Late Great Planet Earth, 59–60, 75
"The Leadership Breakfast" (The West Wing), 139
The Mail on Sunday, 81, 170n1

The Maltese Falcon, 74

The Mark: The Beast Rules the World, 169n16

"The Message," 110, 124

"The Midterm," 140–141

The Miseducation of Hill, 110

The Nation, 124

"The Negro in Art: How Shall He Be Portrayed?," 121

"The Negro Renaissance," 119

The New republic, 140

The New York Times, 20, 65, 171n23

The Onion, 7

The Peacemaker, 60

The Pet Goat, 70

The Plot Against America, 102

The Postman Always Rings Twice, 74

The Powers That Be, 142

The Prairie, 2

The Present Darkness, 60

The Professors: The 101 Most Dangerous Academics in America, 69

"The Proud," 158

The Race, 16

The Remnant: On the Brink of Armageddon, 63, 169n16

The Revisionists, 170n31

The Rise and Fall of the Great Powers, 39

The Rise of the Dutch Republic, 23

The Rising, 57

The Scotsman, 81, 170n1

The Second Coming 1998, 59

The Senator, 142

The Seven Last Years, 70

The Shaking of the Foundations, 61

The Shell Game, 16

The Sopranos, 158

The Source, 110

The Sun Also Rises, 2

The Thatcher Papers, 84

The Times Literary Supplement, 13

The Today Show, 140

The Trial of Tony Blair, 84

The Truth, 84

The United States v. Hip-Hop, 107, 111, 114, 117, 120, 123, 127, 129, 132

The Video, 84

"The Wake Up Call," 164

The Walled Orchard, 26

The Way, 84

The West Wing, 3–4, 6, 15, 53, 72, 79, 81, 97, 132, 137–146, 148, 151, 155, 157–161, 163–164

"The Winter of the Long Hot Summer," 125

The Wire, 157–158

The World Tonight, 84

They Eat Puppies, Don't They?, 85

"Thidwick the Big-Hearted Moose," 13

Thomas, Don, 171n14

Thompson, Fred, 126

Thompson, Judd (character), 68

Thucydides, 5, 23, 25–26, 36, 168n14

Thurman, Wallace, 109

Tilden, Samuel J., 146–147

Tillich, Paul, 61

Time (magazine), 50, 62, 101, 138, 169n15

Time Has an End: A Biblical History of the World 11,013 B.C.—2011 A.D., 60

Tone Loc, 171n3

Tonneson, Stein, 168n28

"Too subtle for the small screen," 172n31

Toomer, Jean, 109

"Transcript: Democratic National Convention," 172n30

Treme, 158

Trend, David, 168n9

"Trends in Large U.S. Church Membership from 1960," 169n17

Tribulation Force: The Continuing Drama of Those Left Behind, 55, 65

Troilus and Cressida, 168n7

Trotsky, Leon, 101

Trudeau, Garry, 142

Truman, Harry S., 77, 119

Tse, Alice, 167n22

Tsion, Ben-Judah (character), 52, 63
Tucker, Delores, 116, 172n7
Turley, Jonathan, 170n12
TV Guide, 139
Twain, Mark, 2, 20, 105, 152
Tweed, William M., 6
Tweedy Bird Loc, 114
Twitchell, James B., 170n30
Tyson, Mike, 122

"Uncle Sam Goddamn," 124
Uncle Tom's Cabin, 15, 64
*Uncovered: The Whole Truth About
    Iraqi War*, 168n23
"US Congress Opts for 'Freedom
    Fries,'" 171n29
"USA President Barack Obama
    Opinion on Hip Hop & Rap
    2008," 172n23
USA Today, 62, 173n34

Valentine, J. Manson, 59
van Rijn, Rembrandt, 22–24, 45
Van Susteren, Greta, 170n8
Van Vechten, Carl, 109, 131
Vanilla Ice, 171n3
Verres, Gaius, 46
Vidal, Gore, 13, 45
Viewing America, 158
Vinick, Arnold (character), 143–144
Vladov, Andrei, 172
Voigt, John, 19
von Clausewitz, Carl, 32

Wacker, Grant, 169n25
Wagner, Alex, 170n19
Walker, Scott, 149
Wall Street Journal, 173n40
Wall, Paul, 121
Wallsten, Peter, 170n19
Walmart, 167n12
Warner, Charles Dudley, 105
Warren, Robert Pern, 105
Washington, George, 10
Washington, Lionel, 68
Watkins, S. Craig, 118, 171n2, 172n32

Watson, Sydney, 169n6
Watt, James, 58
Waxman, Sharon, 172n8
WC, 130
Wear, Ben, 172n4
Weinberger, Caspar, 58
Weiner, Eric, 173n38
Weingarten, Marc, 171n8
Welles, Orson, 19
Welna, David, 170n9
Werrenchuk, Max, 169n4
What Would Jesus Eat?, 62
"What Would You Do?," 125
"When the Revolution Comes," 111
"Where Ya At?," 129
Whisenant, Edgar C., 59
White Dawg, 121
White, George, 108
White, Walter, 119
Whitford, Bradley, 139, 173n32
Whitman, Walt, 121
Why We Fight?, 168n33
Wiarda, Howard J., 168n21
Wigglesworth, Michael, 75
Wilkinson, Paul, 169n4
William of Orange, 23
Williams, Buck (character), 52–55,
    169n6
Wilson, Charles, 168n30
Wilson, Woodrow, 30–31, 88
Winfrey, Oprah, 72
Wolfe, Tom, 25
Wolfowitz, Paul, 37–38
Wolverton, James, 94
Women of the House, 142
Woodward, Bob, 81, 171n22
Wurst, Gregor, 169n11

X-Clan, 124
X, Malcolm, 128
Xenophon, 23

"Yertle the Turtle," 13
Yes Minister, 161
Yes, Prime Minister, 161
Yeskel, Felice, 167n12

Yo! MTV Raps, 110
You Can't be Neutral on a Moving Train: A Personal History of Our Times, 87
Yovanovich, Gordana, 170n34

Zap2it.com, 172n2
Zagorin, Perez, 168n7
Ziegler, Toby (character), 139, 141, 151
Zumthor, Paul, 23
Zinn, Howard, 87, 168n12

Printed and bound in the United States of America